CHOCOLATE ISLANDS

William A. Cadbury, Joseph Burtt, and an unidentified African man in Luanda, January 1909. Photograph in the Cadbury Papers 308, Cadbury Research Library, Special Collections, University of Birmingham, Birmingham, UK.

Chocolate Islands

COCOA, SLAVERY, AND COLONIAL AFRICA

Catherine Higgs

OHIO UNIVERSITY PRESS ~ ATHENS

Ohio University Press, Athens, Ohio 45701
ohioswallow.com
© 2012 by Ohio University Press

To obtain permission to quote, reprint, or otherwise reproduce or distribute
material from Ohio University Press publications, please contact our rights and
permissions department at (740) 593-1154 or (740) 593-4536 (fax).

Printed in the United States of America
Ohio University Press books are printed on acid-free paper ⊚ ™

20 19 18 17 16 15 14 13 12   5 4 3 2 1

Library of Congress Cataloging-in-Publication Data
Higgs, Catherine.
 Chocolate islands : cocoa, slavery, and colonial Africa / Catherine Higgs.
   p. cm.
 Includes bibliographical references and index.
 ISBN 978-0-8214-2006-5 (hc : alk. paper) — ISBN 978-0-8214-4422-1 (electronic)
 1. Forced labor—São Tomé and Príncipe—History. 2. Slavery—São Tomé and
Príncipe—History. 3. Cacao—Harvesting—São Tomé and Príncipe—History. 4.
Cacao—Harvesting—Moral and ethical aspects. 5. Cacao growers—São Tomé
and Príncipe—History. 6. Portugal—Colonies—Africa—Administration. 7.
Burtt, Joseph, 1862–1939—Travel—Africa, West. 8. Cadbury, William A. (William
Adlington), 1867–1957. 9. Cadbury Brothers—History. I. Title.
 HD4875.S36H55 2012
 331.76337409670904—dc23
                              2012009341

FOR KATHY JOINER MILBURN AND JEFF MILBURN

CONTENTS

ILLUSTRATIONS

FIGURES

MAPS

PREFACE

This book is about an Englishman's journey through Africa in the first decade of the twentieth century, undertaken as European colonial powers were tightening their grip on the continent. The traveler's name was Joseph Burtt. He had been hired by William A. Cadbury on behalf of the British chocolate firm Cadbury Brothers Limited to determine—in response to an emerging international controversy—if slaves had harvested the cocoa the company was purchasing from the Portuguese West African colony of São Tomé and Príncipe.

Burtt's voyage took him from innocence and credulity to outrage and activism. Between June 1905 and March 1907, he traveled to the islands of São Tomé and Príncipe, then south along the coast to the large Portuguese colony of Angola, to Mozambique in Portuguese East Africa, and to the Transvaal Colony in British southern Africa. Through his eyes, we learn about the often complacent British and Portuguese attitudes toward work, slavery, race, and imperialism in the early twentieth century. He visited agricultural estates—*roças* on São Tomé and Príncipe and *fazendas* in Angola. He talked to diplomats, journalists, and European and African businesspeople, and he traced the slave route through Angola's interior. He conferred with mine owners in the Transvaal and colonial officials in Mozambique, which supplied most of the labor for the Transvaal's mines. He was not the first man to make such a trip; readers interested in the broader literature into which this narrative of his experiences fits may wish to read "A Note on Sources" at the end of this book.

Burtt wrote a stream of letters to Cadbury recording what he saw and whom he met. He was not a flawless observer, but this should not surprise us, living as we do in an age that has long abandoned the pretense of objectivity. What Burtt wrote prompted Cadbury Brothers Limited to seek alternate sources of cocoa. The report he prepared summarizing his observations was submitted to the British and the Portuguese governments, and it helped reform the recruitment and treatment of laborers. Joseph Burtt was no casual visitor to Africa: he traveled with a purpose, and what he saw and what he did mattered. A century later, his journey echoes in the human rights organizations of our own day, which seek to expose the sometimes oppressive conditions under which workers still produce our foodstuffs. At the beginning of the twentieth century, the observations of this "big, innocent-looking man," by turns idealistic, naive, perceptive, and too often racist, help us understand the cultural blindness of those who sought to improve the lot of African workers. Yet help to improve it, as the following story demonstrates, he did.[1]

ACKNOWLEDGMENTS

I am grateful to the many librarians, archivists, colleagues, and friends who have made this book possible. Dorothy Woodson, curator of the African Collection at Yale University, gave me access to the collection of James Duffy's papers donated by his widow in 2000. They restored to the archival record the set of letters Joseph Burtt wrote to William Cadbury from Africa between 1905 and 1907. Copies of the letters have been deposited in the Cadbury Research Library, Special Collections, at the University of Birmingham, where Helen Fisher and Philippa Bassett assisted me. Sarah Foden gave me access to the small archive still maintained by Cadbury Information Services (now part of Kraft Foods). Two summer Professional Development Awards from the University of Tennessee funded my 2002 visit to Birmingham (I thank Isabel Hackett for her kind hospitality) and my 2003 visit to São Tomé. I am grateful to Augusto Nascimento for introducing me to the staff at the Arquivo Histórico de São Tomé and Príncipe and helping me negotiate the archive at a moment when I was just learning Portuguese. Nascimento and Eugénia Rodrigues (both of the Instituto de Investigação Científica Tropical [IICT]) also graciously hosted me in Lisbon. A 2004 grant from the Luso-American Foundation funded a summer of research at the Biblioteca Nacional in Lisbon. I owe a special debt of gratitude to Helena Grego and Cristina Matias of the Sociedade de Geografia de Lisboa, who in 2006 kindly helped me track down numerous references. My debt to Gerhard Seibert of the Centro de Estudos Africanos (ISCTE-IUL) is considerable. Among many favors over the years, he read this manuscript and introduced me to the great-grandson of Francisco Mantero, who shares his name. I thank Kate Burlingham for her research assistance at the Arquivo Histórico Nacional de Angola, as well as the librarians and archivists at the Rhodes House Library at Oxford University; the Biblioteca Nacional, the Arquivo Histórico Ultramarino, and the Arquivo Histórico Diplomático in Lisbon; and the Arquivo Histórico de Moçambique in Maputo.

The University of Tennessee had just granted me a fall 2005 sabbatical and the American Philosophical Society had awarded me a spring 2006 sabbatical fellowship when Kevin Grant's *A Civilised Savagery: Britain and the New Slaveries in Africa* (2005) and Lowell Satre's *Chocolate on Trial: Slavery, Politics, and the*

Ethics of Business (2005)—both of which explore the controversy over cocoa— were published. In this book, I take a fresh approach, following the advice of Joseph C. Miller and Robert R. Edgar, who encouraged me to write a history of interest to students, scholars, and general readers. I hope I have fulfilled their vision. I thank David Birmingham, William Gervase Clarence-Smith, Douglas L. Wheeler, and Linda Heywood, and also John K. Thornton for his model of a popular history, *The Kongolese Saint Anthony: Dona Beatriz Kimpa Vita and the Antonian Movement, 1684–1706* (1998). Stephen V. Ash, a friend and a noted historian of the American Civil War, taught me how to write narrative history, and he wore out several red pens commenting on multiple drafts of each of my chapters. Among many other colleagues and friends at the University of Tennessee (present and former), I thank especially Kim Harrison and Anne Galloway, Carolyn Hodges, Ann Jefferson, Nancy Schurr, Dawn Duke, Tina Shepardson, Jay Rubenstein, Robert Bast, Rosalind Hackett, Ernie Freeberg, Tom Burman, David Tompkins, Michael Kulikowski, Todd Diacon, and Moema Furtado. Over the years, I have been supported by friends of long standing, including Kathy Joiner Milburn, Jeff Milburn, Marion Taylor, Glen Taylor, Patricia Behre, James Francis, David Godfrey, Ellen Macek, and Sean Redding. This project has also brought new friends, including Ruth Rogaski, Julianna Munden, Todd Cleveland, Eric Allina, Jeremy Ball, and Denise Perreira. Many have kindly read parts of the manuscript, and I have benefited greatly from their insights and suggestions. Two diligent research assistants, Brad Pardue and Katherine Thompson Newell, helped me proofread the text and check the notes. Will Fontanez, director of the University of Tennessee's Cartographic Services Laboratory, drew maps 3 and 5. Finally, I thank Gillian Berchowitz of Ohio University Press for her interest in and encouragement of this project.

Permission to reprint photographic and archival material was granted as follows: for figure 1, by the Cadbury Archives, Kraft Foods, Birmingham, United Kingdom, courtesy of the William Adlington Cadbury Charitable Trust; for figures 2–8 and 10–23, by João Loureiro from his Postcard Collection; for figures 24 and 26–29, by Historical Papers, William Cullen Library, University of the Witwatersrand, Johannesburg, South Africa; for figures 25 and 30, by Francisco Mantero; and for figure 31, by the Cadbury Archives, Kraft Foods. Permission to cite from the William Adlington Cadbury Family Papers, held at the Birmingham City Archives, was granted by the William Adlington Cadbury Charitable Trust; permission to cite from the American Board of Commissioners for Foreign Missions papers housed at the Houghton Library, Harvard University, was granted by the Wider Church Ministries of the United Church of Christ.

GLOSSARY

Banco Nacional Ultramarino	National Overseas Bank
câmara	Municipal Council
creole	Person born in the colonies
curador	Portuguese colonial labor administrator
dependência(s)	Outlying section(s) of an agricultural estate
fazenda	Agricultural estate in Angola
filho(s) da terra	African(s) indigenous to São Tomé and Príncipe, also known as *Nativo(s)* and *Forro(s)*
forma	Roll call
forro(s)	Free person(s) of African descent born in São Tomé and Príncipe, also known as *filho(s) da terra* and *nativo(s)*
liberto(s)	Newly freed slave(s) in Portuguese Africa, 1858–75
mestiço(s)	Person(s) of mixed racial descent
nativo(s)	African(s) indigenous to São Tomé and Príncipe, also known as *Filho(s) da Terra* and *Forro(s)*
prazo	Agricultural estate in Mozambique
prazero	Estate manager in Mozambique
roça	Agriculture estate in São Tomé and Príncipe
roçeiro	Planter and estate owner in São Tomé and Príncipe
serviçal (serviçais)	Contract laborer(s)

Prologue

JOSEPH BURTT AND WILLIAM CADBURY

JOSEPH BURTT and William Cadbury shared a concern for the English worker, an opposition to slavery in any form, and through their membership in the Society of Friends, a long acquaintance. Their paths crossed professionally in 1904 when Cadbury, a director of the chocolate firm Cadbury Brothers Limited, offered Burtt an eighteen-month contract to investigate the working conditions of African laborers in the Portuguese colonies of São Tomé and Príncipe and Angola. Burtt's mission was to determine if rumors that slaves were harvesting cocoa on the island colony of São Tomé and Príncipe were true. The answers he found would forge a friendship and link the two men publicly in what was in some ways an unlikely collaboration.[1]

Joseph Burtt was born in December 1862 to John Bowen and Ann Bevington Burtt in Kettering, England, fifty miles east of Birmingham. He spent a happy childhood in the countryside with his seven brothers and sisters, but since no family records have survived, how John Bowen Burtt supported his large brood remains a mystery. There was enough money for Joseph Burtt to ride horses as a child and for a tutor to visit occasionally and oversee the children's lessons. In his early teens, Burtt spent two years at the private Crypt School in Gloucester, in the southwest of England. In 1879, at the age of sixteen, he went to work for the Gloucestershire Bank in Cheltenham.[2]

Tragedy marked William Adlington Cadbury's early childhood. His mother, Elizabeth Adlington Cadbury, died just before his second birthday in early 1869, and William spent the next two years living with his grandfather, John Cadbury. William Cadbury held tight all his life to the memory of his mother lifting him in "her arms so that he could see a shining candlestick on the mantelpiece." That there was a candlestick there at all was a testament to the hard work of her husband, Richard. The Cadburys had been selling tea and coffee since 1824, but when Richard and his brother George took over the family firm in 1861, it was teetering on the edge of bankruptcy. They almost went under in

1863 but by the next year had made a small profit, in part by moving away from coffee and tea and investing in cocoa. In 1866, they introduced "Pure Cocoa Essence," marketing it as a nutritious hot drink and tapping into Britain's growing consumer culture and to the new concern with "pure" foods.[3]

By the time William Cadbury's father remarried, to Emma Wilson in 1871, the firm was prospering. John Cadbury built a house in Edgbaston's Harbourne Road for himself and a second one for his son Richard. The two gardens became a happy playground for young William Cadbury, his brother, and his two sisters.[4]

With its stately houses and broad, leafy avenues, Edgbaston was one of Birmingham's more affluent suburbs. It sat in marked contrast to the gritty industrial city around it. In Birmingham's poorest slums, housing was crowded, sanitation was often inadequate, and the death rate was double that in Edgbaston. Neither Richard nor George Cadbury was blind to the inequalities; George taught in the Society of Friends' adult school movement, which served the city's poorest residents. As Quakers—members of the Society of Friends—the Cadburys held religious beliefs that influenced how they conducted business. Excluded from politics and the connections that came with membership in the Church of England, many Quakers had turned to business during the Industrial Revolution and acquired wealth in mining, banking, and insurance. Capitalism was acceptable, but Quaker products had to be beneficial to society and priced fairly. In the early 1800s, many Quaker families abandoned the plain dress and speech that had set them apart from mainstream English society and began publicly enjoying their wealth. They also embraced philanthropy, speaking out for prison reform and the abolition of slavery. Cocoa—presented as a healthy alternative to hard liquor—neatly supported another Quaker social cause, the temperance movement, and it was no coincidence that two other large British cocoa manufacturers, J. S. Fry and Rowntree, were also Quaker family firms.

The cause Richard and George Cadbury took up was improving the lot of the worker. An eleven-year-old William Cadbury was dispatched in 1878 to dig holes for the soil inspectors on a piece of land the brothers had purchased at Strichley. It became the site of the Bournville Works, the new factory Cadbury Brothers built in the countryside four miles from Birmingham's industrial center. Housing was built for factory foremen, but the rest of the company's workers continued to travel daily by train from the city. The holes William Cadbury had dug as a child were never filled in, and his gentle boast was that he had turned the first ground on the "factory in the garden."[5]

The growing success of Cadbury Brothers shaped William Cadbury's "no frills" education. He attended Friends' schools in Southport, where he sustained a chronic injury to his hip playing football, and in Hitchin, where he excelled at cricket. An early fascination with the sea was quashed by his rather austere father, who expected him to pursue a "useful career" by joining the family firm. Though an amateur musician and artist—he carried a sketchbook with him on many of his travels—William Cadbury had little time for either pursuit. At eighteen, he took a job in the engineering department at J. J. Seekings in Gloucester. In 1886, he spent eight months studying drafting and machinery at the German chocolate firm of Stollwerck in Cologne. A year later, at twenty, William joined Cadbury Brothers. He maintained the Bournville Works machinery and buildings; he hired male workers; and every six weeks from 1888 through 1892, he traveled the countryside visiting clients.[6]

Late in 1889, William Wilson, the brother of William Cadbury's stepmother, Emma, visited Edgbaston. The eldest of Wilson's children was a precocious six-year-old named Emmeline, who was the same age as William Cadbury's half sister Beatrice. Cadbury was first charmed and then smitten, sending Emmeline small presents, writing her letters, and deciding when she was only nine that he would ask her father for permission to marry her when she turned eighteen. That he could make such a decision when he was twenty-five seems surprising now, but it was not uncommon for men of Cadbury's class to marry late and to wed much younger women. The couple married in 1902, after Emmeline returned from six months at a finishing school in Switzerland and shortly before her eighteenth birthday. William was thirty-five.[7]

In 1895, using his own money, George Cadbury bought 120 acres near the factory and designed Bournville Village's garden cottages, streets, and parks as a model working-class community. There were no restrictions on who could buy a house there, and the only thing missing was a pub, since George Cadbury hoped workers would prefer gardening to drinking. He gave the community to the self-governing Bournville Village Trust in 1900.[8]

The absence of a pub in the village suggests paternalism, but the company took great pains to avoid that label. Cadbury employees sat on works councils and participated in trade unions where their concerns were taken seriously. A minimum wage, sick leave, and a pension plan were among the innovations introduced at the Bournville Works. At the center of the company's business philosophy was the belief that a laborer was not a "living tool." Rather, as one man who left his bank job to work for the company observed, the Cadburys "somehow conveyed the idea that their purpose was to do something *for* one, rather than to get the last ounce in the way of work; I think they generally did get the fullest in service, but they *attracted* it—they did not force it."[9]

Employees were encouraged to continue their education, and the company provided a variety of on-site training programs. Sport was another welcome diversion, and William Cadbury played on the Bournville football and cricket teams and served as vice president of the Bournville (Men's) Athlete Club when it was established in 1896.[10]

While William Cadbury dutifully embraced his responsibilities at the family firm, Joseph Burtt succumbed to a "crisis of conscience." In 1898, after almost twenty years working for the Gloucestershire Bank, he turned down a promotion to manager, quit his job, and helped found the utopian Whiteway Colony near Stroud in rural Gloucestershire. The strikes and industrial violence in several British cities in the late 1890s seem to have influenced Burtt's decision to leave a promising career at age thirty-five. "It is hard to say," he would later recall, "if it was the horror of industrial cities or the degradation of the workers, or shame in my participation in an evil system that gave me a passionate desire to escape to some spot where I and my friends could settle and cultivate the land."[11]

In our age, we might be inclined to think that Joseph Burtt had had a midlife crisis, but his rejection of capitalism and his search for a "practical utopia" had a long history in England. Among the late nineteenth-century experiments was George Cadbury's Bournville Village, his response to the growing recognition of poverty in Britain. His fellow Quaker B. Seebohm Rowntree would publish a statistical study, *Poverty: A Study of Town Life*, in 1901. Ebenezer Howard's town-planning manual, *Tomorrow: A Peaceful Path to Real Reform*, also captured the growing concern with social reform. First published in 1898, it envisioned "slumless smokeless cities" with easy access to public transportation and public gardens. Reissued numerous times under the title *Garden Cities of Tomorrow*, the manual embodied the concerns of many Britons about the potentially dehumanizing effects of industrialization, especially on the working poor.[12]

The founders of Whiteway Colony belonged to a variety of Left-leaning organizations, including the Fabian Society, the Independent Labour Society, and especially the Croydon Brotherhood Church. Minister John C. Kenworthy opened his church—ten miles southeast of London in Croydon—each Sunday afternoon to "every kind of 'crank,' . . . Atheists, Spiritualists, Individualists,

Communists, Anarchists, ordinary politicians, Vegetarians, Anti-vivisectionists and Anti-vaccinationists—in fact, every kind of 'anti' had a welcome and a hearing, and had to stand a lively criticism in the discussion which followed." Members of the Croydon Brotherhood Church embraced a kind of religious anarchism, rejecting the acquisition of wealth and trying to lead lives modeled on those of Christ and his disciples.[13]

The Whiteway colonists looked for their inspiration to Leo Tolstoy, the Russian novelist whose embrace of nature, admiration for the peasantry, and revolutionary reinterpretation of lived Christianity brought him to the attention of English idealists. Tolstoy argued that the Christian message had been distorted by the churches, by the state, and especially by capitalism. Rejecting these three negative influences, he advocated instead "the establishment of the kingdom of God on earth; that is, the establishment of the order of life in which the discord, deception and violence that now rule will be replaced by free accord, by truth, and by the brotherly love of one for another." On his own estate at Yasnaya Polyana, Tolstoy dressed as a peasant and labored in his fields beside his workers. He did not, however, give up the title to his property.[14]

Members of the Croydon Brotherhood founded Purleigh Colony in Essex in 1896, but it fell apart within two years when colonists disagreed over whether to accept two tradesmen—a carpenter and an engineer—who had applied to join the commune. For some Purleighites, this dispute smacked of class bias, of a distinction made between those who had actual wealth to reject and those who did not. In the spring of 1898, William Sinclair, Arnold Eiloart, and Sudbury Protheroe joined Nellie Shaw in searching for a site for a new colony. Their plan in turn attracted Clara Lee, Daniel Thatcher, and Joseph Burtt; the two men were members of the West of England Land Society and of the Society of Friends. Burtt was still working for the Gloustershire Bank in Cheltenham. That August, the group, less Protheroe, cycled or traveled by train around Gloucestershire.[15]

After an extended search, Eiloart and Burtt purchased forty-two acres known as Whiteway and conveniently located near the railway lines connecting Stroud, Gloucester, and Cirencester. They had found a garden surrounded by small cities. Two women and six men, including Joseph Burtt and his brother Gopsill, moved into a rented house in nearby Sheepscombe. In October, leaving Daniel Thatcher and Clara Lee to set up a women's weaving cooperative in Sheepscombe, the rest of the colonists moved to the Whiteway farm.

In February 1899, Jeannie Straughan joined Whiteway, where she entered into a "free union" with Sudbury Protheroe. On the issue of free unions, the English idealists parted ways with Tolstoy, who envisioned abstinence as "the ideal . . . marriage being tolerated but not encouraged." Rejecting chastity, the Whiteway settlers took Tolstoy's thinking to its next logical step, arguing that dedicated Tolstoyans could not seek the sanction of either church or state for a marriage, which in any event made a woman a "chattel, . . . ringed and labelled as man's property, losing even her name in marriage—almost her identity." Instead, women at Whiteway donned "rational" (that is, non-constricting) dress and joined the men in working the fields. The men rarely reciprocated by helping the women in the house.[16]

The unmarried Burtt appears not to have entered a free union during the time he spent at Whiteway, but he did become intimately familiar with hard physical labor and poverty. With no experience farming, he and the others found that "small culture by amateurs" produced "little, and we soon became very poor, in spite of many gifts from friends." Still, Burtt was enormously happy, recalling that

> frost did not chill by night, nor the sun burn by day. I do not remember that rain ever fell in the sweet Arcady. . . . We felt immensely rich, and at peace with all the world. Even the poorest, we hoped, could not accuse us of taking an undue advantage of having been born in a better position than himself. If our feet were down in the potato trenches, our heads were up with the stars. We felt we were gods.

"After a few months at Whiteway," he felt that his "mind and body seemed to be created anew."[17]

After a long day of work, the colonists spent their evenings in rather bourgeois pursuits, playing the piano, singing, and reading: "Shelley, Browning, Shakespeare, Emerson, Carpenter and Ruskin were perhaps the chief favourites."[18]

Of course, all was not idyllic in utopia, as Burtt's reference to digging potatoes suggests. The community's decision to purchase two uncooperative dairy cows proved a minor comedy, and the local *Stroud Journal* included the occasional critical paragraph on the "educated" folk dabbling in the simple life at Whiteway. The commune also attracted curiosity seekers, especially in the summer, who came to gawk at the "settlers." More serious were the persistent financial problems and the personality conflicts that threatened to tear the community apart.[19]

Most of the money to buy Whiteway had come from Daniel Thatcher. Joseph Burtt contributed £100, and £50 each came from William Sinclair and Sudbury Protheroe, who had received payment for their dedication to Purleigh Colony, despite its collapse. The rest of the original Whiteway colonists contributed "what little we had" to the loose change box that sat on the fireplace mantel in the main house. Having embraced a philosophy of "all things in common," none of the men and women wanted to sign their names to Whiteway's title deed. To transfer legal ownership of the property, however, someone had to sign, and after much debate, Burtt, Sinclair, and Protheroe agreed to do so. They then burned the title deed in a symbolic act much like Tolstoy donning peasant dress to work his fields beside his laborers. A copy of the title deed remained in the Gloucestershire county clerk's office, but the symbolism of watching "the neatly inscribed deed" sizzling "in the flames" appealed to Whiteway's settlers, who wished the property "to be at the service of anyone who desired to use it productively." Within a few months, the money in the cash box was gone, and the colonists accepted the offer of financial support from the now-married Clara and Daniel Thatcher at Sheepscombe.[20]

The Thatchers considered joining the community at Whiteway but chose instead to maintain their own home and garden at Sheepscombe, where they "practically lived the life of any middle class couple." A drunken brawl between two community members made the *Stroud Journal*, and the violent breakup of the free union of two of the settlers attracted the Thatchers' attention. In September 1899, they requested a public meeting with the Whiteway colonists. Of the three men who had signed the deed to the property, only Protheroe was present: Sinclair was away, and Burtt had joined his father for a vacation in Yorkshire. Four police officers and a local journalist accompanied the Thatchers to the meeting, where Daniel Thatcher demanded that the deed to Whiteway be signed over to him. Protheroe, supported by the other colonists, refused, and an infuriated Thatcher declared, "Well, we can't take away the land, but we *can* take away the cows!" He then left in a huff. The *Stroud Journal* sided with the Thatchers, in part, Nellie Shaw thought, because of the money the couple had spent in and around Sheepscombe. On his return from vacation, Joseph Burtt visited his friends in Gloucester in an attempt to salvage the colony's reputation, but he made little headway.[21]

In October 1899, John Bowen Burtt fell ill, and Joseph and Gopsill Burtt left the colony after just over a year's residence to care for their father. The quiet and well-regarded Joseph Burtt had emerged as a leader of Whiteway Colony, and he departed at a moment of deep crisis in its history, though the community did survive. The Burtt brothers took their ailing father first to Fritchley and then to Crich, where they built a house and designed and planted the surrounding gardens and orchards themselves. Though no longer in the fields digging potatoes, Joseph Burtt continued to embrace physical labor, perhaps out of necessity. To bring in a bit of extra income, he began managing a building.

The year 1899 was a turning point in William Cadbury's life too. Richard Cadbury died, and his brother George incorporated Cadbury Brothers. William, his brother Barrow, and George's two sons (Edward and George) were appointed directors. In 1900, William Cadbury moved out of the engineering department and into sales.[22]

The Cadburys had embraced the Quaker ideal of "doing good in the world, preferably in full public view," and they did not limit their concern for workers to Britain. George and William were members of the British and Foreign Anti-Slavery Society, established by Joseph Sturge in 1839—three decades after Britain had banned its citizens from participating in the transatlantic slave trade and a year after slavery ended in Britain's colonies. Slavery then still continued in India (where the English East India Company had been trading since the early 1600s), and in many other places not under British control or influence. The society, in keeping with its Quaker roots, sought to end slavery through "moral, religious and pacific" means everywhere it existed.[23]

It was Travers Buxton of the Anti-Slavery Society who brought Joseph Burtt to William Cadbury's attention. In November 1903, Cadbury was casting about for a representative to send to São Tomé and Príncipe, and Buxton suggested Burtt, who had just turned down an offer to become the society's assistant secretary, in part because he thought London too superficial a place to live. The former bank clerk briefly turned utopian idealist and the socially conscious if cautious businessman thus became entangled in a controversy over cocoa and slavery that extended from Britain to Portugal, down Africa's west coast, and around to its east.[24]

One

COCOA CONTROVERSY

ON AN April morning in 1901, William Cadbury sat at his desk in Bournville reading a catalog from a cocoa estate in São Tomé. The catalog accompanied an offer to purchase the *roça* (agricultural estate) named Traz-os-Montes on the island of São Tomé. The estate's 6,175 acres, its buildings, machinery, tools, and vehicles were listed for sale along with two items that caught Cadbury's eye—cattle valued at £420 and "200 black labourers" valued at £3,555. Offering workers for sale along with cattle and machinery made him suspect that the conditions of labor on São Tomé were less than ideal. From cocoa planters in Trinidad in the West Indies came rumors that slave labor was indeed being used on São Tomé's roças. William Cadbury was concerned. In the early 1900s, Cadbury Brothers imported about 55 percent of its cocoa from São Tomé and Príncipe, the world's third-largest exporter after Ecuador and Brazil. The firm would not knowingly use slave-harvested cocoa in the manufacture of its chocolate. Labor, whether at the Bournville Works or on the roças of São Tomé, should by definition be dignified and a worker should be free to leave his or her job.[1]

While Joseph Burtt tended his orchards in Crich, William Cadbury turned his attention to the island colony of São Tomé and Príncipe and to Angola, Portugal's largest colony, which was farther south along the West African coast and the source of most of the labor for the islands. In doing so, Cadbury found himself caught up in the long and complicated relationship between Britain and Portugal. From the Portuguese perspective, it was a relationship that was too often humiliating.

In 1901, Britain claimed an empire that included parts of North America, Africa, and Asia. Portugal, depending on one's point of view, was either "one of history's most successful survivors" or the "sick man of Western Europe." In the sixteenth century, Portugal had acquired its own massive empire, stretching from India to Brazil and including claims to the extensive territories in Africa that would become Angola and Mozambique. Yet it never had the manpower or the resources to control its empire effectively. It was poor at the height of its imperial greatness, poorer when Brazil slipped out of its grasp in 1822, and poorer still in the first decade of the twentieth century.[2]

Britain and Portugal had been allies since the fourteenth century, though theirs was not an equal partnership. Portugal's dependence on Britain dated at least to the 1703 Methuen Treaty, which gave England access to Portuguese ports, granted preference to imported English textiles and clothing, and gave Portugal a guaranteed export market for its wines. The Anglo-Portuguese Treaty of 1810—signed after Britain ousted the French forces occupying Portugal during the Napoleonic wars—extended British access to Brazilian markets. Britain also bullied Portugal to abandon the trade in slaves across the Atlantic. Britain had been the first major European slave-trading power to bar its citizens from participating in the Atlantic slave trade, which it did in 1807. A year later, it set up a naval blockade along the West African coast in an effort to prevent anyone else from trading in slaves. Under considerable pressure from the British to end a still-lucrative slave trade from Angola to its former colony in Brazil, the Portuguese agreed in 1836 to outlaw slave trading across the Atlantic.[3]

In late 1884 and early 1885, representatives of Britain, France, Portugal, Spain, Belgium, and Italy met in Berlin at the invitation of Germany. All the invited parties had banned their citizens from trading in slaves and had outlawed slavery in their colonies, though they generally disregarded its persistence. Germany, the host of the Berlin West Africa Conference, was new to the imperial stage in the mid-1880s, and it took a different approach. Once it established a colonial presence in 1890, it allowed carefully regulated slavery in its colonies to continue. In almost every part of Africa claimed by Europe, Africans, Arabs, Afro-Arabs, and Afro-Europeans continued to trade slaves and to practice slavery. This situation gave the delegates in Berlin the rationale for colonizing. They pledged to end slavery in Africa and to replace it with the civilizing effects of free labor and commerce. Introducing commerce, however, would prove much easier and less costly than ending slavery, especially since commerce demanded labor. Delegates to the 1889–90 Brussels Conference would again take up the pledge to end slavery, with similar "sadly milk and watery" results. Ending slavery was a moral tangent, a sideshow that masked the central reason for the 1884–85 meeting in Berlin—the desire of the participants to clarify their territorial claims and to redraw the map of the African continent in order to best exploit its economic potential.[4]

The Portuguese asserted their right to colonize the African territories where they had first established a presence in the late fifteenth and early sixteenth centuries: Angola, Mozambique, Guinea, and the islands of São Tomé and Príncipe and Cape Verde. The 1885 Berlin Act, however, set a new standard of "effective occupation" for European colonies in Africa. To claim territory, there had to be colonizers on the ground and recognizable administrations. Such a policy favored strong economies and militaries over weak ones. When Portugal nevertheless set out to create a transcontinental empire linking Angola on the west coast with Mozambique in the east—envisioned as a "Rose-Coloured Map"—Britain opposed the move because it would block the equally ambitious British plan to link Cape Town in the south to Cairo in the north. When Portugal then asked Britain's colonial rival, Germany, to support its transcontinental project, Britain issued the 1890 Ultimatum, insisting that Portugal withdraw its forces from central Africa. Weaker strategically than its longtime ally, Portugal withdrew but then spent eighteen months trying to negotiate a more generous settlement before accepting Britain's terms in June 1891.[5]

The 1890 Ultimatum, however, was a turning point in Portugal's foreign policy. Portuguese leaders had little choice but to continue the alliance with Britain; the shift in attitude came in the relationship between Portugal and its colonies. In the Portuguese imagination, both official and entrepreneurial, the country remained if not a great imperial power then an empire that could rise again. In this vision of Portugal, the African empire figured prominently, and British meddling, whether by officials or by businesspeople buying cocoa beans, was greatly resented.[6]

Britain had extensive business interests in Angola and maintained a consulate in Luanda, the colonial capital. In his 1894 report to the British Foreign Office, Consul Clayton Pickersgill described what he considered a slave-labor system practiced on the coffee estates of Cazengo in the north of Portugal's largest African colony. Portugal had outlawed slavery in its colonies in 1858, but like France in Madagascar and Britain in Zanzibar, it struggled with how to legally redefine newly freed slaves and how to compel them to work in a wage economy. In the Portuguese colonies, former slaves, now called *libertos* (freedmen), were obliged to work for twenty years for their masters. The system ended three years early, in 1875, and *serviçais* (singular *serviçal*), literally meaning "servants" in Portuguese, replaced the libertos. In southern Angola, serviçais had their five-year contracts renewed without their knowledge by the local colonial magistrate's consent. Investigating further, Pickersgill traveled north along the West African coast to the equator and the islands of São Tomé and Príncipe, where he found the *"serviçal* system" well entrenched. He was impressed by the good working conditions, but in an 1897 addendum to his earlier report, he quoted a line from a song sung by the contract laborers: "In São Tomé there's a door for going in, but none for going out." As in Angola, contracts were automatically renewed and workers had no mobility; they were effectively slaves. The response from the British Foreign Office was silence.[7]

There were prominent Portuguese critics of labor practices on São Tomé and Príncipe, including Júdice Biker. In the late 1890s, while working for the reform-minded governor-general of Angola, António Ramada Curto, Biker wrote a report on improving the recruitment, payment, and working conditions of African laborers. In a scathing article in the *Revista Portugueza Colónial e Marítima* (Portuguese Colonial and Maritime Review) in December 1897, Biker lambasted a system that brought Angolans from the interior, signed them to five-year contracts to work in São Tomé and Príncipe that they did not understand, subjected them to eleven-and-a-half-hour workdays on coffee and cocoa plantations in a tropical climate where they suffered high death rates, and never gave them the opportunity to return home. Was this, Biker asked, "because the *roceiro* [plantation owner] makes their life so agreeable, dressing them and feeding them so well, instructing them, civilizing them, creating necessities for them? . . . Do they choose to continue to work there, renewing their contracts? . . . Would that this were so." In part, Biker was protesting a system that robbed Angola of labor. On the issue of working conditions on the islands, however, most Portuguese officials—like their British counterparts—chose silence.[8]

In April 1901, troubled by the possibility that the cocoa that went into Cadbury's drinking cocoa and chocolate candy was being produced by slave labor, William Cadbury wrote to William Albright and Joseph Sturge, fellow Quakers active in the Anti-Slavery Society. The context in which Cadbury framed his concerns was revealing: "One looks at these matters in a different light when it affects one's own interests, but I do feel that there is a vast difference between the cultivation of cocoa and gold or diamond mining, and I should be sorry needlessly to injure a cultivation that as far as I can judge provides labour of the very best kind to be found in the tropics: at the same time we should all like to clear our hands of any responsibility for slave traffic in any form." Before he criticized his Portuguese cocoa suppliers, William Cadbury wanted more evidence.[9]

The gold and diamond mines were in what was then the British-occupied South African Republic (the Transvaal) and the British Cape Colony. The Anglo-Boer or South African War had begun in October 1899. The British claimed that the conflict was about restoring the civil rights denied British miners in the gold-rich republic. Residents of the Transvaal, descendants of seventeenth-century Dutch settlers who harbored a deep antipathy to the British, concluded it was all about stealing their gold. George Cadbury, a committed pacifist like all other members of the Society of Friends, publicly opposed the war in the pages of the *Daily News*, the newspaper he had bought for that very purpose—an outspoken position that hardly endeared him to the British Foreign Office. Meanwhile, British-owned mining companies in occupied Transvaal were desperate for labor, and their recruiting practices were sometimes controversial. One of their major sources of workers was the neighboring Portuguese colony of Mozambique. Writing to Albright and Sturge, William Cadbury argued that working conditions in São Tomé were superior to those in the Transvaal mines, but he did note that in both places, "it sounds very much as if the labour was contracted for on the same lines," implying that recruiters had used force to secure workers. Though reluctant to go public without confirmation, Cadbury Brothers Limited would sanction neither slave trading nor slave labor.[10]

The 1902 Foreign Office report on São Tomé and Príncipe, written again by the British consul in Angola, Arthur Nightingale, noted that in 1901, a total of 4,752 contract workers (2,616 men and 2,136 women) had arrived on the islands. Most came from Angola, where they were "ransomed from the black traders who bring them from the far interior." In his public report, Nightingale did not describe conditions either in Angola or on the islands as slavery, nor did he comment on whether workers returned home at the end of their contracts. He did acknowledge the high death rate among serviçais, particularly on Príncipe, which necessitated "constant fresh supplies of labourers." A controversial figure, Nightingale had arrived in Angola in 1898 and at one point managed a plantation of about four hundred workers, where rumor had it he was notorious for his cruelty. Whatever the truth of Nightingale's preconsul days in the colony and despite the reticence of his official report, he pulled no punches in his private correspondence with the Foreign Office: "A repugnant traffic in human beings . . . will not be abolished until some strong influence from outside is brought to bear on the matter."[11]

On January 29, 1903, the Portuguese government issued a royal decree in an attempt to curb the worst abuses of the contract-labor system and, more significantly, to ensure the labor supply for the islands of São Tomé and Príncipe. Five-year contracts were strictly enforced, and 40 percent of a worker's monthly wage was set aside to pay for his or her repatriation. Workers labored nine and a half hours per day, with a half day on Sunday, for a sixty-two-hour workweek. A minimum wage was introduced, with a guaranteed increase of 10 percent at the end of each five-year contract. In a symbolic gesture, twenty-seven Angolan residents—businesspeople and colonial officials among them—were charged with illegal slave trading. Some critics saw the 1903 labor decree as a classic example of the Portuguese strategy of "para o Inglês ver," meaning "for the English to see." In other words, it was "window dressing," and on the ground, little would change.[12]

The Portuguese legation in London went on the offensive in support of the January 1903 decree. Replying to queries from the Anti-Slavery Society about the condition of labor in São Tomé and Príncipe in late February 1903, the Marquis of Soveral conveyed the government's position that "Portugal may justly boast of having completely suppressed the wicked traffic which nowadays only has an existence in the imagination of certain philanthropists." In what would become a standard defense, officials quoted the British colonial diplomat Sir Harry Johnston, who had praised working conditions on the islands. The pragmatic Johnston was a prolific author and a career diplomat who had sidestepped the fierce debate in Britain in the 1860s that portrayed Africans in Portuguese Africa either as completely oppressed or as "savage children" whom "Portugal, or any other white authority, was perfectly justified in dealing harshly with." Johnston had accompanied Lord Mayo on his tour of Portuguese West Africa in 1882. In his pamphlet *De Rebus Africanis* (Concerning African Things), Mayo denounced as slavery the process of recruiting laborers from Catumbela and Benguela in Angola and their shipment to São Tomé and Príncipe. Johnston's assessment was more generous. In a presentation to the Royal Geographical Society in London, he praised the islands' natural beauty; the abundant vegetation and fruit trees; the extensive infrastructure of churches, schools, stores, and hospitals; and the effective system of official apprenticeship introduced following the abolition of slavery in 1875. The islands, Johnston asserted, "might be considered an ideal paradise for the Negroes, and those of S. Thomé might be considered the happiest in the world." Portugeuse officials understandably embraced Johnston's interpretation, twenty-five years out of date though it was, and insisted that the British Anti-Slavery Society's accusation that slavery was still being practiced in São Tomé and Príncipe was "absolutely destitute of foundation."[13]

Portuguese indignation also revealed a fundamentally different interpretation of work. If for the British and especially for the Quaker Cadburys work was intimately linked to notions of the dignity of labor and mobility and the freedom to leave one's job, the focus for the Portuguese was on

FIGURE I. William Adlington Cadbury, c. 1910. By permission of the Cadbury Archives, Kraft Foods, Birmingham, UK, and the William Adlington Cadbury Charitable Trust.

working conditions. Contracted African laborers in São Tomé and Príncipe were housed, fed, and clothed and were paid for their work; their medical needs and emotional health were also attended to. Indeed, as one letter writer to the Lisbon newspaper *O Século* (The Century) would put it, "the servants of São Tomé are much happier than our own peasants."[14]

Still unconvinced, William Cadbury went to Lisbon himself, accompanied by Matthew Stober, a young Afro-Scot attached to the Angola Evangelical Mission who served as his translator. George Cadbury found Stober abrasive and worried about his diplomatic skills. In fact, finding a trustworthy representative of the company who also spoke Portuguese fluently enough to put planters and officials at ease would prove a persistent problem. William Cadbury and Stober stayed at the elegant Hotel Braganza in the city's center. Lisbon must surely have seduced the amateur artist Cadbury. Approached from the Atlantic coast, the city was breathtaking, its streets terraced along the seven hills of the city and its red-roofed houses plastered in white.[15]

As distracting as the city might have proved, Cadbury was in Lisbon on business. Early on the morning of March 17, he went to the offices of Henri Burnay and Company to meet with the English-speaking Baron Carl de Merck, a German who worked for the firm. Henri Burnay was Portugal's most prominent banker in the late 1800s and early 1900s. In 1876, he had saved from bankruptcy the Banco Nacional Ultramarino (National Overseas Bank), which underwrote many colonial ventures. The Burnay Company traded in tropical products, including rubber, cotton, tobacco, and cocoa. Cadbury found Merck charming, a trait that had probably served him well a decade earlier when he had worked with the mining magnate Cecil Rhodes, then premier of the British Cape Colony on the continent's southern tip, to gain control of the Lourenço Marques railway in neighboring Mozambique. By 1895, the Companhia do Nyassa (Nyassa Company) had raised £400,000, but instead of using the money to develop Mozambique's railroads, the company's directors bought European stocks. If William Cadbury was aware of Merck's questionable past, he did not convey it in his letters from Lisbon in 1903. For his part, Merck arranged for Cadbury to meet a handful of the individuals and company representatives who controlled about 80 percent of the cocoa trade from São Tomé and Príncipe.[16]

First on Cadbury and Stober's list was the Count of Vale Flôr, born José Constantino Dias into poverty in northern Portugal in 1855. To Cadbury, Vale Flôr was "a risen man with a kindly face," who "received us with a simple directness and answered all questions with candour." Vale Flôr had gone to São Tomé in 1871 to work as a store clerk. He began farming in 1874 and by 1882 had saved enough to buy the roça Bela Vista, named for its beautiful view. Eventually, he owned more than ten thousand acres and employed forty-seven hundred laborers. When William Cadbury met him in Lisbon, where he lived in luxury on the exclusive Rua Aurea, the onetime poor boy from Murça had a yearly income of £60,000. His wife preferred their apartment in Paris.[17]

Vale Flôr's entry into the titled nobility was remarkable, but the emigrant path he took to achieve it was in some ways typical of Portugal's peasants. At the beginning of the twentieth century, Portugal remained rural; industrial laborers comprised perhaps 10 percent of the population. Urban workers labored twelve to fourteen hours per day, six days a week, for wages so low that one commentator characterized their lot as white slavery.[18]

Most Portuguese workers, however, lived in rural areas. They were peasants, and they could expect to work seventeen to eighteen hours per day, with time off for church services on Sunday. How much access peasants had to their own land depended on the region where they lived. The south was dominated by *latifundia* (large estates). Their owners were usually absentee landlords, often residing in Lisbon. Effectively a rural working class, peasants labored in the "wheat fields and olive groves" for estate owners and sharecropped for themselves. Population density in the arid south was low, and most peasants had no access to landownership.[19]

The experience of the peasantry in the north was different. As in the south, there were rural aristocrats who owned substantial property, but there were also small family farms owned by peasants. Other peasants were tenant farmers or sharecroppers, and some were farmworkers. Then as now, land in the northern region, which produces most of Portugal's wines, was more fertile. Rain was more regular, and population densities were higher. These factors, combined with a centuries-long history of subdividing properties among heirs, have meant that northerners have long emigrated out of necessity. Emigrating, one regional newspaper asserted, rescued the worker from "the misery of slavery." Though there was regular seasonal migration from the north to southern Portugal, Brazil was the destination of choice for most emigrants. Portuguese immigrants to independent Brazil encountered hostility, but labor was scarce and wages were high in comparison to Portugal, allowing some northerners to return home comparatively wealthy.[20]

Decidedly fewer Portuguese went voluntarily to Africa—São Tomé was a penal colony until 1881, and Angola had two thousand white convicts in 1900. Those who emigrated to the islands went as plantation managers, overseers, or clerks, and once they arrived, they found fewer opportunities for social mobility. Indeed, many white workers who went to São Tomé and Príncipe in the late 1800s felt as if they were "orphans of the race." Yet there was an essential distinction between white workers and black workers on the islands. Most white workers could leave, and some of those who stayed did succeed. Among the success stories was José Constantino Dias, the Count of Vale Flôr.[21]

Charmed by Vale Flôr's seeming openness and impressed by his rise from poverty, William Cadbury asked him about the high mortality rate of African workers in São Tomé and Príncipe. The count attributed the situation to the poor physical condition in which many arrived on the islands, and he noted that most returned to good health after they had adjusted to the climate. In other words, it was not that working conditions were harsh; instead, the climate was poor and necessitated a period of "seasoning" for laborers to adapt.[22]

Cadbury next called on Francisco Mantero, second only to Vale Flôr in wealth and influence among the São Tomé cocoa planters. Of Spanish extraction, Mantero was born in Lisbon in 1853, and like Vale Flôr, he went to São Tomé as a young man, though not to work in a store but rather on the coffee plantation of his Spanish uncle, Francisco de Asis Belard. In 1892, in an attempt to encourage investment on the smaller island of Príncipe, the Portuguese government had made trade from the island duty free, and Mantero invested £100,000 to establish the Companhia da Ilha do Príncipe (Principe Island Company). He cofounded a second company, the Sociedade de Agricultura Colonial (Colonial Agriculture Society), on Príncipe, and in 1898, he bought the Água-Izé plantation on São Tomé. His colonial investments grew to include copper mines and coffee plantations in Angola, and coconuts, sisal (used to make rope), cotton, and rubber in Mozambique. Underpinning all these far-flung enterprises was Mantero's need to generate workers for his cocoa estates in São Tomé and Príncipe.[23]

Mantero reminded Cadbury "of some of the old Spaniards I have met on the Trinidad estates—a shrewd colonist with fine features." Where Vale Flôr appeared kind and open, Mantero was forceful. He claimed that in twenty years spent living on both islands, he had never locked the door to either of his houses. He argued that the accusations about labor practices were motivated by jealousy over the productivity of the islands, and he defended the labor reforms of January 29, 1903. He suggested that the reason so few workers went home to Angola was that they wasted their money in the estate stores on alcohol and tobacco, and when given the opportunity to stay on the plantation or return to the oppressive conditions of Angola's interior, they chose São Tomé. Finally, he asserted that the 20 percent mortality rate on Príncipe did not reflect the experience of contract workers but was skewed "by the great mortality among the aborigines who will do no work on the estates but live lives of perpetual orgie and dissoluteness." In other words, part of the problem was that the islands' local (*nativo*) population had not embraced the dignity of labor. Mantero and Vale Flôr encouraged Cadbury to visit the islands to make his own assessment. Both men claimed they had no direct knowledge of how labor was acquired for the islands from the interior of Angola "but were prepared to admit that cruelty probably existed in some cases."[24]

At the Banco Nacional Ultramarino, a very angry A. Mendes da Silva demanded to know why, given the respect with which dead laborers were buried, Cadbury imagined they were not equally well cared for when alive. He too urged Cadbury to inspect São Tomé and Príncipe for himself.

Last on the list of the contacts Merck had given Cadbury was Antonio Ferreira of the Companhia Comercial de Angola (Angola Commercial Company), "the largest trading company in the colony," with major interests in sugar production in the Benguela District. Here, Cadbury encountered what seemed like refreshing honesty. Ferreira admitted that prior to the January 29, 1903, reforms, "the system amounted to slavery because £35 was paid . . . to any chief who would provide a labourer." Under the new regulations, a chief received slightly less than £1, and about £12 went to a labor-recruiting agent to cover the cost of transporting workers to the coast.[25]

If the January 1903 labor laws deprived African chiefs of income and influence and transferred these benefits to Portuguese, Afro-Portuguese, and other European recruiters, William Cadbury was unconcerned. There was little in European colonial efforts in Africa that Cadbury Brothers Limited approved of, but it did support the stated goal of the 1884–85 Berlin West African Conference and the 1889–90 Brussels Conference to end slavery in Africa. If that constrained the power of African chiefs, then it also promised to introduce their subjects to the dignity of free labor, the sort of dignity enjoyed by workers at the Cadbury chocolate factory in Bournville.

Before leaving Lisbon, Cadbury visited Sir Martin Gosselin, the British consul. Gosselin also laid the blame for the rumored Angolan slave trade at the feet of African chiefs, whom he dismissed as "petty kings" who "treated the people as cattle and for liquor or money will readily trade their own people." Yet as a general rule, the chiefs traded their enemies and only sold their own people when they had committed crimes or other offenses that challenged the society's stability. Gosselin also conveniently ignored the question of whether the chiefs would trade anyone in the absence of a demand for their labor. In Cadbury's view, African responsibility was less the issue than the Portuguese obligation as a civilized people to impose order and end the trade.[26]

A meeting with Manuel Gorjão, the Portuguese minister of marine and colonies, was Cadbury's last appointment, arranged for him by Gosselin. Gorjão had just returned to Lisbon from a posting as governor-general of Mozambique. While there, he had struggled to stem the flow of labor across the border to mines in the Transvaal, a British colony since the end of the South African War in 1902. Of West Africa, Gorjão professed little knowledge, except for the allegations that Africans were being forced to collect rubber in the Congo Free State, a large territory claimed by the Belgian king, Leopold II, that stretched from the west coast deep into central Africa. Gorjão doubted that corporal punishment could ever be completely eliminated as a labor practice in Portuguese Africa, but he assured his visitors that he would do his best to punish anyone convicted of cruelty to African workers, as was then happening in Angola thanks to the January 29, 1903, labor reforms.[27]

Cadbury left Lisbon satisfied that "General Gorjão will help us if any Portuguese can," concluding that "no good would come just now of making further complaint." On his return to Bournville in late March 1903, he sent a copy of his correspondence from his Lisbon trip to William Albright and Travers Buxton at the Anti-Slavery Society. Buxton immediately suggested that Cadbury write to Martin Gosselin and recommend that a British consul be posted to São Tomé and Príncipe. Cadbury Brothers Limited, hopeful that the labor controversy would be addressed by Portugal, initially demurred. By May, however, the firm began searching for a private representative to send to Portuguese Africa.[28]

Back in Lisbon, Gosselin was fretting about the diplomatic implications of Cadbury's meetings with prominent cocoa planters and his connections to the Anti-Slavery Society. He would have fretted even more had he known that Cadbury had sought the advice about suitable representatives from H. R. Fox Bourne, the mercurial secretary of the Aborigines' Protection Society (APS). Founded in 1837, the APS shared the Anti-Slavery Society's mission to end slavery, but it also had a broader agenda to protect the rights of indigenous peoples in both British and foreign colonies. Fox Bourne was a thorn in the side of the British Foreign Office; he condemned the contracting of workers for the Transvaal as slave trading and was harsher still in his assessment of the Congo Free State. In June 1902, using the reports by Pickersgill and Nightingale and Consul Roger Casement's report on labor in the Congo Free State, Fox Bourne had written to the Foreign Office to protest the forced recruitment of workers from the Congo basin destined for Angola's coffee estates and roças in São Tomé and Príncipe. Gosselin's fear, conveyed to the Foreign Office, was that the cocoa controversy would "be taken up by the press and Parliament and 'an attempt made to create a feeling against Portugal similar to that aroused against the Congo Free State.'" British South Africa remained dependent on the flow of workers from Portuguese Mozambique, and turning off the spigot was not an option.[29]

In 1903, the treatment of Africans in King Leopold II's Congo Free State was a cause célèbre, with the atrocities reported by the crusading journalist Edmund Morel. The territory was privately owned by Leopold and thus was "free" of oversight by the Belgian government. At the Berlin West Africa Conference, Belgian representatives had persuaded British, French, German, and Portuguese delegates that Leopold's motives were philanthropic, and they pointed to his support of mission schools. By the 1890s, however, large parts of Leopold's African fiefdom had been sold as rubber concessions to European and American speculators and turned into armed camps, where the severing of a worker's hand was just one of the horrific punishments imposed for failing to meet quotas in collecting raw rubber. In the late 1890s, Morel, then a clerk for a Liverpool shipping company, regularly visited Brussels and watched the delivery of cargoes of ivory and rubber from the Congo Free State. The ships returned to Africa filled with armed soldiers and very few trade goods. Morel eventually concluded that slave labor was being used on the concessions in the Congo Free State. In late 1903, he founded the Congo Reform Association to expose the atrocities. Among its supporters—and also a backer of Morel's newspaper, the *African Mail*—was William Cadbury.[30]

Cadbury, Buxton, and Fox Bourne met in June 1903 to discuss possible representatives to send to Africa. The secretaries of the Anti-Slavery Society and the Aborigines' Protection Society suggested three: a big-game hunter who, to his distress, had encountered slave traders in Angola; a Liverpool businessman with extensive interests in West Africa; and Herbert Ward, who had accompanied Henry Morton Stanley to Africa in 1887 and then written a book critical of the adventurer. Stanley, one of the most famous nineteenth-century explorers of Africa, had, with the aid of African guides, "found" the medical missionary Dr. David Livingstone in central Africa. *Through the Dark Continent*, Stanley's chronicle of his voyage down the Congo River, made him infamous for the brutal treatment he meted out both to the Africans working for him and to those he encountered along the way. It was just the sort of brutality that Cadbury hoped was disappearing in Africa, but neither Ward nor four subsequent candidates proved suitable to represent the firm.[31]

In June 1904, William Cadbury wrote again to Lisbon, asking Merck whether the January 1903 Portuguese labor reforms had indeed gone into effect in São Tomé and Príncipe. Merck consulted Vale Flôr and Mantero and several other large plantation owners. They confirmed that although the 1903 regulations had not been implemented, there were so few laborers available that they were exceptionally well treated, better than was any Portuguese worker. They again invited Cadbury to visit São Tomé to see for himself. Cadbury declined the offer, observing without irony, "I am not my own master" because business and family duties meant that he could not leave England for an extended period. He urged Merck to use whatever influence he might have to get the government in Lisbon to enforce the new labor regulations, and he noted that, however well treated laborers on São Tomé's cocoa plantations might have been, if they could not freely leave at the end of their contracts, they were slaves.[32]

Having tried and failed to find a representative who spoke both English and Portuguese and was willing to take an extended trip to Africa on behalf of Cadbury Brothers Limited, William Cadbury finally wrote to Joseph Burtt in July 1904. Cadbury wanted him to spend up to eighteen months traveling in Portuguese West Africa, and he suggested that Gopsill Burtt could take over the building Joseph had been managing. Joseph Burtt spoke French, but he needed to learn Portuguese. Cadbury wanted him to go to the university city of Coimbra, Portugal, where there would be fewer English-speakers and thus less distraction. Instead, Burtt went to Porto in September 1904 to study with Alfredo H. da Silva, a Methodist minister in an overwhelming Catholic country. Silva was of Portuguese, English, and Norwegian descent. How Cadbury came to know Silva is unclear, but the minister was the president of the National Committee of the Young Men's Christian Association (YMCA) in Portugal and had opened its first branch in Porto in 1891 with seventeen members.[33]

Porto was Portugal's second city. It sits north of Lisbon at the mouth of the river Douro along the Atlantic coast. Like Lisbon, it is a port city, though with a difference. The Portuguese people joke that one goes to Coimbra to study, to Porto to work, and to Lisbon *para malandrar*—"to live a scoundrel's life." Porto was about business: exporting wine and importing and distributing manufactured goods, many from Britain. As Burtt entered Porto, he saw the city's terraced streets rising above him, the white-plastered granite buildings giving the city a brilliant sheen on a sunny day. Parks and gardens dotted Porto, and ships of all sorts crowded the shores of the Douro—small steamships, large sailing ships, and numerous barges transporting Douro wines downstream. Like Lisbon, and indeed like parts of Birmingham, Porto was poor. Day laborers and beggars filled the streets, and even though electric lighting and a sewer system had been installed in the late 1800s and early 1900s, transport was still by mule and ox-drawn cart.[34]

In early October 1904, while Burtt studied Portuguese in Porto, Travers Buxton received a visit from Henry Nevinson. Like Edmund Morel, who used the *African Mail* to expose atrocities in the Congo Free State, Nevinson was an activist journalist. He had been an organizer and advocate for the working class in London and a teacher before becoming a noted war correspondent. He covered the 1897 uprising on the island of Crete and reported from Madrid during the Spanish-American War and on the siege of Ladysmith in 1899 and 1900 during the South African War. "One of the most famous journalists of his day," he negotiated a contract in September 1904 with *Harper's Magazine* to write a series of articles about the slave trade in Portuguese West Africa. On October 10, 1904, he wrote to William Cadbury to offer his services and to ask for introductions to planters in Angola and São Tomé.[35]

On the day he received Nevinson's letter, Cadbury was reporting to the firm's board of directors on conditions in São Tomé and Príncipe. He had met with Sir Harry Johnston at the Foreign Office and concluded that no British consul would be appointed to the islands. Johnston had no particular objection to the use of forced labor and thought, in keeping with Vale Flôr and Mantero, that market forces and especially chronic labor shortages would likely eliminate any abuses over time. As Merck, Vale Flôr, and Mantero before him had done, Johnston urged Cadbury either to visit Portuguese West Africa or to send a representative on his behalf. Nevinson, however, was never a serious candidate—and not only because he planned to publish an account of his journey. Cadbury answered his letter politely and gave him the name of A. G. Ceffala, who ran the Eastern Telegraph Company station in São Tomé and whom Cadbury had met in Lisbon. Cadbury doubted Nevinson's seriousness, noting that he spoke no Portuguese, had no contacts in Portugal, and planned a brief tour of just two or three months' duration. To Fox Bourne, Cadbury expressed his concern that Nevinson's "impressions will be all from the surface, and I hope what he publishes will not be of such a sensational character as to injure Joseph Burtt's chance."[36]

Burtt spent eight months studying Portuguese in Porto and acquired a thorough working knowledge though not complete fluency, as he was the first to admit. He enjoyed his time in Porto and made good friends; in April 1905, he confided to William Cadbury, "I don't like the idea of leaving Oporto a bit. I hate leaving people and places. It's a lovely day here, sunshine and shadow like an April day in England but warmer."[37]

As Joseph Burtt prepared to head for São Tomé, Merck sent a very frank assessment of his qualifications to William Cadbury. Merck thought Burtt "an awfully nice fellow and a gentleman" and "quite sweet" but questioned whether he trusted "himself sufficiently to believe in his own judgment." He thought

Burtt's Portuguese good enough; where Burtt seemed "deficient [was] in being altogether quick or sharp enough to grasp any question put before him and to deal with it." In contrast to "Americans who did not know a syllable of the language of the country where they worked and did their task splendidly," he seemed a poor risk. Still, Merck was willing to support him and to provide him "6 or 8 good useful introductions from me to planters, managers, headmen."[38]

Cadbury's reply to Merck was equally frank. Burtt had been chosen because he was "not cut out for a commercial career," because he was straightforward, and because he had no prejudices against the Portuguese; indeed, he had made good friends in Porto. "We believe," Cadbury asserted, that Burtt's "journey will be no less useful because he knows nothing at all about cocoa." Furthermore, Burtt had "no monetary interest in the *result* of his enquiry"—an implied criticism of Henry Nevinson. Finally, Cadbury admitted that Burtt had been the only choice available.[39]

This reply was hardly a ringing endorsement of Burtt's expedition by the man underwriting it, but it captured the contradictions that officials at Cadbury Brothers Limited faced. As Quakers with a strong commitment to humanitarian causes and precepts, including the essential dignity of both labor and the laborer, they would not knowingly buy cocoa that had been produced by slaves. As critics of British colonial policy, they were reluctant to attack Portuguese cocoa planters on São Tomé and Príncipe without sufficient evidence. The directors at Rowntree—which had joined its fellow Quaker chocolate maker Fry in supporting the Cadbury Brothers plan to send a representative—were particularly reluctant to interfere in foreign policy, be it British or Portuguese. As businesspeople, they all sought the finest grade of cocoa possible. William Cadbury was relying on Joseph Burtt's amiability to help him negotiate these contradictions. At the heart of the dispute was the definition of freedom, and mobility was the point where the British and the Portuguese parted company. For William Cadbury and Cadbury Brothers Limited, a worker's right to leave his or her job was fundamental. Without that right, the worker was a slave. Mobility was a right that even the poorest Portuguese peasant did have; indeed, for some, it was an imperative. In the Portuguese view, however, the key factor to consider was working conditions. Where the British saw slavery in Portuguese Africa, the Portuguese saw British ignorance of the dignity of labor in a colonial context. In public and private discourse, the two interpretations seemed to run along parallel tracks. Discovering how they might converge was Joseph Burtt's mission when he sailed for São Tomé and Príncipe at the end of May 1905.[40]

TWO

CHOCOLATE ISLAND

STANDING ON the pier of the Água-Izé plantation on a bright and beautiful morning in June 1905, Joseph Burtt watched twenty men leisurely unload boxes of parts that would become a cocoa-drying machine. Behind him was São Tomé's lush equatorial forest, before him the Atlantic Ocean shining silver with fish. Burtt fell in love with his surroundings, writing to William Cadbury: "As I ride about this wonderful island I dream dreams of what might be with these gentle black people and this fertility, but it is only goodness that could realise them." The gentle black people were at the center of the controversy that had brought Burtt to the islands. Were they *serviçais* (servants)—paid and voluntarily recruited—as the Portuguese maintained? Or did their inability to leave the islands make them slaves? As he watched the men work, his gaze drawn to the sun glinting off the waves, he thought the lives of the laborers "far more agreeable than that of many an English workman."[1]

Burtt's first few days on São Tomé were leisurely. He stayed in the guest quarters at the Eastern Telegraph Company's compound at the invitation of A. G. Ceffala, whom Cadbury had met in Lisbon. A gentle sea breeze cooled the house, curtains around his bed kept out malaria-carrying mosquitoes, and the sound of the surf lulled him to sleep. Though the island sits just north of the equator, the night temperature was in the seventies, pleasantly cool for June. From the rear veranda, palm and banana trees, "with the head of the fruit stalk hanging down like a purple snake," filled the view, and in the distance, he saw the island's low volcanic mountains. Seduced by his surroundings, he spent time butterfly hunting and cataloging the orchids he found growing on coffee trees.[2]

A short walk away—and a study in contrast—was the island's capital, São Tomé City, which was really a small town. Burtt thought it "an awful hole": in the absence of a sewer system, a pervasive stench hung over the city, the water supplied by the Água Grande River was polluted, and housing for Europeans and local São Toméans alike was in a marked state of decay. The wealth of the island lay in its cocoa plantations, and the town's major function was as an administrative center and port. Very little money was invested in public services or infrastructure, in part because taxes and customs duties collected from planters were redirected to less successful colonies and the Portuguese government was unwilling to impose more taxes on the roceiros—the planters—whose productivity had made the islands "the pearls of empire." Colonial officials were also reluctant to upgrade the city for the benefit of local São Toméans for reasons Burtt would soon discover, though not during his courtesy call on the islands' genial governor-general, Francisco de Paula Cid Júnior.[3]

Within three days, Burtt was enthusiastically reporting to Cadbury that he "had met a good man," Paulo Magaltrães, manager of the roça Rio d'Ouro. Its owner was the Count of Vale Flôr, but like most of São Tomé's large planters, the count was an absentee landlord. He maintained homes in Paris and in Lisbon, where William Cadbury had met him in 1903. Magaltrães sent Burtt a large mule and a small boy who carried his luggage and walked behind him as he made his way along a "fine well-kept road with telephone wires running by the side," cocoa trees everywhere, groves of bamboo, and the occasional giant oca, its enormous trunk "buttressed with great flanging roots."[4]

Burtt had met Magaltrães's wife on the boat that had carried them both to São Tomé, and after a two-hour ride, he was ushered into the couple's "desolate looking salon," which Burtt, having spent eight months in Porto, deemed "truly Portuguese in style." After a quick breakfast, the two men took a tour of the roça, and Burtt got his first whiff of fermenting cocoa, an odor only slightly more tolerable than that coming from the serviçais' chicken coops. "These people are like children," Magaltrães told Burtt, adding that "if he made a tidying up clearance of the offending hovels," they would "be very sad." Whatever Burtt might have thought of the explanation just days into his sojourn on São Tomé, he was not going to press his host.[5]

Rio d'Ouro employed fifteen hundred serviçais, or contract workers, and together with another fifteen hundred workers employed on the count's other two roças, they produced fifty thousand sacks of cocoa weighing 128 pounds each per year, for a total of 6.4 million pounds. Both men and women harvested cocoa, cutting the pods from the trees with machetes and then splitting them open. Women extracted the beans from the husks and placed them in baskets that were then emptied into the small iron trucks of the

FIGURE 2. Customs house bridge, São Tomé City, in the early 1900s. By permission of the João Loureiro Postcard Collection.

estate's tramline and delivered first to the fermenting sheds and then to the drying sheds.[6]

The children on the roça occupied themselves collecting the berries dropped by rats—a chronic problem everywhere on the island—after they had eaten the sweet outer husk of the cocoa pod. Singing happily, the children came into the plantation's paved central square carrying five-pound baskets of cocoa beans on their heads and were rewarded for their efforts with biscuits. Burtt was particularly impressed by Magaltrães's rapport with the children, mildly abusive though it appears to have been. After he gave each child a biscuit, the manager "would turn up the little flat faces and clap them with his open hand. Evidently they looked upon this as a sort of religious rite, which though a little trying was highly satisfactory and they would smile and blink their big eyes." After roll call (*forma*), the children and their parents went off to dinner, as did Burtt, who, much to his embarrassment, collapsed into bed early after a long day of watching other people work. He was, he wrote to Cadbury, "well and happy."[7]

Magaltrães, Burtt concluded, would have served Mary Kingsley quite nicely "as a type of an athletic hard working squire." Kingsley, an unmarried Nonconformist at a time when women had few career options, had traveled into the interior of the French Congo and Cameroon in 1893. At one point, the sound of a perfect English accent on the Remboué River prompted her to turn around; she saw "what appeared . . . to be an English gentleman who had from some misfortune gone black all over and lost his trousers and been compelled to replace them with a highly ornamental table-cloth." *Travels in West Africa,* her chronicle of her adventures, proved a sensation when it was published in 1897. Burtt could not replicate Kingsley's wit and talent for irony, but in the descriptions of the places he went and the people he met, he tried to give William Cadbury a sense of what it was like to be an Englishman in São Tomé.[8]

Água-Izé roça took the edge off Burtt's enthusiasm. The most profitable plantation on the island, it had a storied history that captured the complexity of São Toméan society. The Portuguese first encountered the islands of Fernando Po, São Tomé, Príncipe, and Ano Bom as they sailed south along the West African coast in the late fifteenth century. São Tomé rose to prominence with the sugar boom in the 1500s when great swaths of the coastal forest were felled and about a third of the island planted with sugar. After most of the sugar planters relocated to Brazil in the early 1600s, the island became a port in the transatlantic slave trade serving the New World colony. In the two centuries that followed the Portuguese exodus, the descendants of Africans imported to harvest sugarcane emerged as the islands' rulers. The first baron of Água-Izé, José Maria de Sousa e Almeida, was born on the island of Príncipe in 1816 to a Creole mother and a Brazilian father who was a colonel in the island's militia. "Dark-skinned but thoroughly Portuguese in culture," Sousa e Almeida initially traded in slaves in Angola. After the Portuguese abolished the transatlantic trade in 1836, he became governor of the district of Benguela. While living in Lisbon in the 1850s, he secured the leases on several estates in São Tomé that were once owned by religious communities. He set up the roça Água-Izé on the east coast and quickly took advantage of the island's coffee boom, which preceded the boom in cocoa. More trees were cleared to make way for plantations, and eventually, the forest survived only above thirty-five hundred feet, where neither crop flourished.

Sousa e Almeida became the baron of Água-Izé in 1868, the year before he died. His son Manuel da Vera Cruz e Almeida—one of eleven illegitimate children—briefly became the second baron of Água-Izé and then viscount of Malanza after making and subsequently losing his own fortune. Born in 1838 in Benguela, Angola, Cruz e Almeida may have been the son of a slave mother, though his biography describes his mother as a *serviçal,* or servant— one of the terms the Portuguese used to describe newly freed African slaves after 1875. When the first baron died in 1869, his insolvent roça Água-Izé was

FIGURE 3. The first baron of Água Izé. By permission of the João Loureiro Postcard Collection.

purchased by the Banco Nacional Ultramarino, which funded and rescued many colonial ventures. In 1898, the bank sold Água-Izé to the Companhia da Ilha do Príncipe, owned by Francisco Mantero.[9]

Butterfly hunting again at Água-Izé in late June near a railway line where the discarded heaps of the "sweet sticky stuff that covers the beans" attracted insects, Joseph Burtt ran into "an intelligent creole" and "asked him if he liked the place." Inclined as he was to note in his letters when the people he met were black or mulatto (or short and fat, for that matter), Burtt may have been using the narrow definition of *Creole* to describe a European born in the colonies. The man's answer suggested he might have been white: "He said it was necessity not pleasure that kept him here, as to the blacks, they liked the life and did not like it, but he did not seem inclined to explain." Whites, however, were a minority on the island; in 1900, they made up about 3 percent of a population of forty thousand, the great majority of whom were African serviçais. The serviçais were likely the blacks to whom the intelligent Creole was referring. Creoles in the Portuguese colonies were not defined by color but by Portuguese culture, law, language, and religion. The barons of Água-Izé were Creoles, and Burtt's companion might also have been dark-skinned, if not in his own estimation black.[10]

Água-Izé, like Rio d'Ouro, was run by a manager, this one a retired general, Claudino de Sousa e Faro, who oversaw the estate while Francisco Mantero was in Lisbon or visiting his holdings elsewhere in Africa. Something about Água-Izé bothered Burtt, though he could not quite put his finger on it. "The moral atmosphere here seemed different" than that at Rio d'Ouro, and Burtt was not as happy. Unlike the well-maintained road that had taken him to Vale Flôr's roça, the road to Mantero's estate was full of potholes, and Burtt's mule quickly went lame. He hired a fresh horse at a roadside tavern and after a three-hour ride was greeted by the elderly Faro. After lunch in another "large desolate room overlooking the sea," Burtt and the manager took a tour of Água-Izé via the roça's tramline, a narrow-gauge Decauville railway snaking its way along the hillsides, their small car pulled by a team of mules. Though he neglected the road to his estate, Mantero had been an early advocate of railways as an efficient means to traverse the island's rugged terrain and to get cocoa to the coast for transshipment by sea. The large estates would eventually boast hundreds of miles of rail lines, many powered by steam engines. By contrast, in 1905, there were no public railroads on the island. Rail travel was commonplace in Burtt's England, and he did not highlight the significance of this particular business innovation by Mantero

FIGURE 4. Workers at a dependência of Água Izé roça, São Tomé, in the early 1900s. By permission of the João Loureiro Postcard Collection.

and his fellow roçeiros in his letters to Cadbury. After a mere ten days on the island, he was bored: "One gorge is much like another, a stream at the bottom with rocks and bridges and pools and kingfishers, up the sides cocoa and bananas with forest trees rising up from the mass of green below."[11]

Cadbury wanted numbers, and Burtt duly reported them. At the time, 1 million of Água-Izé's cocoa trees were producing; 1.5 million more were expected to reach maturity within two years. In 1904, Mantero's combined estates on São Tomé and Príncipe yielded 4 million pounds of cocoa, and the company paid its investors "12% on the share capital of half a million" pounds sterling. Água-Izé employed 1,668 African workers, and 163 children also lived on the estate. A daily diet of dried fish, rice, beans, bananas, and breadfruit plus meat once a week sustained the laborers. The mortality rate for children was very high (46 had died in 1904) and for adults very low (only 53 had died). Dysentery and anemia were the most commonly reported causes of death and, occasionally, smallpox. Like many other large plantations, Água-Izé maintained its own hospital, and the staff explained the high death rate among children much the same way Francisco Mantero had answered William Cadbury's questions in Lisbon in 1903: it was due to "the unproductiveness of the black races, and their lack of faithfulness to one partner." Angolan contract workers came from polygynous societies, a reality that Portuguese planters tended to condemn as evidence of sexual promiscuity and the cause of laborers' poor health and low productivity. Burtt did encounter hospital patients suffering from syphilis, but that disease affected both black and white workers on the island and was far down a list of illnesses—topped by fever—that reduced workers' productivity.[12]

Charles Hart, the American salesman who had sold Água-Izé its cocoa-drying machine, accompanied Burtt to his next stop, the roça Caridade, set 250 feet above sea level with a dramatic view of the coast. Caridade was owned by a black man, Jerónimo José da Costa, and after the unease he had felt at Água-Izé, Burtt was again charmed. The roça sat in a verdant valley shaded by trees and low mountains and cooled by a fresh breeze. To his surprise, three employees just out from Lisbon had already succumbed to fever—probably malaria—but overall, the death rate among adult workers appeared fairly low. African workers were particularly well fed, with half a pound of meat and slightly more in rice and beans provided per day to fuel eight and a half hours of labor.[13]

Jerónimo da Costa was a *forro*—a free person born in São Tomé and Príncipe—whose ownership of land made him a member of the islands' African elite. A later entry into cocoa cultivation than the first baron of Água-Izé, Costa had owned a shop in a small fishing village on the east coast of São

6. *Taboleiros para secar cacau*

FIGURE 5. Cocoa-drying tables. By permission of the João Loureiro Postcard Collection.

Tomé. In 1895, he clashed with the administrators of Água-Izé, then owned by the Banco Nacional Ultramarino, over the demarcation of property lines and accusations about the theft of plants. By 1905, Costa estimated the value of Caridade roça at £140,000. At Caridade, he invested in new farming techniques, but he also supported a local arts and trade school in the town of São Tomé, and while in Lisbon, he joined the African League, founded to promote the rights of indigenous Africans. His elite status was further reflected in his marriage to a Portuguese woman. Few Portuguese women ventured to the islands during the early period of settlement, though marriages—formal and informal—between African women and Portuguese men were not uncommon. The reverse was much rarer and may have prompted Burtt to note in his letters to Cadbury that he breakfasted with Hart, Costa, "his Portuguese wife and his little mulatto boy."[14]

Though much smaller than Vale Flôr's estate of ten thousand acres and less productive than Mantero's, with its yearly yield of 4 million pounds of cocoa, Costa's operation was substantial by local standards. In the early 1880s, about half of the island's coffee and 60 percent of its cocoa had been produced by African small farmers. By the early 1900s, the farmers' share of exports had dropped to about 6 percent as large entrepreneurs displaced smallholders—often by legal purchases but sometimes violently—and also claimed large stretches of forest to which no one had previously held title. Costa employed three hundred serviçais, whose death rate was about 4.6 percent a year. The death rate for the hundred or so children was slightly higher, 7 percent, but considerably lower than the 28 percent at Água-Izé. Of Caridade's approximately 2,500 acres, 1,730 were planted, and Costa expected a yield of 16,000 arrobas. One arroba equaled 32 pounds and in 1905 netted a market price of 14 shillings. On 528,000 pounds of cocoa, less costs of £5,000, Costa expected a profit for the year of approximately £6,000. Demonstrating the naiveté that had worried Carl de Merck, Burtt was so enchanted by the roça Caridade and its owner that he thought it an ideal purchase for Cadbury Brothers Limited, a prospect the company had declined to consider in 1901 and would not consider in 1905.[15]

At the nearby Bom Reteiro roça, another black planter impressed Burtt even more. Intelligent and agreeable, Manuel Quaresma Dias da Graça employed two hundred serviçais. Like Costa, Graça was a forro, though his family name suggested a status at the top of the forro class. He may well have called himself a *filho da terra* (son of the land), claimed descent from the original late fifteenth-century Portuguese and African settlers, and asserted

MAP 1. Joseph Burtt's map of São Tomé, 1905. In "Copy of Letters Received from Joseph Burtt," following p. 103, James Duffy Collection, African Collection, Yale University, New Haven, Conn.

FIGURE 6. Two São Toméan women. By permission of the João Loureiro Postcard Collection.

S. Tomé – Duas nativas.

that his ancestors had always been free. Portuguese planters, however, generally ignored the distinction between filhos da terra and forros, and Burtt appears to have been unaware of the difference.[16]

Bom Reteiro was well run. Fifty children under fifteen lived on Graça's estate, and pregnant women received both prenatal and postnatal care. Only four workers had died during the previous year. Graça had a son attending university in Lisbon and was particularly attentive to the price of cocoa: at nine thousand reis an arroba, he told Burtt, he could afford a top hat; but the drop to thirty-five hundred reis meant he wore a cap. The fluctuating price of cocoa threatened the profits of large and small planters alike. Beginning in the late 1890s and continuing for a decade, Henri Burnay and the Count of Vale Flôr were among the large planters who tried to stabilize profits by buying and storing cocoa beans in Lisbon, where they had an unfortunate tendency to spoil. That their scheme was largely unsuccessful was evident in Graça's choice of a cap in 1905.[17]

The accomplished and dignified Costa and Graça stood in marked contrast to another forro Burtt met. Out on a walk with Joaquim Gaspar Rodrigues, the acting manager of the Boa Entrada roça, Burtt "came to a small property where a black man opened the door of the yard to us and shook hands." Burtt complained to Cadbury: "This indolent, untidy, drinking S. Thomeite" owned approximately 125 acres "of land in this best cocoa district, but will not sell. He keeps a few serviçais and is content to get a trifle from a property worth £6,000 and that might yield 3,000 arrobas a year and perhaps £1,000 clear profit." The man's laziness offended Burtt as much as, if not more than, his taste for drink. "Father, mother, and son are at the door, a curious family group, the boy looks bright, intelligent and free," and, to his apparent surprise, Burtt reported that "they speak to us as equals"—an odd observation from a man who had so recently rejected materialism and flirted with the idea of a classless society while a colonist at Whiteway.[18]

The indolent São Toméan prompted Burtt to ponder "the influence the possession of land has on character, it is a key to wealth and power whether a man uses it or not." As he and Rodrigues strolled through the groves of cocoa trees, he wondered "if it would be possible to civilise the black through ownership of land." Ignoring the black planters who had so impressed him, he decided it would not: the average black "would only make a bare subsistence and drink and loaf and finally be trampled out by the stronger white." Burtt's prejudices were hardly unique in the early 1900s, and the reality was that small African farmers had been trampled during São Tomé's coffee and cocoa booms, finding themselves gradually pushed out by larger proprietors, some of whom were black but most of whom, by the end of the nineteenth century, were white. By the early 1900s, Costa and Graça were a minority. Burtt was less optimistic about the rest of the islands' black population: "The only chance I can see for the black to keep a place in the world is for him to acquire the habit of regular work."[19]

Still, Burtt's use of the word *black* could be confusing. Costa, Graça, and their lazy counterpart were black, São Toméan, and forros. Yet for Burtt, the achievements of the larger landowners put them in a different class and gave them "a place in the world." Also black were the serviçais, Africans transported from Angola to labor on the roças of Vale Flôr, Mantero, Costa, and

Graça. To distinguish themselves from these imported workers and to assert their own status, the forros refused to do physical labor or even clerical work on the roças, which infuriated Mantero and led him to assert: "There does not exist among the unprogressive natives the necessity to work to clothe or feed themselves; apart from this a poorly conceived pride prevents them undertaking wage labour because they repute this form of work as too humble for persons of their social category." In other words, the forros were not black in the way the serviçais were black, nor were they *nativos* in the way that the serviçais were "natives." *Nativo*, a word the forros also used to describe themselves, translated literally as "native," but in the context of São Tomé and Príncipe, it meant "indigenous to the islands." It referred not only to the era of the original fifteenth-century settlers but also to the two-century period from the early 1600s through the early 1800s when most Portuguese had left and the islands and islanders underwent a period of re-Africanization, albeit with a Portuguese overlay. Burtt was clearly aware of this distinction between *native* and *nativo*. He had little trouble conversing in Portuguese with the forros but found "the gulf between an English visitor and the serviçaes," most of whom spoke only a few words of Portuguese, "very wide."[20]

In his easy use of other common terms to describe Africans and black people—*darkies, niggers,* and even *natives,* used widely and interchangeably by European colonizers in Africa and Asia—Burtt seemed oblivious to the injurious and discriminatory weight of such words. For instance, he complained in one letter to Cadbury that, courtesy of African porters, his "bag was blackened with niggers' heads." Like Mary Kingsley, Joseph Burtt had little doubt that whites were superior and that the terms *black, African, darkie, nigger,* and *native* were synonyms. In the case of Costa and Graça, however, commercial success had trumped color, whereas the indolent São Toméan smallholder, drinking and loafing on his 125 acres, remained black. Although Burtt's elevation of Costa and Graça put him at odds with many Portuguese estate owners who favored the demise of all the landed forros, his broader racism placed him firmly in the orbit of the planters' worldview.[21]

Henrique José Monteiro de Mendonça, owner of São Tomé's model plantation Boa Entrada, had, in Burtt's opinion, properly embraced the European obligation to civilize and protect the African worker. A member of the Geographical Society of Lisbon and a leading agriculturalist, Mendonça had wide-ranging business interests that included textiles and diamonds in addition to cocoa, and he served on the boards of the Burnay Bank, the Banco Nacional Ultramarino, and Francisco Mantero's Companhia da Ilha

FIGURE 7. Angolan serviçal couple, São Tomé, c. 1907. (Editor: José Teixeira Barbosa, Bazar Africano, S. Tomé.) By permission of the João Loureiro Postcard Collection.

do Príncipe. His public service included work for the Museu de Arte Antiga (Museum of Historic Art), one of Lisbon's premier art museums, and a variety of relief organizations for victims of natural disasters. Boa Entrada dated from the 1880s, and Mendonça acquired its forty-two hundred acres through marriage to the founder's daughter. He began upgrading it in the early 1900s, eventually building a hospital, a children's nursery school, a primary school, and a music school.[22]

Joseph Burtt saw many of these improvements when he visited in July 1905. A carriage ride along a well-kept road delivered him into "the large open square of the roça," where everything was "advanced and up to date; the houses of the serviçaes [were] built of brick," with each family allotted an apartment. The new hospital had thirty-six beds, and there was a separate ward for infectious cases. On the far side of the square were stables for the mules and horses and a cocoa-drying shed. In the center was "a large shallow cemented pool of running water with an electric lamp near." Electricity was generated by a water turbine, and the walls of the pool were serrated for washing clothes.[23]

Boa Entrada also boasted a little over ten miles of Decauville narrow-gauge railway lines used to move cocoa around the estate and down to the pier to load aboard ship. The railway lines sat in the middle of six-yard-wide roads cut through the forest to allow room for mules to pull the small open cars and workers to walk alongside. The open cars were also used to take visitors up to the main house; a hand brake in each car controlled the speed back down the gentle incline. Boa Entrada had the added advantage of being only five miles from the capital, and cocoa could also be shipped by road, an option that was not available to many of the roças hemmed in by the island's rough terrain.[24]

Burtt's companion on his carriage ride was Henry Nevinson, who had completed his six-month tour of Angola for *Harper's Magazine* and arrived in São Tomé on June 17, shortly after Burtt. He stayed in the staff quarters opposite the telegraph station house, and Burtt saw little of him. Burtt nevertheless made an impression on Nevinson, who described him in his diary as "a big, innocent-looking man" with too "much luggage." Nevinson also recorded Charles Hart's assertion that "the planters had ordered everything to be carefully arranged for his visits." Nevinson left for Príncipe on June 21, returning to São Tomé five days later after a rough boat trip delayed by bad weather. He and Burtt did find time for a long talk "about the state of things," and Burtt reported to Cadbury that Nevinson admitted "that the

FIGURE 8. Model housing for workers, Boa Entrada roça. By permission of the João Loureiro Postcard Collection.

people on the roças seem comfortable" though he disliked how much power the planters had. Nevinson recalled their talk, as they walked along the coast to a fishing village, rather differently. Burtt, he concluded, was "about the youngest man of 43 that could live—the mind of a youth, confused and interesting and full of dreams and theories." Burtt's time at the communist Whiteway Colony had apparently left him "despising the working man" and convinced that the "slave system" on São Tomé was good for Africans. "All very crude and youthful stuff," the forty-nine-year-old Nevinson thought, "full of contradictions and very astonishing." On a whim and despite his misgivings, he joined Burtt on his visit to Boa Entrada on June 29. He would leave São Tomé just two days later, on July 1. Worn out from his long Angolan sojourn and always sensitive to injustice, Nevinson could not have enjoyed his carriage ride to Boa Entrada, since the bad-tempered Portuguese driver used his whip indiscriminately on the mules, on a black man trying to direct him, and on the dogs they passed along the way. Burtt repeated stories he had heard about Brazil from Ceffala at the telegraph station—of a planter finding his wife with her black lover, killing the man, cooking him, and then feeding him to his wife, who was "chained up . . . in a barn . . . till she died." Nevinson found it all very wearing.[25]

FIGURE 9. Henry Woodd Nevinson in 1901. Photograph in *Changes and Chances* (New York: Harcourt, Brace, 1923), facing p. 344.

At Boa Entrada, José António Salvado Matta, the roça's doctor, joined Burtt, Nevinson, and the manager, Joaquim Rodrigues, for a late breakfast in the estate's garden. Burtt captured the irony of the moment in his letter to Cadbury, noting that they smiled "over lobster salad at the hardships of African travel." Nevinson recorded the "weeping brie" served by the French-speaking manager, the beautiful woodwork adorning the main house, and a tour that included "giant cotton trees and other uninteresting sights."[26]

Harsh news accompanied the good food. Matta pegged the annual death rate at 12 percent; 143 African laborers had died between July 1903 and July 1905, when the workforce varied between 542 and 600. Two Europeans also died—one of anuric fever and the other of malaria—and here, the doctor made the distinction between Boa Entrada's long-term white employees and its transitory white workers. The former, he reported, were well fed, paid attention to hygiene, and followed the doctor's advice when ill. In the view of the latter group, by contrast, "no doctor is any good who prescribes them quinine, and the worst employer is he who does not give them at least a litre of wine at each meal." These people tended to eat badly, preferring "half a dozen green mangos and big draught of bad wine" to the "excellent table" available to them. When ill, they took purgatives and avoided the doctor. Matta did not think Boa Entrada was particularly healthy for Europeans. It was situated in the low-lying and swampier region of the island, five miles inland and without the benefit of the prevailing winds from the south. "The low elevation, the luxuriance of the vegetation, and the sheltered position" all contributed to the heat and humidity of the roça. These factors did not, however, explain the deaths of the two transitory European workers. Such laborers, the doctor said, were "birds of passage—who despise everything connected with hygiene and cleanliness, and never stay longer than a month on any estate." Matta did not think that Boa Entrada deserved the bad reputation it had among European workers.[27]

The great majority of Portuguese workers on the islands were poor migrants, most of them illiterate. Although few white workers on São Tomé and Príncipe rose from poverty as dramatically as the Count of Vale Flôr had, they were nevertheless distinct from black serviçais. For peasants in Portugal and for African contract workers on the islands, to work meant to do hard physical labor for low wages, often in dirty and dangerous conditions. "Agricultural work" was "performed with the body bent forward; most of the time too, the eyes have to be fixed on the ground. . . . A man's independence is vertical, a man's serfdom makes him bend." Overseeing black workers allowed many poor Portuguese on the islands to stand upright, but it did not necessarily spare them the prejudice of wealthier and better-educated whites.[28]

Boa Entrada's location and climate also made it unhealthy for black workers, but Matta noted that what Mendonça had "done for the native establishments is great, and he is still doing more." Despite solid brick houses and a good hospital, serviçais routinely died of anemia, pneumonia, dysentery, and diarrhea. Special care for children and pregnant women and a policy that matched workload to the "strength and capacity of each hand" made no dent in the death rate. Nevinson recorded a death rate of 25 percent for Boa Entrada's children. Twenty-seven of the 143 adult deaths between 1903 and 1905 were undiagnosed, a further 5 were attributed to "general progressive debility," and 2 were described as "sudden death." In Matta's opinion, two self-induced illnesses greatly contributed to the death rate: alcoholism and geophagy, or dirt eating.[29]

Virtually every African worker on Boa Entrada was an alcoholic in Matta's estimate, and the resulting intestinal inflammation made dysentery and anemia that much deadlier. Palm wine was readily available: serviçais would "make a hole in the top of a palm tree and fix a calabash to it," collecting the fermented wine the next day. The doctor also blamed the much-maligned forros for supplying serviçais with the locally produced brandy, *aguardente,* for which they were willing to trade all their rations. What Matta did not acknowledge was that the islands were also a major market for Portugal's wine industry. The Portuguese took advantage of a loophole in the 1899 Brussels Convention that limited colonial imports of alcoholic beverages to those with 23 percent or less alcohol by volume. In the early 1900s, 1 million gallons of wine per year were imported, or 2 gallons per month for every man, woman, and child on the islands. Boa Entrada's roça store sold workers soap, cloth, tobacco, candles, matches, and Portuguese brandy and wine. The wine purportedly was meant to help wean workers off the more potent local brew, but the real advantage went to wine producers in Portugal. Father Rooney, an Irish Catholic priest attached to the Angolan mission whom both Cadbury and Burtt had consulted in Lisbon, went so far as to portray wine as a civilizing tool along with clothing and better food "because work is necessary to obtain these things." But Boa Entrada's manager, Rodrigues, observed to Burtt that alcoholism reduced productivity on the roça, and Matta, even as he ignored the Portuguese wine trade, considered alcoholism "one of the first causes of mortality in S. Thomé." Though Burtt wondered aloud if sadness or depression contributed to the death rate, none of the men breakfasting on lobster salad seemed to see alcohol as a way for the serviçais to figuratively, if not literally, escape their confinement.[30]

Geophagy, which occurred on many plantations, was another matter. Matta did not think the habit was an attempt to redress mineral deficiencies in the serviçais' diets, nor was it a symptom of a physical or psychological illness as it was in Europeans. In his view, it was a way for African laborers to avoid working. A few days' rest in the hospital cured the effects of eating dirt but not the desire to do it, and though serviçais were watched carefully, they often ended up back in the hospital. In Matta's opinion, "one of the highest pleasures open to the black is to trick the white." In other words, whereas alcoholism was a human weakness shared by whites and blacks, dirt eating was a form of resistance distinctive to blacks.[31]

Other forms of resistance were also common on the islands and called into question how content the serviçais actually were. Matta's statistics for Boa Entrada included two suicides, for which he offered no explanation. One homicide also went unexplained, though the motives for murder could be

Roça Agua Izé - Interior de um dos Hospitaes

FIGURE 10. Hospital on Água Izé roça. By permission of the João Loureiro Postcard Collection.

prosaic—a serviçal on the Mont'estoril roça, for example, was murdered when he surprised a local São Toméan farmer stealing pigs. Plantation managers routinely complained to the island's magistrates about lazy, disrespectful, drunken, or absent workers; about the sabotage of equipment; and about theft. The most obvious form of resistance was running away. When slavery was abolished in 1875, six thousand libertos walked to the capital and successfully demanded fair wages and the right to work on a roça of their own choosing. While this mass action proved successful, most workers ran away individually or in small groups. In 1899, the Água-Izé roça lost 10 percent of its workers. In the early 1900s, an average of eight serviçais ran away annually from the São Miguel roça, run by the Companhia Agricola de S. Thomé (S. Thomé Agricultural Company) and owned in part by the Burnay Bank. Running was risky, and fugitives were usually caught; those who did find sanctuary in the forest discovered that there was little to eat besides pigeons and rats. Runaways who survived often stole from the roças and gave managers the justification for tracking and recapturing fugitives. Still, Burtt met only one manager who feared an outright revolt by black workers—and that he attributed to Mario Ferreira Lopes Duarte's recent appointment as manager of the roça São Miguel and his lack of experience on the island.[32]

Morning and evening roll calls were one way plantation owners and managers tried to keep track of their workers, if not necessarily prevent them from running away. The more formas Burtt watched, the more he found them tedious and a little depressing, a sentiment many workers likely shared. Workers did have recourse to the legal system and to an ombudsman, the *curador geral do serviçais* (general curator of servants). Sometimes, the workers refused to renew their contracts, a process the curador oversaw. The problem, as Burtt reported to Cadbury, was that even though workers had the technical right to complain to colonial officials, they needed permission to leave the roça to do it. If serviçais did make it into town, they discovered that the planters were more powerful than the colonial administrators and that laborers who complained were punished for "disobedience" back on the roça. Even those officials willing to listen had trouble doing so in the absence of interpreters who could speak the languages of the Angolan serviçais, many of whom were Ngangela or Wiko. At Boa Entrada, Rodrigues, who had a decent command of several African languages, dealt with complaints on the spot. One evening, a black worker protested that a white overseer had denied him his rations when he had turned up late for roll call. Rodrigues promptly summoned the white and reprimanded him, noting that "a man must eat to work," and sent the black worker to the roça's kitchen to collect his dinner. Other efforts to assert labor control included maintaining roça shops, which swallowed up laborers' wages and thereby prevented them from sneaking off to local bars; rewarding good work with bonuses; and holding regular dances, though Burtt found "the native dance very ugly even with merry children."[33]

Religion was rarely used as a form of control on the roças. Most local São Toméans were practicing Catholics (though few observed the sacrament of monogamous marriage), but the vast majority of serviçais were not Christians. São Toméans did not favor the conversion of contract workers, since being Catholic was a mark of status and another way that forros distinguished themselves from serviçais. Planters nevertheless had a legal obligation to teach their workers about the faith. Roceiros built chapels on their estates but made little effort to convert workers, concerned in part that evangelization would raise workers' consciousness and increase their dissatisfaction with roça life. Burtt encountered only one roça, Monte Café, that held a weekly mass for workers. The largest estate on the island, it was owned by the elderly Claudina de Freitas Chamico, who, like most other owners, lived in Lisbon, where she directed her profits to charity, including the building of a hospital. At the roça Santa Margarida, owned by Francisco Mantero, a

Catholic priest presided over funerals and baptized children but did not conduct marriages because serviçais, in the manager's view, had "no idea of the meaning of marriage as we understand it."[34]

Other owners did seek to control their workers by allowing them to marry. Married serviçais often lived together and thereby acquired a degree of autonomy and personal space. Nonetheless, power remained in planters' hands, since they retained the option of separating husbands and wives and parents and children. On Boa Entrada, Rodrigues registered marriages sealed by "verbal contract," and discouraged the dissolution of the unions except when domestic violence was the cause. Formal marriage, however, was a relative rarity on São Tomé and generally entered into only by high-status forros: only sixty-four church marriages took place between 1885 and 1895.[35]

The opportunity for contract workers to marry or to form a stable relationship was also limited by the shortage of women on the islands. In 1901, 2,616 male and 2,136 female serviçais arrived, and on average, approximately 55 percent of Angolan laborers in the early 1900s were male. Women were often able to exploit the imbalance, trading sexual favors for household goods and for money (they earned only eighteen hundred reis per month whereas male workers earned twenty-five hundred). Portuguese planters and colonial officials may have regarded the exchange as prostitution, but they generally turned a blind eye to it. The shortage of women explained the low number of children born on the islands, but female serviçais also practiced abortion. Avelino Arlindo da Patena, the manager at the Uba Budo roça, thought that one reason women objected "to bearing children is the continency it entails." Like many middle-class Catholic Portuguese and indeed like the Quaker Englishman Joseph Burtt, Patena was culturally conservative, uncomfortable with African sexuality, and prone to stereotype it. The idea that women might have been protesting their effective confinement by controlling their fertility did not occur to him. He acknowledged that "the natives on the island like a large family"—since children were "a source of wealth and care and protection in old age," just as they were for Africans on the mainland—but he added that on a "roça where the necessaries of life are provided these considerations have little weight" and that women serviçais thus preferred not to have children. As with all generalizations, there were exceptions. Monte Café had 330 men, 303 women, and 215 children living on the estate, and the Porto Alegre roça on São Tomé's southern tip, owned by a consortium of Portuguese and Belgian investors including Henri Burnay, boasted 257 children below the age of six out of a serviçal population of

1,093. Women got "two months' rest from regular work" after the birth of a child. There was a dark side to fertility; the *tongas*, as the children born to serviçais were called, were automatically contracted to the roça's owner.[36]

More complicated were the relationships that African women entered into with Portuguese men. The women were almost always São Toméan; indeed, colonial law prohibited sexual intercourse between white employees and African serviçais. (Such interracial sex was nevertheless commonplace.) São Toméan women spoke Portuguese and were at least nominally Catholic and familiar to European men in a way that the non-Portuguese-speaking Angolan women were not. In the absence of European women, a Portuguese man would hire a *lavadeira*, a local washerwoman, who, in addition to cleaning his clothes, cared for him when he had malaria and often bore him children. The man would usually acknowledge the children as his own and, if he had the means, pay for their education.[37]

Burtt encountered two examples of these special relationships between Portuguese men and African women. Felsirano da Cunha Lonseiro managed the four-square-mile Pinheiro roça for a black São Toméan, João Macedo. "A short man with full muscular shoulders, a bullet shaped head, dark beady eyes, and a moustache . . . elegantly dressed in a white linen suit . . . and white canvas shoes," Lonseiro, in Burtt's view, was dedicated but limited. His face "gave no key to anything but vitality and was almost as expressionless as that of a bird, without a single line of thought or suffering. Not a bad man, hardly a good man and a southerner down to his small feet." In other words, Burtt found the manager rather boring and liked him best when he was playing music or with his "little black daughter, mulatto really, but she looked very black." Burtt did not meet the child's mother.[38]

Though formal liaisons between Portuguese managers and female African serviçais were uncommon, Francisco d'Olevares Marin's relationship with his black female servants did pique Burtt's curiosity. A nephew of Francisco Mantero, Marin managed the roça Ponta Furada, halfway up São Tomé's west coast. He had lived on the islands for twenty-two years, including three on Príncipe, and had worked on several roças. A talented linguist, he spoke several Angolan languages and the Portuguese dialects of São Tomé and Príncipe, as well as Spanish, Portuguese, French, German, and quite good English. Ponta Furada was in a particularly hilly area of the island, with a clear view of its tallest mountain, the peak of São Tomé. Burtt spent a week at the roça, and one evening, after a vigorous day of hiking, he returned to a dinner attended by "silent black waitresses with gold beads round their brown necks." He described to Cadbury "one sweet faced child who used to stand with folded arms. I wonder what she thought and half envy her having such a supreme being as Marin to wait on, a man whose word is law in her little world, who possesses unknown power and wealth, giving gold necklaces to whom he will, and speaking strange tongues." Burtt did not suggest that Marin expected any favors in return for his gifts of gold necklaces, though one imagines few managers gave their servants jewelry.[39]

Cape Verdean women were the other group to whom Portuguese men turned. The ten Cape Verde Islands sit off the northwest coast of Africa. The Portuguese first settled the archipelago in 1462; its strategic mid-Atlantic location made it an ideal rest stop for Portuguese ships. The islands did not go through the period of re-Africanization experienced by São Tomé and Príncipe after the early seventeenth-century exodus of European planters. Rather, the long-standing Portuguese presence and the ongoing relationship afforded Cape Verdeans a special status within the empire. The archipelago, however, is at the same latitude as the Sahara Desert and is subject to severe periodic drought and accompanying famine. In 1903 and 1904, sixteen thousand Cape Verdeans died of hunger during a prolonged drought, and another five thousand sought work on São Tomé's cocoa plantations. Instead of the five-year contracts offered to Angolans, Cape Verdeans received one- or two-year contracts, with men earning 3,000 reis per month, 500 more than was paid to Angolan men. Women earned 2,500 reis per month, 700 above the female minimum wage.[40]

About 35 percent of the Cape Verdeans were women, many of whom had accompanied their husbands and children but some of whom had arrived alone. On the roça Pinheira, Burtt encountered "one fine pleasant looking woman working in a shed with her light skinned baby." He had learned that "a white wished to make her his housekeeper, but though it would of course have been a move up in comfort for her, she preferred to remain faithful to her husband in Cape Verde." Assaults were not unknown, but forced sexual encounters were generally not tolerated. Cape Verdean women also resisted advances from lower-status African men. "I so wonder what brought that woman over here," Burtt wrote to Cadbury, "probably poverty, I hear they are very poor in the islands and require assistance from Lisbon." William Cadbury could only have been disappointed by his investigator's reticence. The woman spoke Portuguese, and given a golden opportunity to ask about her experience as a serviçal, Burtt remained silent, apparently tongue-tied by her beauty.[41]

If Burtt missed the implicit violence that accompanied a black woman's decision to become a washerwoman or a housekeeper to a white manager,

FIGURE II. Cape Verdean workers on Príncipe, c.1907. (Editor: José Teixeira Barbosa, Bazar Africano, S. Tomé.) By permission of the João Loureiro Postcard Collection.

he did note the more obvious demonstrations of violence. At the roça Santa Margarida, owned by Francisco Mantero's other large holding company, the Sociedade de Agricultura Colonial, he met Joaquim Mantero, "a smart looking young Spaniard," and the roça's manager, José Mantero, "a quiet pleasant man of the lower middle class." Located more than one thousand feet above sea level, the roça had a very low mortality rate of only 1 percent among its 201 men, 134 women, and 46 children. The hospital was clean and well maintained; the workday was eight hours long; and the rations of rice, dried fish, palm oil, salted American beef, and beans—which Burtt tried—were ample. Life on the roça was nevertheless tedious, both for black workers and for white managers and visitors. Joaquim Mantero accompanied Burtt on his visits to *dependências*—the small substations maintained by many sprawling roças—and to neighboring estates. The rest of his time Mantero spent riding and hunting. Burtt had no aversion to guns or to hunting, and despite his affiliation with the Croydon Brotherhood Church, he was no vegetarian. Still, he found it disturbing to watch a bored Mantero, having failed to hit any pigeons from the balcony of Santa Margarida's main house, take aim at a small goat in the courtyard and shoot it "in the foot. It was an ugly sight to see the poor little beast shake its wounded limb; happily the next shot hit it in the breast. The mother seemed much puzzled at the odd behaviour of her kid."[42]

Although it is tempting to posit that idle violence directed at animals translated into violence against African workers, owners like Vale Flôr and Francisco Mantero insisted that it was simply poor business to abuse a labor force in such chronically short supply that owners attempted—with limited success—to recruit workers from China and India. Nonetheless, like most absentee landlords, Mantero could exercise only limited influence over his managers, even those to whom he was related, such as his cousin José and his nephew Joaquim. In April 1905, following a confrontation, Joaquim Mantero had locked fifteen serviçais in their quarters to punish them for insubordination, and then, finding them impossible to control, he sent them to another Mantero property on neighboring Príncipe. Given the much higher death rate on that island, largely due to endemic sleeping sickness, it was a harsh punishment indeed.

Burtt thought Santa Margarida's manager, José Mantero, uneducated and uninteresting, though "good hearted and practical . . . knowing his people, beating them at times severely for serious faults." Below the level of managers, white foremen and overseers routinely kicked and punched and occasionally whipped serviçais. Particularly unruly workers were struck on the palm of the hand with the aptly named *palmatória*, a heavy piece of wood resembling a large, flat wooden spoon. Formal punishments took place at the evening roll call in front of other workers, both to humiliate the offender and to set an example. All these practices were illegal; punishment technically fell under the jurisdiction of the curador, who was also charged with protecting workers' rights. The curador traveled widely across the island, visiting roças to inspect conditions and to oversee the recontracting of serviçais, but one man, even assisted by clerks, could not effectively attend to forty thousand workers. Everywhere in the Portuguese Empire, colonial officials and civil servants were thin on the ground and planters exercised a good deal of latitude. If they were lucky, they had a manager like José Mantero, who kept "an anxious eye on the death rate" even as he beat his workers.[43]

Despite his misgivings at Santa Margarida roça, Burtt decided that "from a merely material standpoint I imagine the lot of the serviçais is, to them, one of comfort." Moving away from his initial impression that serviçais had an advantage over English workers, he ultimately concluded that their existence "would be a miserable one to a European." His own linguistic shortcomings hampered his ability to speak directly with serviçais and learn what they were thinking. He did not speak any of the African languages of Angola, and by his own admission, he got "on much better with Portuguese when my host is a man of education." Yet these limitations did not stop him from imagining what workers were thinking or assessing the characters of the people he met. At the Benda roça, manager José Joaquim Fontes struck Burtt as "a young, stout, fresh coloured man, troubled with neither brains nor ambition but not lacking in sound sense, and the type of man to make his people very comfortable." The roça was clean and orderly, the technology advanced: zinc hot-air pipes beneath large slate slabs dried cocoa beans on a thirty-six-hour cycle. Most important, "the servicais [were] fat and well" and the death rate low.[44]

Fatness and contentment went hand in hand in many of Burtt's descriptions. Handsome and square-jawed with wavy brown hair and a mustache, he was tall, lean, and athletic. In the early twentieth century, however, being fat demonstrated that one had more than enough to eat, and Burtt took pains to assure Cadbury that the serviçais looked plump. One July morning in São Tomé City's central square, he encountered a "healthy comfortable looking woman . . . sitting a few yards from me. . . . She wore a white cotton handkerchief with red spots on her head . . . a red and white jersey and striped blue and white cotton cloth round her waist," and she smiled when she saw Burtt watching her. Beside her sat a two-year-old baby with "a big stomach, and head, and thin arms and legs like most of these children," signs of malnutrition that he mistook for healthy fatness.[45]

The woman and her toddler had disembarked with two to three hundred other contract workers from Angola that morning. All wore sweaters or jerseys and cloths around their waists issued to them aboard ship, and around their necks a small tin plate on a string with their contract number stamped on it. About twenty of the women had babies tied to their backs with cloth, and when Burtt helped one young woman up on the pier, he noticed "that her arm was hot as with a touch of fever." Still, he saw "no traces of illtreatment nor signs of fear"; indeed, "some smiled as they floundered on to the pier." Nevertheless, he found the whole scene distressing. As he made his way back along the beach to his lodgings at the telegraph station, he found himself "dreaming of some order in which material wealth would be a disgrace." Forgetting for a moment that he was reporting to one of England's most successful chocolate makers, he confided to William Cadbury:

> What I feel so much among these people is the wicked waste of opportunity of making and producing human happiness. With these gentle, patient creatures anything could be done with firm kindness. They are mere clay under the strong white hand. Our comparative

omnipotence and omniscience ought to arouse a feeling of responsibility and a desire to be of use to them, but greed for money and power don't leave room for much else.

Cadbury could agree on the issue of happiness, since it was one of the goals of the reforms undertaken at the Bournville Works. There was, however, an essential distinction: the views of workers at Cadbury Brothers Limited were taken seriously by management. For all his utopian tendencies, Burtt could not fully embrace the humanity of the African serviçais; he could not span the cultural and linguistic divide between himself and the "patient creatures" he had come to observe. The image of the African Burtt produced for Cadbury was a limited one.[46]

It was the sort of confused thinking that had so astonished Henry Nevinson. Nevinson spoke no African languages and no Portuguese, but he argued against the European propensity to "think of 'black people' in lumps and blocks" and stressed "that each African has a personality as important to himself as each of us is in his own eyes." The journalist still managed to objectify Africans, though in a manner less condescending and more romantic: "We profess to believe that external nature is symbolic and that the universe is full of spiritual force; but we cannot enter for a moment into the African mind, which really believes in the spiritual side of nature."[47]

Nevinson returned to England on July 21, 1905, and promptly sent a brief letter to William Cadbury confirming that he had met Burtt. Contradicting his somewhat harsher diary entries, Nevinson assured Cadbury that Burtt was "a thoroughly good fellow [who] will be able to tell you all that you want to know." Also in late July, Cadbury received a bundle of letters and photographs from Burtt that documented "the splendid way in which cocoa cultivation is carried on" and gave a good sense of what the men on the spot—the managers of the roças—were thinking and doing. In his reply, Cadbury admitted that he was unsure what "Nevinson . . . intends to do with his notes," but he assured Burtt he would send any articles that Nevinson published. He asked Burtt to see if he could observe the recontracting process for serviçais as well as determine if there were any cases "where the labourers have been transferred from estate to estate at the convenience of the masters." He also revealed an ambiguity on the subject of slavery that would irritate more ardent antislavery activists, including Henry Nevinson: "I think it is quite possible, as was the case in the West Indies, that on certain estates a state of slavery may be greatly preferable to freedom when there is no law or order with the freedom, but it is very distasteful to an English mind to think of a whole race of men being put on the basis of cattle, and of course the system is open to awful abuse." Even though the sales catalog from April 1901 equating laborers and cattle remained firmly in William Cadbury's mind, he seemed willing to place productivity and discipline above freedom.[48]

Cadbury's letter had still not reached Burtt a month later, and Burtt never found the opportunity to observe the curador recontracting serviçais, perhaps because the planters were carefully managing his appointments—as Charles Hart had suggested to Henry Nevinson. The planters assured Burtt "that when the black is accustomed to this life he does not wish to change it," and though he had heard of interpreters "falsifying the serviçal's reply to the question" of whether he wanted to return home, Burtt remained convinced that "the curador is a true friend of the labourers." The curador was Emeríco d'Alpoim de Cerqueira Borges Cabral, but curiously, Burtt did not mention his name in his letters to Cadbury, nor did he mention the names of most other colonial officials he met. Colonial policy was made in Lisbon; officials in São Tomé, good or bad, were functionaries. Burtt's primary charge was to visit the roças, where planters and their managers had the most direct effect on workers' lives.[49]

In late August, he revisited Boa Entrada, the model plantation that had impressed him early in his tour. After the slovenly and poorly kept Monte Café, Boa Entrada's cleanliness and order were a welcome relief. He watched "an invalid sitting happily on the pier catching fish, he came eight years ago and has never been able to work since his arrival. It gave one the idea he had fallen into good hands." From Boa Entrada on the east coast, Burtt took the boat *Ambaca* around to the west coast, where the image of harmony was reinforced a week later at the S. António roça. Its manager, Arlindo Wenceslau da Silva Marques, told Burtt that "he had worked for so many years with the people that he felt them comrades in labour." As unlikely as it was that Marques spent his days splitting cocoa pods with a machete, Burtt reported the observation without commentary. He also noted that children played on the balconies of the elaborate main house where Marques lived with his family, that a new hospital was being built, and that master-servant relations seemed pleasant. Burtt liked "the human touch that one feels exists on some of these roças," which he thought "a great safeguard against ill-treatment."[50]

From the roça S. António, Burtt joined George Castreuil on a nerve-racking mule ride along rocky, narrow paths to the Porto Alegre roça on the southern tip of São Tomé. Here, the local Africans were not forros but

23. Angolares a suas cubatas

FIGURE 12. Angolares' houses, São Tomé, c. 1910. (Editor: A. Palanque, S. Tomé.) By permission of the João Loureiro Postcard Collection.

Angolares, descendants of a community founded by runaway slaves in the late sixteenth century. They made their living fishing and ferrying mail for the planters by canoe. Much to the irritation of the roçeiros, the Angolares refused to work on the cocoa estates, a decision that led Burtt to conclude, "One would be sorry for these gentle smiling giants to die out but probably that is their fate if they will not bow their necks to labour."[51]

Castreuil was a relative rarity among managers on the island: "of the upper class . . . vivacious, keen, decided" and, Burtt could not resist telling Cadbury, "something of an exquisite" who favored "silk shirts and dainty waist coats." The Société Anonyme Portugaise de Responsibilité Limitée (Portuguese Limited Liability Company [LLC]), a joint Belgian-Portuguese venture again including Henri Burnay, owned Porto Alegre. The estate was divided into sixteen dependencies that together yielded 1.65 million pounds of cocoa per year. The roça boasted several miles of railway lines; an experimental farm growing cinnamon, Liberian coffee, and rubber; and a machine shop stocked with steam-driven saws and planes. Porto Alegre also had a hospital and employed its own physician, Adriano Luíz d'Oliveira Pessa, a pleasant but plodding young man who diligently cared for the workers. Burtt surmised he was not bright enough to find a job in Lisbon and so ended up on the island, separated from his wife and young child. Pessa did give Burtt a clear sense of the risks of working on a cocoa plantation: one of his first tasks on arriving had been to amputate a worker's leg, and he had also treated a man who had been shot in the face with an arrow. Burtt sympathized with the young doctor's loneliness. Despite the estate's beautiful setting just seven miles north of the equator, there was little to do. Burtt entertained himself adjusting his watch each evening at 6:00 p.m. as he watched the setting sun's "green rays of light . . . as it sank into the sea."[52]

Back in the capital in mid-September, Burtt concluded that he had "extracted all that is of importance" on São Tomé and prepared to visit Príncipe. Having finally received Cadbury's July letter, he consulted the curador, Cabral, who confirmed that workers were not moved between roças at the planters' whim, though "sometimes as a punishment a man is sent to another dependencia" on the same estate. If the offense was particularly serious, a worker might be sent by the curador to Príncipe.[53]

"Nevinson's influence," Burtt also noted to Cadbury, "is already being felt here." The second of Henry Nevinson's articles on "The New Slave Trade" appeared in *Harper's Magazine* in September 1905. It included an editor's note indicating that the article had been written in Luanda, Angola, in December 1904, but it began with an extract from a letter Nevinson had written in May 1905, after two months spent tracing the slave route in Angola's interior. After nine weeks of walking, he was thin, ill from fever, possibly poisoned, and still two hundred miles from the coast. Unsure whether he would survive, Nevinson had arranged for his report to be delivered to Benguela and mailed to the magazine's editor. The dramatic opening and the confused time line prompted Cadbury to write to Nevinson and complain about the "somewhat stagey nature" of the article and to note that it gave ammunition to Portuguese interests always inclined to question the reliability of English critics. Nevinson replied the next day, assuring Cadbury that he was disgusted by the inclusion of the letter and the confusion it caused and that he had informed the editors at *Harper's* that if they tried anything similar again, he would withdraw his series of articles. Nevinson's assertion that "of course it will be put right in the book" could not have reassured William Cadbury. As Joseph Burtt sailed for Príncipe, the cocoa controversy also entered new territory.[54]

Three

SLEEPING SICKNESS AND SLAVERY

TWELVE HOURS on a hot, stifling steamer brought Joseph Burtt to Príncipe, and his unabashed romanticism bubbling to the surface. As he stood on the deck,

> faint rosy glimmers in the east stole through the mist, and sought and kissed the gleaming water; and strengthening and growing slowly drew back the curtain of the night from the verdant island of Principe. And as the light brightened the sea became sapphire blue over the rocks, and turquoise in the sandy shallows, while here and there beneath grey precipitous cliffs it lay in pools of deep translucent green that seemed too radiant for mortal eyes to look upon. Beyond this, and as white as silk, the tiny breakers foamed against the line of yellow sand where careless cocoa palms flung up their sloping stems and tossed their plumes in the fresh morning air. Behind were grey rocks, half clothed in tender verdure, and dense masses of tropical vegetation, relieved by the light brown stems of the forest trees. Further still, and higher, the vast dome of Papagaio stood out against the pale blue sky, veiling one purple side in diaphanous clouds that rolled and rose like incense to the mountain gods.

At seventy-one square miles, the tiny island was a mere "speck on the map," one-seventh the size of São Tomé, though similar in geography and climate. Burtt's contact on Príncipe was B. W. E. Bull, "a coloured man" who managed the island's telegraph station. Burtt thought him a "capital fellow" and assured William Cadbury that he "knows everybody here, from the governor downwards, and everything about the island. He mixes on equal terms with all the planters, and is a capable, manly fellow." It was a high compliment in an age when many were uncertain—Burtt often but not always among them—that a "coloured

Ilha do Principe — Vista geral da bahia e cidade

FIGURE 13. Príncipe—view of the bay and city. By permission of the João Loureiro Postcard Collection.

man" could be capable and manly. Bull's house in the capital, Santo António, functioned as a sort of club for the town's residents. He also owned a small roça on the island and, like Francisco Marin on São Tomé, he was multilingual: he spoke Portuguese, Spanish, English, and French, though no African languages.[1]

The morning after Burtt arrived, Bull took his guest to meet Príncipe's governor—unnamed in Burtt's letters—an "agreeable . . . intelligent man . . . keenly alive to the interests of the island." But Burtt was disappointed by the town of Santo António, which was desolate, with "tumbled down wooden houses and deserted buildings and churches." It had enjoyed a century-long heyday, long past by the time Burtt visited in September 1905. In 1753, Portuguese officials had left São Tomé City and relocated to Santo António after a series of rebellions led by landed forros and supported by the *câmara*, the municipal council. Príncipe had no câmara; the island was the "private fiefdom of the Carneiro family by grant of the Portuguese crown in 1502." There was thus no local elite with the power to oust Portuguese governors, as had happened regularly on São Tomé. The Carneiros were compensated for their loss of power with a large estate in Portugal, though they also maintained extensive landholdings on Príncipe. In 1852, the Portuguese moved the capital back to São Tomé and in 1858 began the process of recolonization, prompted in part by the promise of coffee and cocoa.[2]

The factor that most shaped Príncipe's history, from the mid-nineteenth century forward, was a disease: sleeping sickness, carried by the tsetse fly (*Glossina palpalis*). It likely accompanied shipments of cattle, which were "brought over in small, shallow-bottomed boats" from nearby Gabon beginning in the 1820s. The disease spread slowly across the island from north to south, and few cases were recorded before 1890. In the early 1890s, Angolan serviçais recruited in Cazengo, where sleeping sickness was endemic, also began working on the island, and some may have arrived already infected. Sleeping sickness devastated the local population, even as many refused to believe that their symptoms were caused by the bite of a fly, attributing them instead—to the despair of colonial medical officers—to "fetish." The Portuguese tended to dismiss African religious beliefs as superstition, which proved a particular burden for serviçais. In the absence of religious practitioners from their home communities, they secretly improvised healing rituals for the sick and services for the dead in their quarters after a long day's work on the roça. Resistance to Western medicine was not, however, unique to Africans: at Boa Entrada on São Tomé, the resident doctor also struggled to treat white employees who ignored his advice. In 1844, there were 1,122 local islanders, descended, as was the case in São Tomé, from slaves imported to cut sugarcane in the early sixteenth century. By the early 1900s, their population had dropped to 550. The 4,219 African workers and 169 Europeans on the island were also at risk, as Burtt was well aware. One manager he planned to visit had fallen ill with sleeping sickness. Burtt professed both dread of and fascination with the tsetse fly, which he reported to William Cadbury "is rather larger than a house fly and when at rest folds one wing over the other. It does not buzz but flies noiselessly and very swiftly."[3]

The first estate he visited was the eastern section of the roça Porto Real, owned by the Sociedade de Agricultura Colonial, whose major shareholder was Francisco Mantero. Burtt was struck by the slow pace of life, centered on the balcony of the main house: "Smoking cigarettes on the balcony seemed the important business," and "children skip about on the balconies, and shout for bread after meals, and altogether I have never been at a roça where there seemed a better relation between men and masters." In the afternoon, he sat with the manager, José Manuel dos Santos Abreu, on benches shaded from the sun by the balcony, "and the children would play about or pick the grass seeds from Abreu's legs." Abreu returned the affection; that July, he had founded a choral group for the roça's children. A resident doctor—a fat Spaniard—busied himself riding a "large Spanish horse as sleek and comfortable as himself but a trifle more lively," smoking fine Spanish cigars on the balcony, and occasionally checking on patients in the roça's hospital.[4]

Abreu, "a kindly pleasant young man," took the time to show Burtt around the roça, where he "did the usual things, visited the dependencias . . . travelled about on the tram, and rode one of the most steady-going mules I have yet met, a sort of patient hairy riding machine; one cannot imagine anything short of a thunder bolt exciting it." Promised a hike up Papagaio, Burtt was disappointed when they arrived at the foot of the mountain and Abreu merely pointed out the peak, in "his gentlemanly and truly Portuguese way." Heavy forest denied Burtt his climb and his view, but they did visit "a fine plantation of young cocoa trees of three years and under, the whole work managed by a tall serious looking black whom one fancied was feeling something of the white man's burden of work." The reference to Rudyard Kipling's famous imperialist poem "The White Man's Burden," which urged white men to embrace their destiny and "civilize" the "new-caught, sullen peoples, / Half-devil and half-child" in their recently acquired empires, captured Burtt's own evolving belief, after four months on the islands, that blacks were "mere clay under the strong white hand." But the confusion in his worldview that had so puzzled Nevinson was present too. Francisco Mantero and the Sociedade de Agricultura Colonial had hired a black man to oversee black workers harvesting cocoa. Skill had trumped race, and very likely the man spoke Portuguese, but given the opportunity to interview him about the burden he had taken up in his strong black hands, Burtt again demurred.[5]

Caring for workers, especially on an island beset by tropical diseases, required a hospital. Porto Real's well-maintained facility had forty-four patients the first day Burtt visited, or about 10 percent of the estate's adult working population of 404. Achiness and fever marked the first stages of sleeping sickness. Burtt met a woman in the second stage who "appeared dull and stupid, but was walking about." At another roça hospital, he encountered a man "in the last stage, lying on his back almost unconscious." The victim had been ill for two and half months, and his caregivers expected him to live another two weeks. Lapsing into a semicoma made death from sleeping sickness relatively painless, but the long decline prompted many sufferers who had maintained their wits in the earlier stages to contemplate suicide. The standard treatment for ox, mule, donkey, and human alike was high doses of atoxyl, administered by injection at the onset of the disease or, if a person knew he or she had been bitten, as soon as possible afterward. Atoxyl did not cure sleeping sickness—the trypanosome parasite remained present in patients' blood—but it seemed to work as a tonic, especially in animals, rendering them "strong and vigorous, and prolonging their life."[6]

The better solution was getting rid of the tsetse flies, the policy advocated by Bernardo F. Bruto da Costa, who first visited Príncipe in 1905 and led the medical commission charged with eradicating sleeping sickness on the island. The flies favored the swampy, low-lying parts of the island and took "refuge in shady places, damp and frequented by animals, chiefly pig, insensible to the sting of the insect, which allow it to settle on them in large numbers and carry it about from place to place." The insect sucked the blood of its host; it was not uncommon for a hunter who had shot a pig to find "as many as thirty *glossinas*, gorged with blood, hanging on the dead body." Another major host for tsetse flies was the dog, and Bruto da Costa complained that every local "hut sheltered a dozen dogs, running wild, as if for the feeding" of the fly. The proposed solution, the "slaughtering of pigs and other mammals running wild," initially met with strong resistance from both local Principeses and Portuguese planters, as did the plan—still in development in September 1905—to clear scrub, clean streambeds, and drain swamps. At Porto Real, that plan ultimately entailed the hard work of draining three square miles of swampland, though the manager was rewarded with a dramatic drop in the roça's death rate from sleeping sickness.[7]

After five days at Porto Real, Burtt traveled with Abreu on horseback to the Monte Alegre roça, where he encountered a relative rarity on the islands—a resident Portuguese owner, Alipio José de Carvalho. His still-unfinished house was paneled with the island's tropical hardwoods, and to Burtt's delight, the planter gave him eight samples. Building the house and developing the property, including the hospital, was slowed by the dearth of serviçais. Monte

Alegre had only fifty-eight workers, whom Burtt thought well treated. He noted that they did not have to cook after a long day's work; rather, their evening meal of meat, gravy, potatoes, and rice was prepared for them. Only four workers had died in the previous year, two from sleeping sickness. Carvalho took Burtt for two walking tours of the estate, "pointing out everything of interest," including kola nut, which was dried and shipped to Lisbon as a medicine and used on Príncipe as a tonic for anemia. "Owners," Burtt concluded, "seem to have a keener appreciation of the beauty of a crop than managers."[8]

On tiny Príncipe, Cadbury's representative encountered a good deal of Portuguese hospitality, encouraged by Bull and admittedly in the planters' interest. After a day at Monte Alegre, Carvalho and Burtt rode over to the western section of the Porto Real roça, "the most important in the island," where they met the acting manager, Pedro Augusto Rocha. Energetic, frank, and kindly, Rocha took Burtt on an extensive tour of the estate, which had lost 139 of its 616 adult workers to illness in the previous year, the highest death rate Burtt had yet encountered. Rocha opened his books and summoned António Damas Mora, the district medical officer, from town. Together, they identified eighty-eight deaths from anemia, nine from sleeping sickness, and fourteen from "debility." When pressed for an explanation, they told Burtt that the weakest serviçais ended up on Príncipe; the healthiest stayed in Angola, and São Tomé got the next healthiest. Plantation owners in Angola begged to differ, protesting that "all the best labor [went to] the rich island of San Thomé," never to return. Rocha's efforts at transparency impressed Burtt, but he confided to Cadbury, "I have little doubt that many of the cases described as anemia are really sleeping sickness."[9]

Burtt stayed on the estate for five nights, noting that "but for that ugly record it was a pleasant place." From the house, he looked out "over an expanse of cocoa, with the ridge of mountain peaks beyond where the clouds lay like smoke." In the evening, he watched parrots flying home to the mountains and bats, "ghostly brown vampires," emerging in the night air. He dined on pigeon, parrot, beef, and dried cod and talked with Rocha about "agriculture, or England, or Herbert Spencer's *Education*." The foremost English sociologist of the mid- to late nineteenth century, Spencer saw in scientific rationalism the solution to society's ills and supported the social Darwinist defense of imperialist expansion, though he opposed colonial wars. Reading Spencer likely reinforced Burtt's view about black inferiority, though that view was challenged somewhat on two excursions around the roça, during which he encountered a gang of women singing as they cleared brush and men laying railway ties. Both groups, to his surprise, were working without European supervision. The railway line built by black hands would eventually link the western and eastern sections of the Porto Real roça and extend across the island, "a costly and valiant undertaking," given the declining price of cocoa and the lower crop yields on Príncipe.[10]

After a brief stop back at the cable station in Santo António and a game with the chess-obsessed Dr. Mora, Bull and Burtt rowed around to the northwest coast of the island to visit the roça Abade, owned by Nicolau McNicoll and his Portuguese partner, António Alves Affonso, and managed by McNicoll's son. Burtt had met a French planter on São Tomé, but the younger McNicoll—very likely a Scotsman—was the "only Britisher administering a roça in these islands." Sleeping sickness had hit roça Abade hard; McNicoll had lost 4 workers in 1903 and 9 in 1904, and by the time of Burtt's visit in September 1905, 16 workers out of 146 had died, 14 "of whom were victims to this dreadful malady." Distracted perhaps by the opportunity to speak English freely, Burtt did not press McNicoll for the usual details of acreage, crop yields, rations, and working hours for laborers, but he noted that the children appeared "healthy and happy, with a very low mortality." The presence of Bull—"a genuine straightforward fellow"—whose numerous contacts made Burtt's mission on the island so easy may also have dulled his observation skills; he remained unconcerned that decisions about where he went and whom he met were being so carefully managed.[11]

Back in Santo António, the two men discussed Bull's plans to raise capital for his own roça and to find a partner, and Burtt gave him an introduction to a London banker. They also discussed repatriation, which Bull favored. The idea that workers on São Tomé and Príncipe would be repatriated to their homes elsewhere in the Portuguese Empire was codified in the January 29, 1903, labor decree. Forty percent of a laborer's monthly salary was set aside to defray the cost of his or her repatriation. But Henry Nevinson's September 1905 article in *Harper's Magazine* asserted—correctly—that no workers had yet been repatriated. Under the 1903 law, serviçais retained the right to renew their contracts if they wished. Like the Portuguese critic Júdice Biker, Nevinson considered this an empty privilege. Most contract laborers spoke no Portuguese and would answer "yes" regardless of the question posed, be it "Will you have a drink?" or "Is it your wish to go to hell?"—Nevinson's play on *"okalungo,"* an Angolan term for the islands meaning "abyss of hell." A serviçal knew only "that he has fallen into the hands of his enemies, that he is being given over into slavery to the white man, that if he runs away he will

A. C. Ilha do Príncipe — Rua S. Antonio   registado

FIGURE 14. Santo António, Príncipe. By permission of the João Loureiro Postcard Collection.

be beaten, and even if he could escape to his home, . . . he would probably be killed, and almost certainly be sold again." Serviçais were effectively slaves who never returned home. The *Harper's* article prompted outrage in Lisbon, where defenders of Portugal's empire took particular offense at Nevinson's assertion that workers renewed their contracts in the same way that sheep went voluntarily to the butcher's shop. Portuguese commentators insisted instead that serviçais signed and renewed their contracts freely. It was in this context that Bull advocated repatriation to Burtt and argued that "it would be better for the laborers to live away from the plantations."[12]

The conversation continued at the roça Ribeira Izé, where Bull and Burtt breakfasted with Miguel Rendondo Jimenez, a Spaniard who managed the nearby Sundy roça. Burtt had trouble following the "very eager and excited discussion on serviçal matters," but it seemed Jimenez was "a great advocate of repatriation and . . . prefers to have free men and not slaves." The two planters blamed the government for its lack of oversight. Labor recruiters—Nevinson implied in his *Harper's* articles that they were slave traders—brought men and women from the interior of Angola and contracted them to planters at the rate of £30 pounds each, a sum that "almost makes it a purchase" and was much closer to the £35 fee common before the January

1903 labor decree than to the £12 quoted to William Cadbury when he visited Lisbon in March 1903.[13]

At the roça he managed, Jimenez appeared singularly unconcerned with money. He showed off his large warehouse "and waved his hands over a great heap ready for export as much as to say 'our output of cocoa is so great here I can hardly calculate it, but that will give you some faint idea of the yield of Sundy.'" The roça was old and unproductive, but Jimenez "seemed supremely contented with everything," and Burtt decided "it would have been indecent with such a man to have asked for exact figures of production." English reticence combined with a dash of acquired Portuguese courtliness distracted Burtt from the collection of statistics. Instead, he entertained Cadbury with colonial vignettes. As they left one roça, he related, "a creek we had crossed coming in was now too deep to ride through, so we got on the boys' bare shoulders and they waded through, we holding on by their heads, with another boy at the side to help steady us." At Sundy roça, Burtt's companions included "a beautiful parrot [which] stood on a perch near his master," who "dined like a gentleman, a servant holding a wineglass for him to drink from." The large dining room opened "on to a balcony where the women wash the dishes, the other girls and children waiting at table, the air of ample spacious dirty comfort—you can imagine it all made a typical plantation dinner."[14]

In all, Burtt visited thirteen roças during the five weeks he spent on Príncipe. The statistics he collected suggested a mortality rate—largely from sleeping sickness—that varied from a low of 4 percent to a high of 22 percent. The official mortality rate was 11 percent. Sleeping sickness was largely confined to the northwest section of the island, including Porto Real and Bom Bom roça, where the resident doctor "puts the mortality at 30% thanks to the tsetse fly." As on São Tomé, everything was an estimate, since "there isn't a soul in the place knows the population," though Mora confirmed that 647 people had died the previous year. Burtt concluded that "the condition of the serviçal in Príncipe is quite as good as in S. Thomé and, but for" sleeping sickness, "some of the roças would be healthy." Good working conditions seemed not, however, to discourage workers from running away: eight had stolen a small boat just before Burtt arrived on Príncipe in mid-September; loaded it with fresh water, bananas, and a roast pig; and headed for the coast of Africa. Many runaways perished on the open ocean, but occasionally, the currents carried them north to Fernando Po, where they soon found themselves returned "to their masters in Príncipe." Burtt had seen no obvious violence directed against workers on the island and found "something very pathetic

MAP 2. Joseph Burtt's map of Príncipe, 1905. In "Copy of Letters Received from Joseph Burtt," following p. 131, James Duffy Collection, African Collection, Yale University, New Haven, Conn.

in these poor simple people," insisting that they were not running away but undertaking a rescue of a relative wrongly imprisoned on the mainland.[15]

His assessment contrasted starkly with that offered by Henry Nevinson's articles in *Harper's*, the first two of which Burtt had read by the time he returned to São Tomé at the end of October. He thought Nevinson's writing "very clever" but did not like it. "You can't turn out devils with the lash of the tongue any more than with the lash of the whip," Burtt wrote to Cadbury. The man who had retreated, however briefly, from the material world to the sanctuary of Whiteway Colony seemed now to conclude cynically that neither the pen nor the sword could accomplish much. Still, his latent anticapitalist tendencies also surfaced: "The grievous and terrible thing is that in Angola as all the world over, there are people who are willing to buy gold with some other person's blood." Burtt nonetheless thought Nevinson a "brave man" and noted that his articles were "certainly making a great impression on the public."[16]

William Cadbury's letter of October 11 awaited Burtt when he returned from Príncipe to São Tomé. Cadbury had yet to receive Burtt's letters from Príncipe, but he concurred on Nevinson's bravery and enclosed the third *Harper's* article, published in October 1905, which flatly accused the Portuguese of running a slave trade from the Angolan hinterland to Catumbela and then to Benguela on the coast. Cadbury had sent the articles to Carl de Merck in Lisbon and got an aggrieved response in which Merck protested that "Englishmen have quite enough [work to do] to clean their own slate" in Africa, a position with which the chocolate maker agreed. Yet he thought the articles "of a high standard" and did not think the accusations of slave trading could "be really controverted." Cadbury's reservation remained that Nevinson spoke "no Portuguese and that the Portuguese cannot be expected to accept his articles as a fair statement of the case." He was also concerned that Burtt's observations could be open to criticism, especially from the mercurial H. R. Fox Bourne of the Aborigines' Protection Society, a supporter of Nevinson and often a thorn in Cadbury's side. "As far as I have gathered you have made almost all your visits by appointment," Cadbury wrote to Burtt, and then he reassured them both by adding: "It would be very difficult to remove all signs of ill-treatment even with a week's notice, and I should suppose that you are fairly satisfied in your own mind that most . . . of the estate owners have dealt honestly and straightforwardly with you."[17]

Burtt did feel that he had been treated cordially and on occasion with "much openness," though he remained suspicious of the figures he collected. "At one large roça where I was surprised at the good records I took from the books, I since suspect, though I have no proof, that the records are falsified to make better annual reports for Lisbon." The motive for tampering with mortality statistics for the benefit of shareholders in Lisbon baffled him; shareholders knew little and cared less "about the labor that produces the dividend." It seemed not to occur to Burtt that the books might have been altered for his benefit or for other foreign critics interested in how many workers fell ill or died harvesting cocoa. Quick to defend his Portuguese hosts, he added that gossip was the currency of São Tomé and that it was possible the false rumor had been spread by a competitor. Ultimately, he concluded that he had been a victim of such a rumor and that the roça had not misrepresented its records.[18]

With a reservation to sail for Angola on December 1, Burtt occupied himself on São Tomé by checking his notes and revisiting a few of the larger estates. A review of the ledgers at Rio d'Ouro revealed that Vale Flôr paid considerably above the rates mandated by the 1903 labor law, which guaranteed a minimum monthly salary of 2,500 reis for men and 1,800 reis for women. Many workers at Rio d'Ouro, however, were earning 3,000 reis, and in some cases, bonuses brought their wages to 5,000. A third visit to Boa Entrada confirmed that "the treatment of the people is particularly good" and prompted in Burtt "something of a personal friendship for a planter who has bestowed such care on his people." A return visit to Monte Café, where profits in the thousands of pounds per year were directed to charities in Portugal, proved less uplifting. Burtt attended evening mass and thought the hundred men and women at the service "looked particularly slovenly in dirty clothes and pieces of old sacking and smelt unpleasantly." They paid little attention to the service, and one man sat intently digging "the jiggers out of his feet." For Burtt, "the whole scene suggested many painful thoughts," though it was at Monte Café that he read the glowing newspaper accounts by Augusto Chevalier, director of the colonial laboratory at the Paris Museum, who had visited São Tomé in August and September 1905 to study innovations in its tropical agriculture. Chevalier's letters, praising the treatment of black workers on the island—particularly at Boa Entrada but also at Monte Café—became ammunition for the Portuguese in their battle against Nevinson's sensational accusations in *Harper's Magazine* that a colonial slave trade continued.[19]

In December 1905, Burtt remained loyal to Emeríco Cabral, São Tomé's curador, "the only man that has shown any indignation at cruelty to the negro." Once convinced that Burtt's agenda was humanitarian and not commercial, Cabral returned the confidence. The curador reviewed the statistics Burtt had collected and suggested that the mortality rate was a little higher than the Englishman's numbers indicated. Cabral even arranged for "his own servant, a happy smiling fellow, once a serviçal," to talk to Burtt and give him "the negro side of roça life." That Burtt did not include the man's observations in his letters could only have dismayed Cadbury. Burtt assured his employer that five months of watching serviçais working had persuaded him that "they looked orderly, well fed and contented." He remained hesitant, however, to offer "an opinion of the labour question of the islands till I had seen the method of procuring labour."[20]

The two-week trip down the west coast to Luanda aboard the *Sobo* gave Burtt the opportunity for further reflection. The interim report he sent to Cadbury acknowledged some of the concerns raised by Nevinson. The majority of the Angolan serviçais, Burtt concluded, had been forced into five-year contracts; they were not freely recruited. Others had been "driven by poverty from the Islands of Cape Verde," and the same might be said of the failed attempts at recruiting Chinese and Indian labor. Mortality rates varied dramatically from a low of 2 percent to a high of 22 percent. Birth rates were similarly skewed. On one roça, Burtt encountered a very low ratio of one child to every ten adults, but another roça had a very high birth rate of 5 percent per annum. Food was adequate; clothing was distributed twice a year; and on the newer estates, houses with "tile roofs and raised floors" were commonplace. Sleeping sickness regrettably continued to ravage Príncipe, but most estates had hospitals, many of which were being upgraded. Wages remained problematic, with Cape Verdeans being offered shorter contracts and paid higher wages even as Angolans, who never returned home, were locked into five-year terms that were automatically renewed. The nine-hour workday began at 6:00 a.m. and ended at 5:30 p.m., with two and a half hours allotted for breakfast and lunch. Resistant workers found themselves punished with the palmatória and occasionally with the *chicote*—a short, hippo-hide whip—though both were "inflicted at the planters' risk, as they are contrary to law, and white men have been ruined through beating a negro." Most troubling, in Burtt's opinion, was that "practically no attempt is made to supply the serviçal with anything beyond his physical needs, and he has no life beyond the plantation." No child attended school, and few workers had the opportunity to attend church. "The life of the serviçal spent under constant rule and authority does not develop character," he concluded, "and the prospect before the children born on the estate, although one of security as regards food and shelter, is at its best but a mild form of slavery."[21]

William Cadbury had his answer: no matter how attentive Portuguese planters were to the housing, food, and working conditions of their serviçais, the majority of contracted workers never left the islands. They lacked mobility, and thus, no matter how mild the terms of their servitude, they were slaves. The other side of the equation—the recruiting of labor—had been described forcefully by Henry Nevinson's articles in *Harper's Magazine*. A slave trade in Angola produced workers for São Tomé and Príncipe. Joseph Burtt might well have returned to England had Cadbury's letter of November 7, 1905, reached him, for it suggested "that the firms who sent you out may feel that Nevinson's report is so thorough" that it was unnecessary for Burtt to go to Angola. When next Burtt wrote to Cadbury, it was from Luanda, "bankrupt and beautiful," a phrase lifted, tellingly, from Nevinson's September 1905 article.[22]

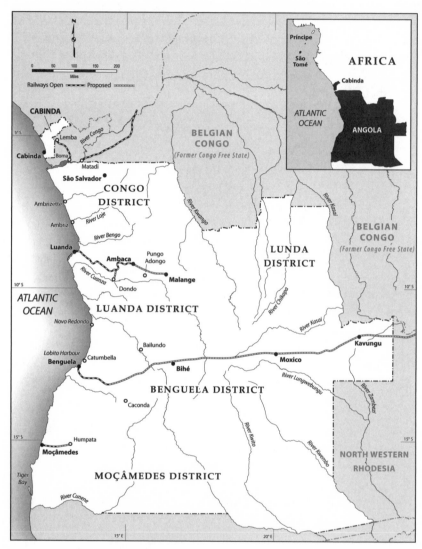

MAP 3. Angola, c. 1910. Adapted by Will Fontanez from the map in William A. Cadbury, *Labour in Portuguese West Africa*, 2nd ed. (London: George Routledge and Sons, 1910), following p. 187.

Four

LUANDA AND THE COAST

JOSEPH BURTT arrived in Luanda in December 1905, his vision of the capital city already shaped by Henry Nevinson's sonorous prose. *Harper's* readers imagined Luanda from the sanctuary of Our Lady of Salvation, a church built in 1664, its walls adorned with blue and white tiles depicting the occupation of the bay by Christian soldiers in 1575. Nevinson thought Luanda "a city that would hardly look out of place upon the Mediterranean shore. It has something now of the Mediterranean air both in its beauty and its decay." The upper town swung "round in a wide arc to the cemetery, and on the cliff are built the governor's palace, the bishop's palace, a few ruined churches . . . and the fine big hospital—an expensive present from a Portuguese queen." On the flats at the base of the cliff sat the customs house, military barracks, the cathedral, stores and restaurants, and scattered among them the "houses and huts" of Africans living in the lower town. For Nevinson, Luanda was beautiful because "she is old, and because she built her roofs with tiles, before corrugated iron came to curse the world."[1]

The city was bankrupt for reasons on which Burtt and Nevinson could agree. Chosen for its "calm lagoon, at the entrance of which the biggest warships can lie," Luanda was hemmed in by dry, sandy soils, and residents had to go north to the Bengo River or south to the Cuanza (Kwanza) River valley to import freshwater and food crops. Of more immediate concern was the 1902 Bailundo war, an uprising by eight Ovimbundu kingdoms in the central highlands that the Portuguese put down with overwhelming force. Portugal's campaign to conquer the central highlands had begun in 1890, in response to the consensus reached at the Berlin West Africa Conference that European colonizing powers had to demonstrate effective occupation of territories claimed in Africa. The Ovimbundu mustered forty thousand soldiers but fell to the superior technology and tactics of the Portuguese and their allies. Victory came at great financial cost, and Nevinson sensed the unease of colonial officials fearful of further rebellion.[2]

Burtt thought Luanda "a decaying emblem of a decaying race . . . a city of unfulfilled hopes, unfinished enterprises, and vague futile endeavour. . . . Here is a huge unfinished municipal building . . . fine wide roads lead to nowhere in particular." Like those of São Tomé City, Luanda's smells were overwhelming, especially on a hot summer day. A single drain carried sewage out to the ocean, and women with babies tied to their backs swept the streets. "Judging of the result by the smells," Burtt suspected that "the whole scheme of sanitation is directed by one of the more casual babies that with their tiny black hands pat their mothers' backs and bob their heads up and down to the movement of the broom."[3]

Burtt arrived in Luanda at a turning point in Portugal's more than three-century-long relationship with Angola. The explorer Diogo Cão had reached the mouth of the Congo River in 1483, and by 1491, the Portuguese Crown was negotiating with representatives of the Kongo kingdom and seeking a monopoly over trade to and from the hinterland. The Kongo elites proved surprisingly receptive to Christianity as kings manipulated the new "spirit cult" to extend their authority via appointed officials who had converted to Catholicism. By the middle of the sixteenth century, Afro-Portuguese Creole traders had established themselves as a group distinct from the Kongo kingdom.

FIGURE 15. Luanda—partial view of the lower city and the African quarter, c. 1906. (Editor: Eduardo Osório, Luanda.) By permission of the João Loureiro Postcard Collection.

Physically indistinguishable from the broader African population and usually speaking local languages, they nevertheless identified themselves as Portuguese. An attempt by the Portuguese Crown to conquer the Kongo kingdom outright in the 1560s failed, but with the establishment of Luanda to its south in 1575, the Afro-Portuguese acquired "their own sovereign territory." Many made their fortunes selling slaves to Brazil's sugar plantations, a business so lucrative that in 1617, another port was established at Benguela, three hundred miles south along the coast from Luanda. By 1700, approximately eleven thousand slaves were being exported each year from the two coastal towns.[4]

Most of the slaves exported through Benguela were brokered by traders from the Ovimbundu kingdoms of the central highlands. Though loosely organized, the Ovimbundu were quick to see the opportunities offered by Afro-Portuguese living in the interior and on the coast. Between 1741 and 1828, Ovimbundu traders sent an average of 4,869 slaves annually to Benguela for export to Brazil. Ovimbundu military coordination and trading networks ensured a degree of stability in the interior that began to unravel with the final prohibition on slave trading in 1836. In the 1840s, Afro-Portuguese entrepreneurs at Luanda started growing coffee in the Cazengo valley. Plantation owners faced difficulties both in pressuring local Africans to work and in protecting their *fazendas* (agricultural estates) from the raids launched in opposition to forced labor.[5]

Planters were competing for labor with local African societies, many of which held slaves. The transatlantic trade had favored male workers, and it initially offered rulers the opportunity to get rid of difficult subjects, including debtors, criminals, and war captives, though the escalating demand for slaves ultimately increased warfare. Slaves who remained in Africa were mostly women. They tended to crops and ideally—from the masters' perspective—helped increase the size of a lineage by bearing children. In the hierarchical Ovimbundu kingdoms, a royal household included the king's immediate dependents—wives, children, and slaves. Also resident were the retainers and titled officials who advised him and made up his inner circle. This privileged group could buy slaves and had preferential access to land, trade goods, and trading networks. Free commoners also lived in the kingdoms, but the largest portion of a ruler's subjects—clients and slaves—were not free. When the Atlantic slave trade ended, some African states responded by increasing their reliance on slave labor to harvest palm oil and rubber for external markets. Slave porters carried ivory, beeswax, and animal skins to the coast. Afro-Portuguese merchants, whose fortunes had waned with the collapse of the external slave market, continued to supply local labor markets and also shifted their focus eastward to supply captives to Arab and Afro-Arab traders in the still-active Indian Ocean trade. The market for captive labor in Angola thus survived and even thrived after 1836.[6]

In his articles for *Harper's*, Henry Nevinson "drew a firm distinction between 'domestic'" slavery practiced within African societies and the abuses of the "foreign" slave systems supplied by Atlantic and Indian Ocean traders. The relation of African rulers to their subjects, the journalist argued, was more akin to feudalism than to slavery. Nevinson offered the example of the Kroo, who lived along the Liberian and Sierra Leonean coasts. Men took short-term contracts on steamships plying the West African coast, and when they returned home, they gave "the chief a share of their earnings as a tribute for his care of the tribe and village in their absence." Nevinson was not defending indigenous African slavery; he acknowledged that "the power of the chiefs is often despotic." Labor relations in many African societies, however, were fluid. If well liked and hardworking, both male and female slaves could improve their status and acquire a degree of mobility in the society that had enslaved them.[7]

Slavery was officially abolished in Portuguese Africa in 1875. Portugal's reach into the interior, however, remained limited. For most Africans, the real shift came in 1899, with the introduction of labor laws that asserted (in keeping with British and French policies) "that conquered peoples had a legal obligation to work." If they could not demonstrate that they were working, "vagrant" Africans often found themselves sentenced to "corrective labour" on road-building projects. Those Angolans who under Portuguese law had been slaves in 1875 became libertos and then serviçais. As had happened in São Tomé and Príncipe, they found themselves locked into five-year renewable contracts that usually became life sentences.[8]

Like their island counterparts, plantation owners in Angola also struggled with labor shortages. Compared to São Tomé and Príncipe, however, the population of Angola was enormous. In 1900, an estimated 4.8 million people lived in the province, dispersed over an area thirteen times the size of Portugal, which had a population of 3.5 million. The 9,198 whites and 3,112 *mestiços* (people of mixed race) made up a mere 0.25 percent of Angola's population, in a colony where both military conquest and building an effective bureaucracy remained ongoing processes. Plantation owners struggled to find crops to rival the cocoa produced by the "pearl of empire." They experimented with sugar, rum, tobacco, and grapes; in the 1890s, they enjoyed some success with coffee. African farmers cultivated grain crops, raised cattle, and also struggled with Angola's uneven rainfall and dry, infertile soils. Beginning in 1906, Africans faced the added burden of taxes levied on their huts (houses) by the Portuguese to help pay for the development of the colony. African and Afro-Portuguese brokers, meanwhile, continued to send laborers to the west coast. Of the 7,363 serviçais contracted in 1899, half stayed in Angola and half went to São Tomé and Príncipe, a reflection of the economic significance of the much smaller colony.[9]

In 1902, Roger Casement, then serving as British consul to the Congo Free State, spent a week at an Angolan fazenda and described the horrific conditions serviçais endured. Contract workers were purchased for a hundred thousand reis each. They were forbidden to leave the estates and were paid not in cash but in vouchers they could use only at a "wretched shell of a store with shoddy goods and rum." As Burtt would discover, their diet, which consisted largely of sweet potatoes, was much poorer than that of workers on São Tomé and Príncipe. As a result, most serviçais suffered from intestinal worms. Angola's contract workers may have been called serviçais, but they were slaves, and no one—legal regulations notwithstanding—pretended otherwise.[10]

Serviçais also worked in Angola's towns. One morning at breakfast in Moçâmedes, Burtt chatted with his waiter, named Bango, and then described the young man's remarkable attitude to Cadbury. Bango, Burtt explained, "is a slave, but his view of the affair is this; one has to work to eat, and one may as well work here as anywhere else." Contract workers also labored in the town's commercial warehouses, through which goods were imported and exported. As on São Tomé and Príncipe, serviçais ran away, and when recaptured, they were whipped or subjected to the palmatória. Burtt marveled at Bango's ability to laugh at such punishments; he was, Burtt told Cadbury, "a good willing boy, and with him, I imagine, beatings do not amount to much."[11]

Burtt also encountered free blacks in the towns and cities he visited. They included farmers, traders, carriers, and artisans. The majority of Luanda's ironworkers, potters, and stonemasons at the end of the nineteenth century were Africans. Black Angolans also held key positions in the army and the colonial government. In 1900, twelve of the thirteen employees in the office of the secretary-general—second only to the governor-general—were Africans. They spoke Portuguese at work and Kimbundu at home. Most were self-educated, although a few had graduated from university, still a rare accomplishment for a Portuguese. Some of Angola's civil servants were the children of Portuguese fathers and African mothers, but many traced their ancestry to a pattern of intermarriage dating back to the fifteenth century.[12]

The further decline in the status of the Afro-Portuguese coincided with the Portuguese attempt after 1890 to demonstrate the effective occupation of Angola and to encourage white settlement, particularly in the agricultural sector. In the Portuguese imperial imagination, modern Angola would be built by white men and women. Planners faced an uphill battle as they worked to assure potential colonists that the areas targeted for settlement were safe, the climate was healthy, fertile land was available, efficient and affordable communications existed, and a recognizable European community was already in place. A variety of schemes met with little success as the mostly unskilled and illiterate white immigrants joined convict laborers living in poverty in the towns.[13]

Nevertheless, Portuguese attitudes toward the Afro-Portuguese who had for so long staffed the military and the civil service had shifted. Writing in 1902, the ethnographer F. X. da Silva Teles argued that "secure racial superiority is disrupted by the silent, implicit threat of African women diluting Portuguese blood and the explicit threat of pollution from an African physical and cultural environment." By the time Joseph Burtt arrived in Luanda in December 1905, the marginalization of the old Afro-Portuguese elite was well under way. An Afro-Portuguese business community would survive longer in the smaller towns south of the capital—Benguela, Catumbela, and Moçâmedes—but eventually, its members too would find their path to advancement blocked.[14]

In Luanda, Burtt met with W. S. R. Brock, who had served as acting consul in 1904 while Arthur Nightingale was investigating labor conditions on São Tomé and Príncipe for the British Foreign Office. Brock told Burtt that the process of recruiting labor in Angola was improving. The newly arrived consul, Horatio Mackie, assured Burtt that Nightingale's report would shortly be published. The available figures suggested that an average of 3,446 laborers per year had been exported to São Tomé and Príncipe between 1901 and 1904, which was about one-third the number exported to Brazil at the height of the slave trade. Burtt remained determined "to investigate the methods of procuring labour which is evidently the worst part of the system. I feel," he wrote to Cadbury, that "I have only taken one step and that I can form no opinion till I go further."[15]

In early February 1906, Burtt finally received the letter Cadbury had posted three months earlier. The fourth of Henry Nevinson's *Harper's* articles

FIGURE 16. Afro-Portuguese elites, Benguela, c. 1905. (Editor: Colecção Tavares, Benguela.) By permission of the João Loureiro Postcard Collection.

had just appeared when Cadbury wrote in November 1905. Burtt remained generous in his assessment of the journalist: "I do not attach quite the importance that you do to the fact of Nevinson not speaking Portuguese, as I think his knowledge of French and keen powers of observation would in measure compensate for this." Burtt did think Nevinson's understanding of working conditions on São Tomé and Príncipe—where he had spent a mere two weeks—was superficial. But what really put Burtt off was Nevinson's "utter lack of sympathy with and understanding of the Portuguese character" and his delusions about being poisoned by Portuguese opponents, "brought on by his arduous toil and sufferings in the interior." Burtt's contacts in Luanda's British community—diplomats, railway men, and harbor officials—assured him that Nevinson's "fears of assassination were entirely imaginary," though "common . . . to persons who have been overdone in Africa." Cadbury's representative felt that he owed the firm an opinion rooted in his own discreet observations of the recruiting process so that his employer would "have something more substantial than the brilliant journalism of a man unhinged with fever and fatigue." Beyond this obligation, Burtt admitted to another motive—a desire to "see the mountains and hear the lions" and, in a long tradition of British travelers, to visit Angola's interior.[16]

Arranging to visit Angola's hinterland, however, took patience and persistence. Though he planned to abandon the excess baggage that had amused Nevinson in São Tomé, Burtt still needed supplies and food for several months. Most important, he needed African porters, who were in high demand to carry ivory, rubber, and beeswax from the interior to the coast. Almost as soon as he arrived in Luanda, he wrote to the Reverend Robert Shields, an American Methodist missionary, to see if he could hire African carriers from Bihé, just to the east of Benguela, to accompany him on his trek along the slave route to Kavungu on the colony's eastern border.[17]

While he waited for a response, Burtt gauged opinions in Luanda on the buoyant market in contract laborers for São Tomé and Príncipe. He wrote that "an intelligent coloured clerk" who was working at the city's telegraph station thought "it quite impossible for a visitor not speaking the native language to get the serviçaes' view of the matter." Here, Burtt might have been admitting his own shortcomings to Cadbury. Even when he had encountered Portuguese-speaking workers on the islands, he had been remiss in soliciting their opinions. In Luanda, a local newspaper editor critical of the trade in serviçais told Burtt that Africans so feared being sent to São Tomé and Príncipe that family members conducted a "service for the dead" on behalf of the contracted worker. The newspaperman nevertheless identified African acceptance of slavery as a factor blocking its complete abolition: "It has gone on here for so many generations that submission flows in the blood, the child drinks it at its mother's breast." The solution, in the view of the telegrapher, was to reduce the price paid for recruited laborers by planters on São Tomé and Príncipe and to encourage repatriation to Angola after workers had fulfilled their initial five-year contracts. The islands would cease to be seen as a graveyard and instead become simply a place to work, made more attractive by the relative decline and subsequent job losses in Angola's coffee and rubber sectors.[18]

Still in search of porters, Burtt headed down the coast in February 1906 to Benguela, Angola's second city. The centuries-old city and its population of thirty-three hundred (about one-fifth that of Luanda) left him unimpressed. He was struck by the town's emptiness and by "wide streets run out into a great plain of sand and bush and bleaching bones of man and beast." At the edge of the desert were the mountains, and from them emerged a long line of carriers; most were men, but there were some young women and children too, "their loads lashed between two sticks, and carried on the shoulder or head." At the local store, they purchased maize flour and rum for the return trip and occasionally manufactured goods; one man "bought a little trunk made of coloured metal." Burtt's visit to a local labor agent, however, yielded the disappointing news that there were no porters available to hire.[19]

Burtt's impression of the city was strikingly different than that presented by Francisco de Paula Cid, whom Burtt met in São Tomé in 1905 while Cid was serving as the colony's governor-general. From 1889 to 1893, Cid had been the governor of Benguela District. In his 1892 report, he praised the town's spacious government buildings and noted that the old fort of São Filipe had been renovated and its exterior walls replastered. A municipal slaughterhouse had opened on the coast, and the town's marketplace boasted two new warehouses. The postal and telephone services were functioning efficiently. Yet Cid had to admit that Benguela's climate was not healthy. Under the circumstances, the local hospital, which dated from 1774, urgently needed to be upgraded.[20]

Joseph Burtt fell desperately ill in Benguela, an ironic turn of events given his suggestion to William Cadbury that Henry Nevinson's articles in *Harper's* had been distorted by fever and fatigue. Trapped in a hot, expensive, and dirty hotel room, Burtt struggled first with a skin infection he had picked up on board the *Sobo*, the ship that had brought him to Angola from São Tomé. Next, he feared that he might be coming down with sleeping sickness. He finally succumbed to malaria. After five sleepless nights, he checked into Benguela's hospital, where he was assigned "a large clean room with a cool breeze blowing in from the sea through the great windows." The staff was kind, he reported, "but the food and attention were incredibly bad." After ten days in the hospital, Burtt felt well enough to leave, only to fall victim to a second attack of malaria. He recovered after an injection of quinine. A young English railway man in the next bed at the hospital, brought in with fever and unable to speak Portuguese, died.[21]

The young man had been working for the English contractor John Norton-Griffiths at Lingue, nine miles east of Benguela, constructing the Benguela railway. Building railways was expensive, and despite Portugal's sensitivity to outside interference in its empire, much of Angola's rail system was funded by foreign capital. Like the call for colonists, the search for investors was perennial. Private Portuguese companies did invest, but so too did British and Belgian firms. The railways were seen as the key to solving Angola's transport crisis and encouraging its economic development. Africans performed the unskilled labor, but foreigners held many of the skilled jobs. Construction on the Benguela line had started in 1902 at the new port of Lobito, about twelve miles north of Benguela. Robert Williams provided the major funding, and he envisioned a railroad that connected Lobito to the copper mines

Benguella   Hospital D. Carlos I.

5 Colleceçaõ Tavares & Cia., Benguella.

FIGURE 17. D. Carlos I Hospital, Benguela, c. 1902. (Editor: Colecção Tavares, Benguela.) By permission of the João Loureiro Postcard Collection.

in which he had invested in Katanga Province, in the southern part of the Congo Free State. So costly was the undertaking that it nearly bankrupted Williams, and he ultimately lost control of his mines.[22]

In 1906, African porters remained central to Angola's transport network, but they could only walk so far and carry so much. The other major players in the carrying trade in the late nineteenth and early twentieth centuries were Afrikaners (Boers) who had immigrated from the South African Republic (the Transvaal) in the 1880s. About two hundred families settled around Humpata, a hundred miles east of the port of Moçâmedes, in southern Angola. In their large, slow-moving, ox-drawn carts, they carried bulky bales of cotton and heavy ivory tusks to the coast. They also helped build roads into the interior from Benguela and Moçâmedes. Their open antipathy toward black people concerned Portuguese officials, who also worried that the Afrikaners might try to establish a separate state within Angola's borders, similar to those they had left in southern Africa.[23]

Portuguese insistence in February 1905 that the Afrikaner settlers license their guns and pay their taxes prompted many to consider trekking further east into Barotse territory. That African state was claimed by both Portugal and Britain, and in one of a series of humiliations, it would ultimately fall under

FIGURE 18. Boer (Afrikaner) transport riders, Moçâmedes, c. 1908. (Editor: Mário Pizarro, Moçâmedes.) By permission of the João Loureiro Postcard Collection.

British sovereignty. Nevinson thought the Portuguese treatment of the Afrikaners in Angola was shortsighted. Though hardly generous in his assessment of the "slouching, unwashed, foggy-minded" Afrikaner transport riders he met while traveling in Angola, the journalist found them "a strange mixture of simplicity and cunning, but for knowledge of oxen and wagons and game they have no rivals, and in a war I should estimate the value of one Boer family at about ten Portuguese forts." With Africans threatening war along the Cunene River, which formed part of the colony's southern border, the Afrikaners were, in Nevinson's opinion, Portuguese Angola's best line of defense.[24]

Burtt's encounters with Angola's Afrikaners left him with a better impression. On a visit to Humpata, he drank strong coffee in "a primitive little house with mud brick walls incased in lime & whitewashed, & [with] a galvanized tin roof." At a Sunday service at the Dutch Reformed Church, standing in a congregation of "fine looking men, brown & bearded, some of the younger ones . . . magnificent specimens of strength and activity," he felt that he had stepped back in time. "The matrons in black dresses," he observed to William Cadbury, "with huge hoods reaching to the shoulders might have walked out of an old Dutch painting." By contrast, Philip Pienaar, another young Afrikaner Burtt met, proved "a daily wonder to me, so utterly is he unlike my preconceived idea of a Boer." Pienaar spoke five languages, including fluent Portuguese and English. His "sound judgment, right feeling and simplicity of manner" reminded Burtt "of a well-educated young Friend." Burtt quizzed him about labor conditions in the newly conquered British Transvaal Colony and about the recruitment of labor from the nearby Portuguese colony of Mozambique. Pienaar assured him that African miners were well treated and well paid—they earned about £3 a month—and that they left freely at the end of their six-to-nine-month contracts.[25]

In contrast to the genial Portuguese and the gracious Afrikaners, Norton-Griffiths, the English railway contractor, left Burtt feeling uneasy. Rumor had it that Norton-Griffiths had been one of five hundred men to take part in the Jameson Raid, an illegal 1895 invasion of Johannesburg (and the mines surrounding it) in the Transvaal. The raid was indirectly supported by the British Foreign Office. Leander Starr Jameson's purported goal was to secure voting rights for the mainly British miners working and living in what was then an independent Afrikaner state, but no European miners came out to support their own supposed liberation. Jameson surrendered to the Transvaal authorities in 1896. Six years later, following its defeat in the second South African War (the Anglo-Boer War), the Transvaal would become a British colony. Norton-Griffiths, however, seemed happy exiled in Angola; stopping at his home at Lingue "was like a little visit to England."[26]

Burtt found Norton-Griffiths and his wife, Gwladys, agreeable hosts. The railway man was a "striking personality," tall and handsome, "with clean cut features and cruel blue eyes" that reflected his abusiveness as an employer. William Cadbury and Cadbury Brothers Limited were hardly naive about the brutality of British practices in southern Africa. The company had publicly criticized the more abusive policies, especially during the recently concluded war. Still, Burtt was taken aback by the Englishman's harshness. Norton-Griffiths "was so violent with the niggers," he reported to Cadbury, "that I spoke about it. Of course he said it was necessary with them and so forth. He appears to be cordially hated by nearly all his men, some 1,700 in all." Such brutality, in Burtt's view, could only "bear a plentiful harvest of thorns and thistles, and Africa has so much of this already." At the railway yard, Burtt watched two workers being whipped: "One man was tied up to a post and the lash was laid on to his bare shoulders with great force. . . . It was a horrible sight to English eyes."[27]

Norton-Griffiths was not alone in his excesses, as Burtt reported to Cadbury: "The depravity of this place steadily grows on one, and our countrymen seem worse than the Portuguese." English workers on the railway had reportedly "flogged a man to death," and a friend told Burtt that he had witnessed a well-known Englishman "knock a drunken man down & kick him in the stomach and face." In addition, the English doctor working for the Benguela railway had lost his hospital privileges over accusations of fraud. It was hardly an uplifting picture of the British presence in Portuguese colonial Africa. When Burtt received an invitation from a Dutch merchant to visit nearby Catumbela, he gladly accepted.[28]

Catumbela sat at the "foot of barren mountains" that to Burtt looked "like huge sand heaps sharply bevelled down by torrents of rain." The Catumbela River wound its way across the plain below, and seen from above, the city was "picturesque, blue and red and white, with the full river gleaming between its leafy banks." In 1906, Catumbela had a population of perhaps twelve hundred. The town was the end point of the carrying trade route from the interior. Africans sat in the shade of the baobab trees in the market square, "their burdens bound between two long sticks at their side," and swarmed "into the shops exchanging sticks of rubber for the trifles of civilization." "For something over a pound of second quality reddish rubber," Burtt informed Cadbury, "one man got an old coat, a mouthful of spirit, and a spoon." Wild rubber from the east had briefly made Benguela District—if not the Africans who carried it—rich. In his 1892 report, Cid noted to his astonishment that fourteen thousand porters had passed through tiny

FIGURE 19. View of Catumbela, c. 1904. (Editor: Osório and Seabra, Luanda.) By permission of the João Loureiro Postcard Collection.

Catumbela in February 1891 alone, and he worried about the threat to public order. By 1900, the rubber trade had largely collapsed, though Burtt watched as sticks of rubber were loaded at Catumbela for the eight-mile train trip to Lobito, whence they were shipped to brokers in Lisbon.[29]

The other commodity processed at Catumbela, once a stop on Angola's slave route, was serviçais. Burtt identified three large dealers, two smaller dealers, and two contracting agents working there to supply workers to planters on São Tomé and Príncipe. For *Harper's* readers, these men were slave traders. Henry Nevinson described a Portuguese trader who openly drove his captives to the coast, "shackled, tied together, and beaten along with whips." The man lost six hundred of the original nine hundred along the way. At Catumbela, "the slaves were rested, sorted out, dressed," and then marched the fifteen miles to Benguela, "usually disguised as ordinary carriers." Burtt met with a local Portuguese judge critical of the labor-recruiting process and left convinced that "the whole city and district is eaten out with slavery and rotten to the core." First prize in a recent raffle, ostensibly a bicycle, had in fact been a young woman. "A phrase used in the description of the bicycle when taken in a 'slang' sense," Burtt explained to Cadbury, "was very descriptive of her, and of course everyone saw through the thin disguise."[30]

Burtt's Dutch host regretted the drain of local labor to the islands but thought the repatriation of workers from São Tomé and Príncipe a waste of time. In the absence of effective law enforcement in Angola, he argued, returned serviçais would simply be recaptured and recontracted. Burtt countered that if the judges "were strong enough, the whole system could promptly be crushed at the ports by liberating all negroes who said they did not wish to go to the islands." The judge at Catumbela, however, had thirteen cases of slavery before his court, and he thought it "hopeless to attempt to do anything through the Portuguese government." Instead, he recommended that Cadbury Brothers "make an appeal through [your] king to Don Carlos himself."[31]

The judge's suggestion was an odd one because the British king, Edward VII, was a constitutional monarch who exerted no direct influence over government policy. The Portuguese constitution allowed King Carlos I more leeway. He functioned as a "moderating power," an executive meant to serve as a neutral negotiator between the branches of the government. But the king's dominant personality undermined his ability to be an effective power broker. That Portugal was mired in debt while struggling to reassert its place on the world stage only made the king's position shakier. In the Cortês, the

Portuguese parliament, antimonarchist Republicans—still in the minority in 1906—loudly criticized government incompetence and corruption. The Catumbela judge may have been a monarchist; there were devoted royalists in the Angolan civil service, even if there were few in Lisbon. In 1906, however, Catumbela, along with the small coastal town of Novo Redondo, elected a Republican municipal council. If repatriating workers to Angola from São Tomé and Príncipe was a waste of time, so too was making appeals to a distracted and increasingly isolated Portuguese king.[32]

Catumbela was not quite as rotten as Burtt imagined. To determine who was living in the district, the municipal council undertook a survey in 1906. The resulting report was less a census—it did not include a population count—than an attempt to identify the political structures, the commercial relations, and even the character of the people living in and around Catumbela. The questionnaire had very practical goals. Portuguese officials were trying to determine which communities among the local Ovimbundu people were the most "warlike"; which *sovas* (chiefs) exercised the most power; and, significantly, how they organized for war. Surveyors were also interested in how Africans viewed whites and mestiços and whether—when the Ovimbundu dealt with these outsiders—they understood the contracts generated by the purchase and sale of land. Understanding how Africans regarded the Portuguese and Afro-Portuguese was essential to Portugal's continued commercial and political success.[33]

Many of the questions in the Catumbela council's questionnaire revealed an attempt to acquire a deeper understanding of how African societies worked. What were the rights of mothers and fathers over their children? What were the rights of a husband with respect to his wife? Did a woman have the right to divorce her husband? An appendix listed 450 words of Umbundu translated into Portuguese, adding to the linguistic studies by J. Pereira do Nascimento and Ernesto Lecomte. Slave traders may have poisoned the atmosphere in Catumbela, but the municipal council boasted in its chairman, Luíz Maria Duarte Ferreira, an amateur ethnographer who demonstrated more curiosity about the Africans among whom he lived than Cadbury's representative had yet to display.[34]

At Catumbela, Burtt fell ill again with fever. So did George, the young itinerant German laborer Burtt had encountered "half starving" and begging for work in Benguela and had hired as a servant to accompany him into the hinterland. George had worked as a "cook and steward at sea," and despite a weakness for alcohol, he seemed to Burtt to be "a smart, intelligent man, very different from a negro." George was nevertheless a servant; Burtt did not use the man's last name in his correspondence with William Cadbury. When George's temperature rose to 105.5 degrees, Burtt arranged for his care and complained to Cadbury: "This place is not fit to live in, and these constant attacks of fever are weakening and depressing. The food is so bad that it seems impossible to pick up strength."[35]

The constant battle with illness, which he had avoided during the six months he spent on São Tomé and Príncipe, likely inspired the florid poem Burtt included with his March 17, 1906, letter. Rudyard Kipling had described the brown and black people of Europe's colonies as "half-devil and half-child." Burtt's poem, "The Wanton of the South," was slightly more complimentary. The bachelor Burtt depicted Africa as a sensual woman:

> Has she ever stooped and kissed you,
> With her warm and clinging lips,
> Till you fell back, hot with fever,
> Throbbing to your finger tips?

The imagery was undeniably sexual, and Burtt was attentive to the physicality of the people he encountered. But while ready at all times to note the beauty of a young African woman, he was also ready to describe, for example, a small boy with a "solemn air" waiting on his table at Ambrizette who reminded him of "a ponderous but well-meaning gorilla." Burtt's social intercourse with most of the Africans he met was limited. There is no evidence in his correspondence with Cadbury that the reticent and racist Burtt engaged in sexual intercourse while in Africa—although had he done so, it seems unlikely that he would have admitted it to his employer. "The Wanton of the South" was mostly about the fauna and flora that had seduced Burtt in Angola: elephants, lions, and leopards as well as flowers, deserts, and plains. Still, after three bouts of malaria in three months, Africa seemed a "cruel woman" to him. Like Nevinson before him, Burtt had been worn thin by illness in Angola.[36]

Once George recovered, Burtt headed three hundred miles down the coast to Moçâmedes, which had a cooler climate and "practically no fever." There, he got to read the last installment in Nevinson's series for *Harper's*. The evocatively titled "Islands of Doom" appeared in February 1906. Burtt found the article "so unfair" that he could barely contain his irritation. "On page 328," he complained, "the guest who says 'The Portuguese are certainly doing a marvelous work for Angola' must have been myself." The balance of the quotation in *Harper's*, which Burtt declined to repeat, read: "Call it slavery if you like. Names and systems don't matter. The sum of human happiness is being infinitely increased." In March 1906, Joseph Burtt was outraged at the implication that he supported slavery. "I need hardly tell you," he assured Cadbury, "that what I did say conveyed an entirely different meaning." When he met Nevinson in June 1905, however, Burtt had just arrived on São Tomé. He was naive, but it seems unlikely—given his mission for Cadbury Brothers—that he would have openly supported slavery. Nevinson had just spent five months trekking through Angola. Physically and emotionally spent and convinced that slave trading continued in Angola, he was probably incapable of coming to any other conclusion during his two-week sojourn on São Tomé and Príncipe. The islands of doom were the place Angolan slaves went to die.[37]

That Burtt made the journey in reverse, first spending six months on the islands before going to Angola, shaped his own view of conditions on São Tomé and Príncipe, as well as his reaction to Nevinson's article. The overall death rate, he reminded Cadbury, was 11 percent, not the 20 percent claimed by Nevinson. Burtt also rejected the journalist's assertion that "the prettiest girls are chosen by the agents and the gangers [as] their concubines." White men did forge relationships with black women, but they were "chosen almost exclusively from the natives of S. Thomé." Nevinson's assertion that children were encouraged to engage in bestiality for the amusement of the planters deeply perturbed Burtt. To the contrary, he recalled that one boy had been "severely flogged" for his outrageous behavior. Flogging, Burtt reassured Cadbury, was nevertheless rare; workers were not routinely whipped to death as Nevinson implied, nor had Burtt found any evidence that runaways were hunted for sport. For him, the final article in the *Harper's* series was an abomination that pointed "clearly to this, that Nevinson writes authoritatively on matters of which he knows practically nothing." Despite the six months he himself spent on the islands, Burtt still struggled "to get at the truth amongst strangers, and if I found it difficult in six months it is quite impossible for Nevinson to have learnt much in as many hours, which was about the time he spent at the roças."[38]

Of another bit of flawed logic in "Islands of Doom," Burtt said nothing. Nevinson argued that Britain had lost any right to take a moral stand on the issue of slavery. It had rejected home rule for Ireland, stood by as Armenians were slaughtered, and crushed the two Afrikaner republics in southern

Africa. If slavery in Portuguese Africa was to end, the United States would have to intervene. Only in the United States, Nevinson argued, did "the sense of freedom still seem . . . to linger, and the people are still capable of greater actions than can ever be prompted by commercial interests and the search for a market." His assertion ignored the Jim Crow segregation laws introduced in the American South beginning in the 1890s, which had increasingly denied civil rights to former slaves and their descendants. American readers of *Harper's* were likely flattered by Nevinson's words, but two years earlier, an American chocolate company, Walter Baker, had declined to support the English chocolate companies' decision to send a representative to investigate the conditions of labor in Portuguese Africa, since so little of its cocoa came from São Tomé and Príncipe. For Burtt, the reality that Nevinson's "loose statement of what sounds like facts . . . will be accepted as such in England and America is to be deplored."[39]

At Moçâmedes, Burtt caught up on his reading and relaxed. He played tennis, went running, and recovered his "health and appetite . . . in this beautiful air." Compared to overpriced Benguela, Moçâmedes was cheap, and the temperature in his pleasant hotel room, at 73 degrees, was a good 10 degrees cooler. For him, it was "like being in England," but he knew few workers enjoyed such pleasures. As much as Burtt disagreed with Nevinson's depiction of São Tomé and Príncipe, his visit to a nearby fazenda confirmed the journalist's portrait of the laborer's lot in Angola. The estate was owned by the Viscount of Giraúl, Joaquim Cardoso Botelho da Costa, and its workers had no time for tennis. In 1903, Giraúl owned twenty-seven thousand acres of land, or just over a third of the land being cultivated in Moçâmedes District. At the fazenda Burtt visited, serviçais harvested bananas, sugarcane, and oranges to supply the steamships anchored at the port. The manager showed him around and told him that workers earned about nine hundred reis per month and were provided with food, clothing, housing, and medical care. The claim was disputed by an old brick maker Burtt talked to after his tour. The serviçal told him he made only six hundred reis a month, about one-quarter the salary earned by a male worker on São Tomé and Príncipe. The manager also admitted that workers were "not free to conclude their contracts at the end of five years."[40]

The town of Moçâmedes had been founded in 1840 to take advantage of the ivory trade. This initial development plan stumbled because of poor communication with the interior, and most trade continued to flow to Benguela to the north. An attempt to settle white farmers in the Huíla highlands in the 1850s failed when it proved too cold to grow tropical crops. In the 1860s, the Portuguese government set out to defeat and then tax the African peoples of the hinterland, but that attempt too was abandoned when it became clear that the cost of conquest exceeded the potential revenue from taxation. In the mid-1880s, following the Berlin West Africa Conference, Portugal again sent white settlers to Huíla and built a chain of forts, with the goal of extending its colonial sphere of influence from Angola in the west to Mozambique in the east. That dream was threatened by Germany's claim to South West Africa on Angola's southern border and then dashed by the British Ultimatum of 1890.[41]

Moçâmedes thus remained a backwater, even though in 1900, it had a population of 6,918, more than twice that of Benguela. African peasants did pass through Moçâmedes on their way to São Tomé and Príncipe, but Benguela continued to dominate the southern export trade in labor. As Burtt discovered at the Viscount of Giraúl's fazenda, farmers at Moçâmedes provisioned passing ships. The other major good produced in the district was aguardente (brandy). In the early 1900s, the viscount's holding company, Viúva Bastos e Filhos (Widow Bastos and Sons), accounted for 31 percent of the legal aguardente produced in and around Moçâmedes.[42]

Legal or illegal, aguardente had as devastating an effect in Angola as in São Tomé and Príncipe. In the Huíla highlands, one chief complained to Portuguese officials that his people had become starving drunks after trading their cattle and grain for hard liquor. Farther south, Ovambo chiefs tried to limit the access of their subjects to imported alcohol. In Angola's northern districts, many Africans smoked *diamba* (marijuana), but the bigger problem was imported rum. Burtt discovered that it was "quite a common thing to pay for everything, labour included, almost entirely in rum," with disastrous results for the local population.[43]

In the first week of June 1906, Burtt traveled from Moçâmedes in the far south to Ambrizette in the far north, "to fill up time" while he waited for porters. He had been in Angola for a little more than five months and with dogged persistence had managed to secure enough carriers for the fifteen hundred–mile return journey to Kavungu, now scheduled for mid-July. The long delay was not unusual. It had taken Dr. Ansorge, a zoologist working for the British Museum whom Burtt had met briefly in São Tomé, four months to plan his excursion, at a cost of £700. Burtt had managed a three-week trip to visit the Afrikaner community at Humpata, a hundred miles to the east of Moçâmedes and five thousand feet up in the mountains. That small adventure had given him a taste of the African wilderness imagined by the readers of Victorian and Edwardian travelogues. He wrote to Cadbury, "Once we . . . halted to sleep near the recent tracks of elephants, which looked as though someone had been dabbing huge flat, cake loaves down into the dust of the road." Tracking the elephants was Jan Harm Robberts, who had tapped his fellow Afrikaners' talent for hunting and transport riding and made a fortune selling ivory. At Robberts's two thousand–acre farm— the largest in the Huíla highlands—Burtt bought a goat to feed George and their five African carriers. Burtt's party also stopped at the Portuguese fort at Mininho, in lion country. Burtt did not see any lions, but he met an Afrikaner who showed him "the marks of a lion's teeth in his knee [and] a pale little storekeeper" who proudly displayed the "rifle he had shot two lions with."[44]

Compared to the dry and sandy south, Ambrizette, in the Congo District 150 miles north of Luanda, seemed verdant. Burtt asked Cadbury to "picture . . . bushes, and great Baobab trees with their swollen trunks, and plantations of millet 10 feet high." He stayed with Matthew Stober, who had accompanied William Cadbury to Lisbon as his translator in 1903. Stober had founded the nondenominational Angola Evangelical Mission, which maintained a station in Ambrizette, in 1897. Coffee and ivory were traded through the nearby port, as were contract workers, many of them drawn from the Congo Free State.[45]

Stober's open opposition to the trade in serviçais to São Tomé and Príncipe drew the ire of Portuguese officials at Ambrizette. The Portuguese government had officially approved the founding of "self-supporting industrial missions" in Angola in 1885. African rulers also welcomed the missionaries and hoped that they would counterbalance Portuguese influence. For their part, Protestant missionaries remained uneasy about their status in Catholic Angola. Even as they funneled information about labor recruiting back to Europe, missionaries feared that their vocal opposition might lead to their stations being shut down. Stober told Burtt that Africans were warned "to have nothing to do with the mission" and that officials had "at times taken away the black servants in the employ of the missionaries." Stober had also written to William Cadbury to tell him about Arthur Oliveiro, who was running a labor-recruiting agency a stone's throw from the Ambrizette mission. During the second week of February 1906, a group of serviçais that Oliveiro had recruited rebelled, severely wounding the agent and his assistants. Twenty slaves, as Stober described them, escaped.[46]

Henry Nevinson, who shared the missionary's views and had met him in 1905, thought Stober "a very unusual man—thin, elegant, polite almost to affection, and much inclined to pray over me." George Cadbury thought Stober was a fraud, and though his nephew William did not agree, the younger Cadbury thought the missionary "about as foolish as a man could be: doing his best to make it impossible for anything like a diplomatic and friendly appeal." Stober's language in his February 1906 letter bore out William Cadbury's assessment: "May Heaven have mercy upon and forgive those who are protracting and making more difficult the speedy end" of the "sorrow in this land, and who write of well treated men, contented women and laughing children—these, the captured and captive slaves of the white man in the plantations in these parts." That Burtt might have been among the transgressors, as implied in Stober's observation that "we have heard much of . . . Mr. Burtt, and though we disagree with some of his methods taken in this enquiry—we are united and earnest for him in much prayer," was firmly denied by Cadbury. The chocolate maker assured the missionary that "with regard to Joseph Burtt, he started his enquiry with the fullest wish to be fair to both sides, and up till now you may be interested to know that he practically confirms Nevinson's more serious accusations, though of course he has not yet had much experience on the mainland—he has, however, seen more of the estates in the islands than perhaps any other European."[47]

Fairness was what the members of the Geographical Society had sought when they met in Lisbon in March 1906 to discuss Dr. Strunk's report on the island of São Tomé, first published in the *Gordian* (a journal for German chocolate manufacturers). The attention paid to Strunk and to the earlier articles by Augusto Chevalier of the Paris Museum were part of the defense of Portuguese colonialism mounted in response to the publication of *A Modern Slavery*, the edited collection of Henry Nevinson's *Harper's* articles. Strunk's concerns had largely been technical; he toured São Tomé on behalf of businesspeople who had invested in cocoa in the German West African colony of Kamerun (Cameroon). Strunk did visit many of the major roças on the island, including Boa Entrada, Monte Café, and Rio d'Ouro. For his *Gordian* readers, he praised the ample and varied diet of the serviçais, observing that if such a diet were introduced to Cameroon, it could only increase the productivity of workers. He also explained the five-year contract system, noting that workers acquired experience and the beneficial habit of labor. Workers' interests, the journal's readers learned, were protected by the curador, a government official who also served as a moderator between serviçais and planters. In Strunk's view, as the members of Lisbon's Geographical Society were happy to publicize, the serviçais on São Tomé were hardly doomed.[48]

Strunk did not suggest that São Tomé's workers were slaves, but then, slavery remained legal in Germany's African colonies. Nor did Strunk's narrative deviate much from what Burtt had found, though Burtt had not hesitated to describe the island's serviçais as slaves. The problem, in Burtt's view, was less the treatment of workers in São Tomé than how they were recruited in Angola.[49]

A visit to Cabinda offered Burtt a welcome respite from the stories of abuse that abounded elsewhere in Angola. The enclave of Cabinda sat just north of the Congo River estuary and shared its northern border with the French Congo colony. South of the port lay a twenty-mile strip of the Congo Free State and, below that, the rest of the colony of Angola. Portugal's claim to Cabinda, which had been a slave-trading post, was recognized at the Berlin West Africa Conference in 1885. Burtt stayed at the Angola Evangelical Mission station, where the house was "surrounded by orange and mango trees" and the "rich and tropical vegetation" that characterized the Congo River basin contrasted strikingly with the "waterless plains of sand" typical of much of Angola's coast. Like the Kroo, men from Cabinda worked on Portuguese steamships or took limited, one-year contracts in São Tomé. In 1905, a total of 213 Cabindas had disembarked at the main island, and 90 were working for the government of São Tomé, many as porters for the customs house in the capital. They were not serviçais, and their short-term contracts were a concession to the district government in Cabinda, which also needed laborers. Burtt thought the system "a good one," well suited to the Cabinda, who struck him as "a superior race of negroes."[50]

Back in Luanda to meet up with his servant George, Burtt was again confronted by the travails of the common worker in Portuguese Angola. George's landlord kept two house slaves, a young boy and girl, whom he regularly beat with both chicote and palmatória and whom he offered to sell to his tenant. Burtt stayed with John W. Lethaby, the manager of a British firm in the capital. He learned that Lethaby had watched as a newly arrived serviçal, unaccustomed to heavy labor, stumbled as he carried a load of firewood. His punishment for tripping was thirty strokes of the chicote.[51]

Lethaby proved a helpful resource in other ways: he lent Burtt a frock coat and top hat. Suitably dressed and with a letter of introduction from Carl de Merck, Burtt called on Angola's new governor-general, Eduardo Costa. Costa had been appointed only in May but was well versed in Angolan affairs; in 1903 and 1904, he had served as the colony's top official. Burtt as always was forthright and made no attempt to hide his agenda. His meeting with Costa, however,

FIGURE 20. Governor-general's palace, Luanda, c. 1906. (Editor: Eduardo Osório, Luanda.) By permission of the João Loureiro Postcard Collection.

proved disappointing. It was "a formal sort of affair amounting to nothing," though Burtt promised to visit again when he returned from the interior.[52]

In Luanda, Burtt also welcomed Dr. Claude Horton to Angola. Burtt's poor health had prompted him to search for a companion to accompany him into the interior. He had considered approaching the zoologist and onetime physician Dr. Ansorge but found him unsympathetic on the labor issue. A Portuguese-speaking American dentist who had studied medicine was interested in accompanying Burtt and was willing to pay the £100 Burtt needed to purchase extra supplies. But in the end, the dentist could not wait for porters, and Burtt wrote to Cadbury to see if he could find him a suitable companion, preferably with medical training. Somewhat apologetically, Burtt explained that the expense of adding another man to the trip would not be great and that such a man, "if he were reliable, would add weight to evidence, a servant and blacks scarcely count, and I can't shut my eyes to what big issues may hang on this trip." Cadbury found Horton, who spoke no Portuguese but made up for it, in Burtt's estimation, with charm, intelligence, and robust good health.[53]

At the beginning of July, Horton, Burtt, and George headed south to Benguela to prepare for their inland journey. Their ship stopped at Novo Redondo, 125 miles north of Benguela, and Burtt and Horton went ashore to explore "the bright little town with its roaring beach and . . . rich green . . . sugar cane plantations hemmed in by bare mountains." A trader Burtt had met in his travels gave them a tour of the town and observed that "so many blacks were shipped away" from the port that "he did not think they could all be needed in S. Thomé." The stop at Novo Redondo also demonstrated how well known Burtt and his mission had become in Angola. The town's medical officer—a friend of the American dentist—sent a servant to bring the two visitors to his house. There, they received "a most cordial reception" from a host who "set champagne, mineral waters, grapes, cake, etc. before us, and was as charming as a Portuguese gentleman can be."[54]

"That little visit to Novo Redondo," Burtt admitted to Cadbury, "should be a warning to us to beware of appearances." They "had seen laughing natives, . . . taken a photo of a girl whose beauty and modest grace we shall not easily forget," and been treated with "the utmost kindness" by the trader and the doctor. Still, Burtt had to concede, as Nevinson had asserted in *Harper's Magazine,* that Novo Redondo was "one of the worst places on the coast," where torture reminiscent of the Inquisition was still practiced. An implicit apology for dismissing the journalist's fear of being poisoned by his enemies also made it into his letter to Cadbury. Burtt had come to understand that "a merchant known to give me information would be obliged to leave the country." One informant had begged him, "Don't let anyone know or they might kill me."[55]

From Benguela, Horton hoped to depart immediately for the interior, but Burtt had not managed to retain the carriers he had hired, though he had arranged for new porters to be sent from Bihé. Horton, who planned to start a new job in England in February 1907, had allotted six months for his Angolan adventure, with a buffer of two months to accommodate unexpected delays. He quickly learned that in Angola, "two months are but as a day."[56]

The delay at Benguela gave Burtt and Horton the chance to have breakfast with William E. Fay, a missionary of the American Board of Commissioners for Foreign Missions (ABCFM) who was stationed at Bailundo, a hundred miles to the east of Benguela. The ABCFM station had been established in 1881. Fay and Wesley M. Stover arrived the following year; by 1885, Fay had helped prepare a preliminary dictionary of Umbundu. Though he had no formal medical training, he also managed the clinic at Bailundo, and he quizzed Horton enthusiastically about the latest medical advances. Fay and Stover and their families had lived in Angola for twenty years by the time war broke out at Bailundo in 1902. Suspicious Portuguese authorities accused the missionaries of encouraging the rebellion. The greater threat, however, proved to be Portuguese and Afro-Portuguese traders, drawn by the opportunities presented by Africans living around the ABCFM missions at Bailundo and Sakanjimba to its east. By 1905, traders and white convicts

FIGURE 21. View of Novo Redondo, c. 1904. (Editor: Osório and Seabra, Luanda.) By permission of the João Loureiro Postcard Collection.

settled by the government had overrun Sakanjimba, and the ABCFM moved its station to Ocileso, forty-five miles to the north.[57]

Stover and Fay preferred not to comment publicly on the trade in contract workers that passed by their station at Bailundo. Privately, Fay told Burtt exactly what he thought. The missionary praised the kindness with which many Portuguese treated Africans, and he agreed with Burtt "that under a similar system the English would probably be worse, we having a stronger racial antipathy to the black." But like Matthew Stober of the Angola Evangelical Mission, Fay had misgivings about Burtt's agenda in Portuguese Africa. He refused on principle to drink cocoa and directed Burtt to "tell Mr. Cadbury from me that cocoa is blood."[58]

Burtt did not and could not—given his contract with William Cadbury—claim the missionary's position as his own. He confessed, however, that "at times I get so wroth" over the abuses in the labor-recruiting system that "I forget my Quaker breeding." His inclination was to offer a more balanced analysis. At the root of the problem was the tremendous profit to be made on a worker contracted for £6 in Ambrizette and then recontracted in São Tomé for £36. The inability of officials in Luanda to govern the hinterland effectively, the low salaries of bureaucrats in rural districts, and a broad tolerance for corruption combined to tempt many to traffic in labor. By tracing the slave route himself, Burtt hoped to acquire some understanding of how the contracting process might be improved.[59]

Five

THE SLAVE ROUTE

THE 750-MILE journey from Benguela to Kavungu on Angola's eastern border took Joseph Burtt and his party along a path familiar to local African traders, soldiers, slaves, and slave dealers. Portuguese had joined the parade of travelers beginning in the late fifteenth century. When Burtt set out in mid-1906, he bought his provisions at an English store in Benguela and was accompanied by his English physician, his German servant, and fifty African porters. Managed by two "petty chiefs," the carriers provided their own food and would be paid in cloth. Several spoke a bit of Portuguese, and two had a little English. As far as Burtt knew, they were all free. Burtt had purchased "food for 3 white men for 22 weeks, which with what we shoot and can (if necessary) buy on the road, should be ample." With a mule and two donkeys at their disposal, the white men could, if they wished, travel in relative comfort. Along the way, they could enjoy the hospitality of Portuguese colonial officials and American, British, and Swiss missionaries. The road to Kavungu, for all the darkness associated with slave trading, was hardly unknown.[1]

On July 31, four days after leaving Benguela, Burtt, Horton, and George pitched their tents on a bluff overlooking the Catumbela River. While George baked bread in a large iron pot, Horton counted the provision boxes and trunks. A passing Portuguese trader on his way to Benguela marked all the best rest stops on Burtt's map and promised to mail his letters. The end of July was the dry season in an arid country, and everyone went to sleep thirsty. Burtt shared a tent with Horton; they found the "brilliant moonlight nights so cold that we find it hard to keep warm." The next morning, after a three-hour march, they reached the banks of the river and stopped again for tea and porridge. The road, Burtt wrote to William Cadbury, was good and wide. Better yet, "strolling along with camera and umbrella . . . at the rear" of his caravan, he managed to encourage his carriers to walk twenty miles a day under a hot sun. Horton, meanwhile, stepped off the road and with the help of a young African went hunting for antelope in the "strong stalks of grass" that had "not burnt away in the fires."[2]

Lugar da estampilha

BENGUELLA
Um grupo de
gentio em um
quintal, ouvindo
tocar „chingufo"

FIGURE 22. Group of Africans and two Europeans at Benguela, c. 1905. (Editor: Colecção Tavares, Benguela.) By permission of the João Loureiro Postcard Collection.

The bucolic scene was disrupted just outside the town of Catumbela by Burtt's discovery of an ankle shackle abandoned "down in the bushes by the steep path." In the town, where slaves and rubber had once dominated the economy, serviçais were now funneled on their way to São Tomé and Príncipe, as Burtt had learned when he visited Catumbela the previous March. The shackle, designed for two captives, was "a rough piece of wood some 14 inches by 6 with an oblong hole in the centre, just large enough to admit the ankle of each man. A couple of pegs passed through it from the side to tighten it." In a scene reminiscent of Henry Nevinson's articles for *Harper's Magazine,* Burtt also passed five skeletons. At the spot where his party stopped to eat, a strong odor led them to "a decomposing corpse, parts of the scalp & body were gone but the feet & limbs were intact." The man "lay on his back with his limbs spread out, . . . a small basket, a large wooden spoon, a mat & a few filthy clothes" by his side. Whether the man was a slave freed from the shackle or a free carrier Burtt could not say, though he had been told that "when a free carrier dies on the road he is buried by his relatives, if in company with them." He added, "We saw many such graves."[3]

In his letters to Cadbury, Burtt did not identify the source of his admittedly narrow knowledge about local burial practices. In Ovimbundu villages, funerals were held for those who had died without kin, but whether that practice was extended to kinless slaves and consistently followed by caravans of traders and porters is less clear. Nevinson, describing a virtually identical scene for *Harper's* readers in November 1905, explained his Ovimbundu Bihéan porters' refusal to bury slaves: they considered it "burying money. It is something like their strong objections to burying debtors. The man who buries a debtor becomes responsible for the debts; so the body is hung up on a bush outside the village, and the jackals consume it, being responsible for nothing." The contrast between Nevinson's porters—moral (at least when it came to debt), pragmatic, and even a bit callous—and Burtt's porters was striking. The fifty men and boys with Burtt were from Quilengues, a village on the trade route to the southeast of Benguela. Ever patronizing, he described them as "gentle willing fellows," contented by "cheap tobacco" and carrying "old guns which they load up and let off with great interest from time to time exactly like children."[4]

East of Catumbela, the road narrowed, and the porters struggled with their loads along rocky paths that were sometimes less than a foot wide. Over seventeen days, the party climbed 6,000 feet through the Benguela highlands before descending to the 4,800-foot-high plateau at Bailundo. The settlement there included a small contingent of Portuguese officials and African soldiers at the nearby fort, as well as a few American missionaries. It was surrounded by the larger Bailundo kingdom. The Ovimbundu at Bailundo had long traded in slaves, ivory, and beeswax; the arrival of Portuguese traders in 1600 introduced European cloth, guns, and liquor. In the late nineteenth century, the kingdom traded in rubber and in serviçais bound for São Tomé and Príncipe.[5]

Missionaries from the American Board of Commissioners for Foreign Missions (ABCFM) had arrived in 1881, and after a brief expulsion in 1884, they were allowed to return under the protection of *Sova* (King) Ekwikwi. By 1903, more than two thousand African students were enrolled in ABCFM schools in Bailundo and in Bihé, five days' walk to the east. In 1890, following the terms of the Berlin West Africa Act, the Portuguese set out to occupy the empire they had claimed in 1885. They first defeated the sova of the nearby Bihé kingdom and then turned their attention to Bailundo. In the 1880s, Ekwikwi had viewed the Portuguese as potential allies, even investing in a trading house in Catumbela. What the Ovimbundu "thought of as an alliance, the Europeans understood as subjection." In the Bailundo memory of the occupation, the Portuguese entered the kingdom first by stealth as "traders" accompanied by African soldiers "disguised as porters with loads of goods." By 1896, the Portuguese had built a fort near Sova Numa II's village

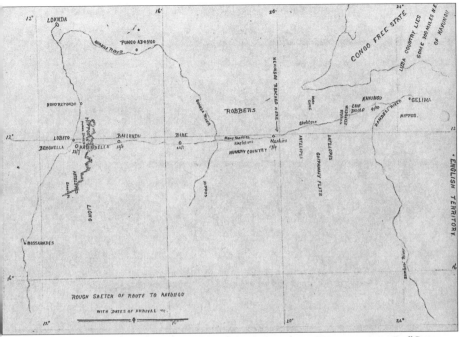

MAP 4. Joseph Burtt's map of his route from Benguela to Kavungu, 1906. In "Copy of Letters Received from Joseph Burtt," following p. 273, James Duffy Collection, African Collection, Yale University Library, New Haven, Conn.

complex. The fort and the ABCFM mission attracted merchants; at the beginning of 1902, there were five hundred trading firms in the area.[6]

Burtt and his porters rested for two days at Bailundo, and he took the opportunity to talk to the ABCFM missionaries about the uprising that had begun in April 1902 and continued sporadically for nearly two years. Whether the missionaries he spoke with included William Fay and Wesley Stover, with whom he and Horton had breakfasted at Benguela in July, is unclear. The missionaries' letters do not record Burtt's visit, and Burtt, convinced that his letters were being opened before they were mailed from Benguela, had become even more opaque in the descriptions he offered William Cadbury.[7]

Burtt's caution was justified, given the web of connections that linked missionaries, traders, and colonial officials. Walter T. Currie, who ran the ABCFM mission at Chissamba in the Bihé District, was particularly disliked by Bailundo's traders—African, mestiço, and Portuguese—because he had established a successful trading firm to fund several industrial schools. In 1901, the resident Portuguese *capitão-mor* (chief constable) at Bihé, Alexandre Malheiro, complained that ABCFM schools not only taught Africans English but also taught them to write their own languages using English orthography. As in São Tomé, ties between colonial officials and traders could be close. Before he left the west coast, Malheiro had presented his credentials to Pedro d'Almeida Leal at the office of the Companhia Comercial de Angola (Commercial Company of Angola) in Benguela, where Leal advised him on what supplies he should take with him to Bihé. Stover, who did not approve of Currie's trading activities, drew official Portuguese suspicion when, with Father Gapon, a Holy Ghost priest, he negotiated a prisoner exchange at Bailundo's fort during the early stages of the war in June 1902. From the African perspective, both Americans and Portuguese could be problematic guests.[8]

The competing demands and agendas of colonial officials, missionaries, Christian converts, mission students, and traders—many of whom (with the exception of the missionaries) trafficked in labor and liquor—increased the stresses within the Bailundo kingdom and contributed to the outbreak of war in April 1902. The collapse in the price of rubber undermined an already fragile economy. Outside traders competed with the Ovimbundu for slaves and for serviçais destined for São Tomé and Príncipe. Some Bailundo leaders particularly resented Portuguese involvement in the rum trade, which they claimed debilitated Africans more accustomed to drinking home-brewed beer. When a Portuguese trader accused a minor chief of not paying for his rum, the ensuing dispute drew in the colonial authorities at Fort Bailundo, who arrested the reigning king, Sova Kalandula, when he visited the fort in May. His successor, Mutu-ya-Kavela, besieged the fort, burned traders' houses, and killed the owners—mostly mestiços but including some "civilized blacks" and Europeans—and tried to blockade the roads leading out of Bailundo territory. Bailundo had watched as the Bihé kingdom, its "principle commercial rival," fell in 1890, and it had not intervened. Bihé was under Portuguese occupation in 1902, and though some fought, most Bihéans did not go to the aid of Bailundo. By July 1902, the Portuguese had mustered three columns of soldiers, about 770 men in all. Most were Africans, but the force included 142 soldiers from Portugal and some Afrikaners. The Ovimbundu may have fielded as many as 40,000 men over the course of the conflict. The Portuguese outgunned the musket-wielding Bailundo with repeating rifles, but even more effective and much more terrifying was the artillery that the Portuguese forces used "to blast the survivors out of their rocky hill or mountain retreats." This conflict marked the end of the independence of the Ovimbundu kingdoms of the central Angolan plateau.[9]

The commander of the Portuguese northern column was Captain Pedro Francisco Massano de Amorim. In 1901, he had investigated what his government officially viewed as an illegal trade in guns and labor along the border with the Congo Free State in eastern Angola. Along the frontier—still the property of King Leopold II at that time and not yet officially a colony of the Belgian state—authorities responded to competition from African and Portuguese slave traders by building a series of forts, designed to keep African workers inside the Congo Free State and block the importation of foreign guns. The forts were staffed by the African soldiers and white officers of Leopold's private army, the Force Publique. By 1900, there were 183 forts, each with about thirty-five to forty soldiers. Amorim investigated the claims of illegal arms and slave trafficking on the Portuguese side of the border and, in Henry Nevinson's recounting, "showed real zeal," even liberating slaves "with special 'letters of freedom' signed by himself." He earned the abiding enmity of Angola's traders, who tore up his letters and reclaimed their slaves when he left. During the 1902 war, Amorim "promised protection to loyalists and death to 'rebels.'" After a second investigation late in 1902, he dismissed the resident captains at Bailundo and at Bihé and prohibited traders from living within nine miles of either fort. Yet in the complex and often ambiguous circumstances faced by colonial officers on the ground, Amorim saw no contradiction between opposing slavery in 1901 and bombarding Africans resisting Portuguese occupation in 1902. The Portuguese Crown honored him for his bravery at Bihé and at Fort Moxico (Moshico) to the east with the Ordem da Tôrre e Espada (Order of the Tower and the Sword). Nor, for that matter, did Joseph Burtt see any contradiction in Amorim's actions. In his opinion and in the view of many British antislavery activists—including William Cadbury—the Portuguese had an obligation to occupy Angola effectively and to bring an end to both domestic slavery and the trade in unfree labor.[10]

The last skirmish took place in March 1904. When Burtt and his party arrived in Bailundo two and a half years later, memories of the war were still fresh. Burtt met traders who had lost everything, and ABCFM missionaries told him that the local people remained terrified. The Ovimbundu nevertheless continued to hold slaves. In the immediate aftermath of the war, the Portuguese did temporarily suspend the trade in serviçais and require all Europeans to register their firearms, but when Nevinson visited Bailundo in early 1905, the trade in laborers destined for São Tomé and Príncipe was operating openly. He saw no evidence of torture and no direct evidence of flogging, but he did hear thirdhand of a "gang of two hundred and fifty slaves" passing "through the Nanakandundu district"—of which Kavungu was part—"bound for the coast, in the end of February (1905), shackles and all." For the most part, however, caravans heading west tended to be smaller, and overseers mixed slaves in among the free carriers. In August 1906, Burtt encountered one such group carrying rubber in the Bihé district. His porters identified twenty-five individuals as slaves "put here & there in the long file" and "conspicuously different in appearance from the well nourished free carriers. The lean limbs & boney bodies told a tale of long hunger." They reminded Burtt of "a number of new arrivals on a roça at Príncipe" whom he had seen "in much the same condition."[11]

By the time Burtt and his carriers reached the mission station at Ochilonda in the Bihé District on August 22, five days after leaving Bailundo, they were all in bad shape. Sore feet hobbled the Africans, who took turns carrying Burtt in a *tipóia*—a hammock tied at each end to a pole and carried by two men. It had been twenty-five days since they had left Benguela on the west coast. With cooperative weather and reliable carriers, the trip could be made in sixteen days; it could take thirty during the rainy season. Only Horton was "well and happy," though "very busy looking after the carriers." Burtt was suffering again from his skin condition, and his legs were still so inflamed after marching from Benguela to Bailundo that he could neither walk nor ride. Forty-three of the fifty carriers he had hired in Benguela at the end of July refused to go any farther. He scrambled to find replacements but managed to hire only twenty-two men and two boys. With regret, he dismissed his manservant, explaining to Cadbury that the reduced number of porters made it "quite impossible to take George with us, as a white man must be well cared for in this country." The German returned to the coast with some of the departing carriers and planned to continue on to England, where he had agreed to deliver some boxes to Gopsill Burtt in Hull. Burtt's other concern was that Africans would decline to travel after mid-September because that was when the planting season began. Burtt and Horton could find themselves stuck in Bihé for months. It was an unwelcome prospect, for even though Burtt's rough sketch of his route to Kavungu identified Bihé as a town, there actually was no town. Rather, Bihé was a "wide district of forest and marsh" with "no big rivers, except the Cuanza, which separates it from the land of the Chibokwe to the east." If they were delayed too long, Horton would have to leave for England and his new job, and Burtt would be forced to abandon his journey.[12]

The nine days that Burtt and Horton spent at Ochilonda were dedicated to securing new porters. Burtt also got a clearer sense of the pressures missionaries faced. Plymouth Brethren missionaries maintained stations at Bihé and Capango in addition to Ochilonda. The ABCFM had missions at Ocileso, Kamundongo, and Chissamba. There were also two Portuguese forts in the district. Fort Belmonte was about twenty-five miles southeast of Ochilonda; Fort Neves Ferreira overlooked the Cuanza River on Bihé's eastern border, four days' walk away. Portuguese suspicion—both official and commercial—of Protestant missionaries had only increased since the Bailundo war. Despite the freedom of religion guaranteed under the 1891 Anglo-Portuguese Treaty, some Portuguese officials even questioned the right of foreign Protestant missionaries to be in Angola. The ABCFM station at Kamundongo, located just six miles to the southeast of Fort Belmonte, had burned to the ground in 1904 and again in mid-April 1906, but Portuguese administrators did not investigate what appeared to be arson, likely by Portuguese traders. On July 4, 1906, the ABCFM missionary Wesley Stover was formally expelled from Angola. The atmosphere in Bihé district in mid-1906 was fraught with suspicion, and Burtt himself was not immune. Even as missionaries offered him a place to stay and helped him find new porters, they questioned whether his openness with Portuguese officials—which Cadbury considered essential to the investigation—prevented him from obtaining the "desired true information."[13]

Ochilonda nevertheless offered Burtt new insights into the complexities of local slavery and the export trade in slaves. The station had been founded in 1893 by Plymouth Brethren missionaries. They had earned the ire of traders first by rescuing an old woman abandoned on the side of the road by a passing caravan and then by taking in a young girl left at the mission after she injured her feet crossing a river. In general, missionaries opposed redeeming slaves from passing caravans, arguing that paying traders only increased their ability to buy supplies and more slaves. In August 1906, however, Burtt and Horton observed as missionaries listened sympathetically to the story of a young girl who had been claimed by an African trader seeking payment of an old debt and then sold to a Portuguese trader. As Burtt explained to Cadbury, a young man named Ngumba asked the missionaries

> what they could do about his wife's cousin Neyambi, a girl about 15 years of age, who had been made a slave. Amorin once told these people that the king had done away with slavery and Ngumba asked if the king did not approve of its being stopped. It seems a wicked old native named Saulamba stated that his uncle once loaned some

goods to the girl's family, creditor and debtor are both dead, but on this ancient grievance Saulamba has actually taken the girl Neyambi, an Ochibundu and an absolutely free woman, and exchanged her for another slave to a Portuguese trader. The poor girl is now a slave for life, and her mother is breaking her heart over it. If her relatives were rich enough they might redeem her by giving the trader two or three slaves from the interior. The more anxious the relatives are to free a slave the higher the price demanded. Unfortunately Neyambi has no elderly male relative to take up the case.

The incident was striking in part because of the amount of detail that Burtt provided to Cadbury. All the participants—Ngumba, Neyambi, and Saulamba—in the small drama that unfolded at Ochilonda were named. For the first time, Burtt gave his employer a glimpse of the inner lives and struggles of the Africans he had been observing for over a year. Neyambi's experience was not unique; individuals did, on occasion, find themselves enslaved because of debt, and Burtt rightly emphasized that without a senior male protector, Neyambi would remain a slave. Cadbury's commissioner was deeply offended by the actions of Saulamba, but what Burtt objected to most was "the evil practice of raking up old offences" and bringing complaints for adjudication to the Portuguese fort, where "too often the judge has some share in the spoil." The fine was routinely paid in slaves, even though the Portuguese had outlawed slavery and slave trading. Poorly paid officials were easily bribed, and the profit to be made from the market in labor for São Tomé and Príncipe was so large "that clean-handed trade cannot compete with slaving. The system," he concluded, was "below the recognised standard of morality and is detrimental to the interests of the Portuguese" and the Africans. Ochilonda awakened in Burtt a "strange new feeling, half sorrow, half anger" that ran "riot in his brain, touching outlying regions of his nature hitherto unexplored." But even though his "indignation rose as he thought of the 'damned nigger' attitude towards the native, still so common in Africa," he could not bring himself to embrace Africans as equals.[14]

Missionaries, motivated to rescue Africans from the "darkness of idolatry" by spreading the Christian gospel, also harbored ambivalent attitudes. Their task, from their point of view, was extraordinarily difficult. To a list of obstacles increasingly topped by official Portuguese opposition could be added inhospitable terrain, deadly diseases—including malaria and blackwater fever—isolation, meager funding, and Africans unwilling to convert.

Even as missionaries learned Umbundu and Lovale (Lwena), they attempted to induce Africans to embrace Western schooling, technology, and cultural norms including monogamy. They worried that their converts were merely "Rice Christians," drawn by the prospect of "free hand-outs" and refuge from local rulers and Portuguese traders. At the ABCFM station at Chissamba, a reluctant Walter Currie found himself cast as "Chief Currie," whose village complex included a farm and an industrial school. He conducted services with the assistance of Ovimbundu deacons, and he spent most evenings "settling disputes among the villagers" and consulting with his neighboring chiefs. The actual African chief of Chissamba village remained deeply suspicious of Currie and never converted.[15]

Burtt's letters to Cadbury do not suggest that he was aware of the challenges missionaries faced in ministering to their congregations. Nor was he, as a rule, interested in the daily lives of Africans living along the road to Kavungu. The focus of Burtt's mission was narrow: to determine if slave trading continued in Angola and if those slaves ended up as serviçais on São Tomé and Príncipe. For a more dramatic sense of what might have happened to Burtt and Horton after they left Bihé on September 1, crossed the Cuanza River, and passed through the Hungry Country, William Cadbury could turn to, among other sources, Nevinson's articles in *Harper's,* written to inform but also to entertain.

Three days' walk east brought Burtt and company to the Cuanza River and the border of Bihé district. When the English Brethren missionary Frederick S. Arnot had made the crossing in 1890, the Portuguese had not fully conquered the kingdom of Bihé. Travelers had to seek permission from the chief, whose village sat atop the steep hill overlooking the river. "This village is so much the key to the crossing," Arnot observed, "that you must enter by its front gate, pass through the village, and make your exit at the back ere the shore can be reached." Getting one's party and supplies to the other bank required hiring a dugout canoe and competing for the available space with traders leading large caravans. Each canoe, piloted and powered by one paddler, held a maximum of four men, who were usually so unnerved by the choppy waters that they lay "flat on their faces in the bottom of the canoe for very dread." In early 1905, Nevinson had reached "the Cuanza rapids, where the river divides among rocky islands and rushes down in breakers and foam." It was the rainy season, and he stared "across the river's broad valley" at a "country steaming with damp." But Bihé was under Portuguese control, and no death-defying feats were required for Nevinson to cross the river—he boarded one of two ferries that regularly made the journey.[16]

From the deck of the ferry, he watched Africans crossing the river from east to west in dugout canoes much as Arnot had done fifteen years previously. The journalist, however, was convinced that the men and women were slaves, trapped by an illegal trade taking place a mile upstream from the Portuguese fort Neves Ferreira and thus conveniently out of view of its commander. Nevinson's suspicion was confirmed when he crossed the river west to east and found in "the trees on the western edge of the Hungry Country . . . shackles in profusion—shackles for the hands, shackles for the feet, shackles for three or four slaves who are clamped together at night." He hypothesized that slave traders abandoned the wooden shackles because they were no longer needed. To get home, captives would have to cross the Cuanza River and then trek through the Hungry Country. Both Burtt and Nevinson found the path between the river crossing and Fort Moxico, about 170 miles to the east, littered with shackles and more than a few decomposing bodies. So had Colin Harding, an administrator in British North Western Rhodesia on Angola's eastern border, who had traveled to Bihé in 1901. Nevinson found the shackles something of a mystery, for they were "so numerous that if the slaves died at that rate even slave-trading would hardly pay, in spite of the immense profit on every man or woman who is brought safely through."[17]

At first glance, the Hungry Country—the effective barrier to captives' escape—also seemed mysterious. Numerous streams and rivers crossed the region, carrying the promise of fertility. Yet the soil was "loose white sand from end to end," and the area suffered from periodic droughts. A swarm of bees attacked Nevinson one afternoon while he was soaking his feet in saltwater. A few simple experiments with salt and honey convinced him that all living things in the Hungry Country—bees among them—craved salt. That included the local Chokwe people, who Nevinson discovered would "sell almost anything" in return for coarse salt.[18]

In Nevinson's view, the Chokwe were "savages of a wilder race," quite distinct from and even superior to the Ovimbundu Bihéans, whose dedication to trading had made them soft and robbed them of any culture worth admiring. The Chokwe, by contrast, were to be respected and feared. Three Chokwe armed with shields and spears followed Nevinson's caravan and tried to rob him. He scared them off "by making a great display with a jammed rifle." Beyond the stereotype emerged the journalist's admiration: "In the arts they far surpass all their neighbours on the west side. They are so artistic that the women wear little else but ornament." The Chokwe excelled at song and dance, decorated everything from their canoes to the iron weapons and tools they forged themselves, and built square houses with "a straight beam along the top, like an English cottage." Chokwe country, however, was poor. People subsisted on a diet of black beans, millet, "a beetle about four inches long," and occasional wild game. When food became scarce, the Chokwe moved. In 1905, Nevinson could not find the large village of Peho, visited in 1890 by Arnot, though it was still marked on the journalist's map.[19]

A more dramatic encounter awaited Nevinson near Fort Matota, where the Portuguese had assigned "a black sergeant and a few men to police the middle of the Hungry Country." When his caravan was fired at, the last carrier in line caught the "would-be murderer, . . . a big Luvale man, with filed teeth, and head shaved but for a little tuft . . . at the top." Nevinson blindfolded him and was about to knock him out with the butt of his rifle when his Bihéan carriers pushed him aside. They took the intruder's gun, "beat him with the backs of their axes, and drove him naked into the forest, where he disappeared like a deer." Only later did Nevinson discover that his porters thought he planned to kill the man, who worked for the Portuguese fort at Moxico, on the eastern edge of the Hungry Country. With memories of the Bailundo war still fresh, the carriers feared that they would suffer Portuguese punishment for Nevinson's actions.[20]

When Burtt passed through the Hungry Country a year later, the district was largely deserted and his journey decidedly less eventful. His caravan included several Chokwe carriers who had joined the party at Ochilonda station in the Bihé district. Burtt's attempt at buying food at a Chokwe village nevertheless fell flat. Offered "a small half-starved fowl for 8 yards of cloth," he left "in despair of 'doing a deal.'" Porridge, hot cocoa with diluted condensed milk, and biscuits became the standard morning meal. The caravan started at 6:00 a.m., covered about twenty miles, and camped at noon, the porters worn out by carrying sixty-pound loads under the hot sun along sandy footpaths. By the time they reached the Brethren mission at Cinjamba, near Fort Moxico, on September 16, they were all, as Claude Horton reported to Cadbury, "very hungry." The trek from Ochilonda had taken fifteen days.[21]

Cinjamba station had been the end point of Nevinson's journey in 1905. After a brief rest and a visit with the two medical missionaries stationed there, he had turned around and begun the walk back to Benguela. In September 1906, Burtt and Horton stayed for two days at the mission to give their carriers a much-needed break. Burtt's health had improved sufficiently that he was able to walk for short periods. Though he remained weak, he amused himself at Cinjamba by "felling a couple of trees." He also bought a

FIGURE 23. Bom Jesus fazenda on the Cuanza River, c. 1904. (Editor: Osório and Seabra, Luanda.) By permission of the João Loureiro Postcard Collection.

pig at a local village for his carriers to eat. The missionaries, as always, were gracious in sharing their stories of the ongoing slave trade with Cadbury's commissioner. Nevertheless, Horton wrote to Cadbury, it was "extremely difficult to get any first-hand evidence of the actual conditions here though there can be no doubt that it is simply slavery under another name."[22]

That slaves had been renamed serviçais was the conclusion of the August 1906 report Arthur Nightingale submitted to the British Foreign Office on labor conditions in Portuguese West Africa. From the Portuguese perspective, however, there was no firsthand evidence to support allegations of slavery. In September 1906, Augusto Ribeiro of the Geographical Society in Lisbon defended Portuguese labor practices in the colonies, condemning the "malevolent ignorance" of investigators motivated more by treachery than by a desire for the truth. Under the 1903 labor regulations, laborers migrating from Angola to São Tomé and Príncipe were registered and numbered. They received a copy of their contract, which could not exceed five years, and a portion of their wages went into a repatriation fund to pay their passage home. Workers were freely contracted and enjoyed the same rights as laborers who migrated to the farms and factories of Brazil and the United States. Indeed, as Ribeiro implied, Portuguese Africa was the more attractive destination—for among the programs introduced after 1903 were access to medical care, nurseries for young children, and care for the elderly. During his tour of the islands in 1905, Burtt had visited hospitals and crèches, and he had met contented, elderly retired workers. In the view of the Geographical Society, the government's plan to introduce professional schools for Africans, tailored to each colony's needs, would only enhance their appeal to workers. Portugal's plans for its African colonies, Ribeiro assured his readers, "is not a chimera." The vision may not have been impossible to realize, but for Burtt, deep in Angola's hinterland in September 1906—and for Nevinson before him—it seemed far removed from reality.[23]

The rainy season began as expected in mid-September, just as Burtt's caravan left Cinjamba. With delays to cross rivers and stops to buy food, it took another sixteen days at an average of sixteen miles per day to reach Kavungu. The party passed through "wide open plains" and struggled across the Chipamajy Flats, not yet the shallow lake it would become later in the rainy season. Herds of antelope—usually oribi—were a common sight. "One day," Burtt wrote to Cadbury, "I turned up five orabi in less than an hour, quite near the road, and shot one. . . . Antelope flesh in practice," however, proved "very tough." Though now more substantial, his party's diet remained monotonous: "maize mush," biscuits, "eggs in abundance which have been a pleasant addition to our meals," and tea consumed "in vast quantities."[24]

The party also encountered local people, most likely Lovale, though Burtt did not identify them in his letters. He did find "some of these interior villages . . . delightful, with their neatly thatched well-built huts." When the caravan camped in the afternoon, women would visit to exchange manioc for cloth; men sold "carved combs or axes." Burtt found them "gentle and friendly," as had the Brethren missionaries who passed through the same area in September 1890.[25]

Burtt and Horton arrived at Kavungu on October 4, 1906. They were welcomed by the Brethren missionary Fritz Schindler, a Swiss who spoke "four or five languages," very likely including Umbundu and Lovale, which Burtt thought gave him "a wider outlook than some of the others." Much of the information Burtt relayed to Cadbury—about the Bailundo war and about events at the Brethren stations at Ochilonda and Kavungu—came from this missionary. Schindler had first settled at Kavungu in 1891 but regularly traveled west along the road to Bihé. In the early 1890s, Portuguese influence along the far eastern frontier of Angola remained tenuous. The Brethren station at Kavungu fell under the jurisdiction of the Lovale queen, Nana Kandundu, who in turn considered herself "tributary to the Barotse" kingdom to the southeast. In mid-1891, after the negotiations that followed Britain's 1890 Ultimatum to Portugal, the Barotse came under British control. When Arnot and Schindler and their fellow missionaries met Nana Kandundu in October 1891, "she seemed very doubtful as to our real intentions, and was fearful of losing her position as chiefess." In the unsettling circumstances in which she found herself, she gave the missionaries an ox and announced that "she and the whites would be friends for ever." Arnot presented her with ninety-six yards of calico. The next day, "arrangements were at once made . . . for getting a house built."[26]

It was Brethren missionaries, Arnot and Charles Swan among them, who would draw attention to the extensive slave routes "from the deep interior, Katanga, Kasai, and Barotseland . . . down to Catumbela." In the 1890s, Ovimbundu oversaw the trade, and Portuguese officials could neither exercise effective control over the border they had claimed at Berlin in 1885 nor police the frontier beyond. Portuguese merchants were, however, heavily involved in the Atlantic coast trade. The independent Swiss missionary, trader, cartographer, and antislavery activist Heli Chatelain reported to the *African News* in 1890 about the short trip he shared on a steamer delivering mail with "200 contract workers . . . in their new striped cotton clothes." Arnot's and Swan's letters in the Brethren journal *Echoes of Service* further drew the attention of British antislavery activists, as well as that of Nevinson and Burtt.[27]

By the time Burtt arrived in Nana Kandundu District in 1906, the Portuguese had built a fort at Kavungu. Its commander, Manuel de Metto Lindo, was a rather questionable character in Fritz Schindler's estimation. Lindo owned slaves and had successfully hidden them from Amorim's investigation of illegal trading along the Congo Free State border in 1901. When Amorim allowed a small community of freed slaves to settle between the Brethren station and the fort, Lindo did not object. But in August 1906, two months before Burtt reached Kavungu, Lindo arrested them all. Insisting they were criminals and runaway slaves, he sent them west under guard to Fort Moxico.[28]

After the arduous journey from Bihé, Burtt found the mission station at Kavungu delightful. Houses with "thick mud walls and thatched roofs" were cool and quiet after weeks spent camping in tents. From his window, he looked out on "a garden with bananas and pineapples bright in the afternoon sunshine." With guides supplied by Schindler, Horton and Burtt briefly played tourist and hiked a day south to the Brethren station at Kazombo on the Zambezi River. "We did not," Burtt wrote to Cadbury, "like being so near without seeing it." At Kazombo, the Zambezi was about seventy yards wide. They crossed in "a shaky little dug-out," watching nervously for crocodiles. "Heavy thunder clouds" greeted them on their return, and a rejuvenated Burtt kept up with his guide as he ran back to camp. Ill health, however, plagued the residents of Nana Kandundu District. Horton and Burtt took quinine daily to guard against malaria, and blackwater fever proved a constant threat. At Kavungu, the missionaries looked "white and delicate." Schindler was "evidently far from well."[29]

Physically frail though he may have been, Schindler possessed a steely resolve when it came to opposing the slave trade. He had arranged sanctuary for the old woman and the young girl cast off by passing slave caravans whom Burtt had met at Ochilonda station. At Kavungu, the missionary repeatedly complained to officials about the activities of three Portuguese traders—Martins, Castro, and Tavares—and even sent Pokanwa, an African convert he had trained as a preacher, to investigate their activities. A former slave trader, Pokanwa was from the island of Zanzibar on Africa's east coast. He eventually settled near Kavungu, where Schindler redeemed his wife, Mwewa, after she was captured during a raid on a nearby village. This was a breach of Brethren policy, but Schindler's rationale was that she was "very lame and of no value." It nevertheless cost him two dozen yards of calico to secure Mwewa's release. At Chipamba, near Moxico, Pokanwa found people being sold for debt and traders raiding villages. The trader Martins had left for the west coast with a caravan of fifty slaves.[30]

At Kavungu, Burtt wrote to Cadbury, "We seem to be in the middle of the traffic." Just to the north, six Portuguese trading firms sat along the Angolan border with the Congo Free State, conveniently out of sight of the Portuguese fort, rather like the ferry that Nevinson had taken across the Cuanza River. With Amorim long gone, traders hired Batatela mercenaries from the Congo side of the border to supply slaves. The Batatela were among the soldiers in King Leopold II's private Force Publique, an army that also included former slaves. In addition to patrolling the border, these soldiers fought other Africans who opposed Congo Free State authority, among them Chokwe living within the Congo's borders. In 1897 and 1898, however, it was members of the Force Publique who rebelled after the execution of several African chiefs. "The rebels," Burtt wrote to Cadbury in mid-October 1906, "have been joined by various outlaws and malcontents and are well supplied with arms and ammunition. The Congo authorities have tried to suppress them . . . without success, and they still continue . . . taking slaves, and supplying them to the Bihean and Portuguese traders."[31]

Many of the authorities of the Congo Free State were openly complicit in slave trading and in procuring the forced labor used to collect rubber. These were among the horrors that Edmund Morel's Congo Reform Association—avidly supported by William Cadbury—sought to end. For Burtt, the atrocities committed by the rebel African soldiers were particularly disturbing. "They are cannibals," he told Cadbury. When Schindler "asked a man whom they had sold, why they had not eaten him, he replied that he had a companion with him and they had scratched their arms, and having tasted the blood, sold him, and ate the other." The story would seem more evidence of Burtt's naiveté, but the decidedly less credulous Nevinson also regaled his audience with the tale of a former Batatela cannibal he had encountered working as a cook for Ovimbundu traders in Bihé. The charges of cannibalism cut both ways: white officers commanding the Force Publique supervised the severing of heads and hands of Africans who resisted occupation or who did not produce the required quota of rubber, and many Africans were convinced that Europeans ate the body parts. For his *Harper's* readers, Nevinson added what Burtt did not—that the young Batatela cook had rebelled "against the atrocious government of the Belgians on the Upper Congo."[32]

At Kavungu, Burtt obtained clear evidence of questionable Portuguese behavior along Angola's eastern border with the Congo Free State and North Western Rhodesia. On September 25, E. A. Copeman, an administrator in North Western Rhodesia, arrested three Portuguese traders "on the charge of trading in slaves, arms, powder and caps on British territory." Texeira, one of the traders about whom Schindler had repeatedly complained, was also implicated. Burtt wrote to Copeman for further details and could not have missed the irony when he accompanied Schindler to Fort Kavungu. The missionary translated Copeman's letter of protest into Portuguese for the fort's slave-owning commander, Lindo.[33]

On October 14, Burtt posted a long letter to Cadbury, sending it across the North Western Rhodesian border. It would take "a couple of months or so" for the letter to reach Birmingham, via mail steamer up the east coast of Africa. In fact, the last time Cadbury and his commissioner appear to have directly exchanged letters was in July 1906, when Burtt's caravan left Benguela. On October 19, Cadbury sent a letter to Burtt's Benguela address, stressing "how important it is that your outline report and summing up should not be delayed." Cadbury asked that Horton bring a draft report with him when he returned to England as expected in December. Burtt could "supply further details" when he returned "home in person."[34]

Officials in Portugal were also keen to read Burtt's report. Addressing parliament on October 31, the colonial minister, José Francisco Ayres de Ornellas, observed: "Not long ago one of the greatest cocoa merchants, Mr. Cadbury, ordered an investigation" into "whether the labour in that colony was regular or if it was slavery, as in the latter event his sentiments would not allow him to have any dealings with it. The result, however, was in our favour." Ornellas was not an uncritical apologist for Portuguese colonial policy. There were, he noted, "modifications and improvements to be introduced in the present regulations, above all the manner in which recruiting is conducted." Yet his assertion about Burtt's report was premature. Under pressure from H. R. Fox Bourne of the Aborigines' Protection Society earlier in the month to publicize Burtt's findings, Cadbury had explained that his representative "has written us many letters, but specially requested that we would consider them as private until he could sum up his whole experience." Burtt and Horton had just begun marching back to the west coast of Angola. From Bihé, they headed north, stopping briefly at the Methodist mission station at Pungo Adongo. At nearby Lucalla, they boarded the train, traveling the remaining 150 miles back to Luanda in relative comfort and arriving on December 7. Neither appears to have written any letters documenting their return journey.[35]

On December 14, the stack of letters Cadbury had sent to Benguela arrived in Luanda. The next day, along with Horton and one of his multilingual "hammock boys," Burtt visited a ship docked at Luanda. While the two Englishmen drank tea, the young man "had some talk with the serviçaes on board." He confirmed that three young men from Quilengues, "caught in Benguella, . . . were now going north to the plantations." Given how well known Burtt's mission was, it seems remarkable that his desire for a cup of tea aboard a Portuguese ship carrying contract laborers was not greeted with more suspicion. Perhaps more surprising is that it had not previously occurred to Burtt to ask an African to collect information for him. That intelligence made it into his preliminary report, along with his meeting with Governor-General Eduardo Costa on December 22. Like Ornellas, Costa thought "a better system might be adopted than the present." Reassured but apparently unaware that the governor-general's two-year term ended on December 31, Burtt left feeling that "however willing" Costa might be, "he would be quite incapable of taking any definite anti-slavery action on his own account." With a day to spare, Burtt finished his report on December 24, 1906. Horton took a copy with him when he sailed for England via Madeira the next day.[36]

Not surprisingly, Burtt's twenty-two-page preliminary report drew heavily on the more than three hundred pages of letters he had written to Cadbury over the year and half since he first landed on São Tomé in mid-June 1905. No longer the innocent admiring orchids and chasing butterflies, Burtt still aimed for balance when assessing the chocolate islands. Workers—most of them from Angola—were, he wrote, "generally, well housed and fed." They had access to medical care when ill. The five-year contracts under which they labored were "nominally free, and controlled by good laws, including the admirable law of 1903 relating to serviçaes." Planters, however, found it all too easy to circumvent the laws, especially if they had powerful friends in Lisbon. The average serviçal was "taken from his home against his will, . . . forced into a contract that he does not understand, and never returns to Angola. The legal formalities," Burtt concluded, "are but a cloak to hide slavery."[37]

In Angola's hinterland, the worst abuses of the slave trade had been checked by the Bailundo war. Yet "the unspeakable horrors of slavery, such as our grandfathers heard of, were openly carried on at the beginning of the twentieth century under a European Government." Slave caravans were smaller, but they still made their way from Kavungu in the east to Benguela in the west. Part of the reason was that "the arm of the Portuguese law is short," whereas the money to be made, including by poorly paid, overstretched colonial officials, proved all too tempting. In Burtt's view, "the wonder" was not "that there is so much slaving in Angola, but that there is so little."[38]

For all of William Cadbury's misgivings about Henry Nevinson, Joseph Burtt's December 1906 report placed Burtt firmly in the journalist's camp. When Nevinson arrived in São Tomé in mid-1905 for a two-week stay, exhausted after his four-month trek along Angola's slave route, he had been incapable of seeing the working conditions on the island as anything but slavery. Burtt spent five months on São Tomé, five weeks on Príncipe, and a year in Angola. He took Nevinson's journey in reverse and over a longer time span, but he ultimately reached the same conclusion. Africans were enslaved in Angola in a still-active trade. Shipped to the islands, they found themselves "doomed to perpetual slavery." Among Burtt's suggestions for improving the "existing conditions" in Portuguese West Africa were informing the British public—as Nevinson had done—and insisting that the Portuguese government enforce its own labor laws.[39]

The question still unanswered in December 1906 was how Mozambique fit into the humanitarian criticism of Portuguese labor policy in Africa. Burtt's third proposal in his preliminary report for improving the contracting process was to recruit "labour from the Portuguese colony on the east coast of Africa, where labour is voluntary." Subject to the same 1903 labor decree that governed Angola and São Tomé and Príncipe, Mozambique supplied tens of thousands of miners each year to Witwatersrand gold mines in the British colony of Transvaal. In October 1906, José Paulo Cancella had asked his fellow parliamentarians why no one was protesting labor contracting in Mozambique when the legal process was identical to that practiced elsewhere in Portuguese Africa. In the same session, the colonial minister, Ornellas, praised the transparency of recruiting across the border between Mozambique and the Transvaal. Not everyone, however, was convinced. As early as April 1901, William Cadbury had wondered if force was being used to recruit mine workers from Mozambique. Henry Nevinson had no doubts: "In Mozambique, the agents of capitalists bribe the chiefs to force laborers to the Transvaal mines, whether they wish to go or not. . . . We may disguise the truth as we like under talk about 'the dignity of labor' and 'the value of discipline,' but, as a matter of fact, we are on the downward slope to a new slavery." Joseph Burtt's final task as Cadbury's commissioner to Africa was to determine the truth of that charge.[40]

Six

MOZAMBICAN MINERS

LOURENÇO MARQUES, on Africa's east coast, was a young city with an old name that honored the Portuguese ship captain who had traded for ivory with Africans at Delagoa Bay in 1542. The development of the port and the town began in earnest only in 1877, after Britain conceded Portugal's right to Delagoa Bay, which lay just north of Mozambique's border with the British Natal Colony. In March 1877, Joaquim José Machado arrived in Lourenço Marques with orders to construct a hospital, a church, a barracks, and a jail. The hospital topped the list because endemic malaria plagued the town. Conditions were still grim a decade later when the town was incorporated. A British visitor described "a land of loveliness, surrounded by rich vegetation" but inhabited by "lazy people who wallow in their filth." Like São Tomé City and Luanda in the late nineteenth century, Lourenço Marques was poorly maintained, and it stank.[1]

Machado's plan to upgrade the port and railways would also achieve the larger goal of displacing the African traders, mostly Tsonga, who transported goods over land and by raft along the coast and in the bay's estuaries. In addition, colonial authorities hoped to undercut Indian traders, whose presence on the east coast predated that of the Portuguese. An 1894 census of Lourenço Marques counted a population of 1,059, including 591 Europeans, 245 Indians, and 39 Chinese. In October of that year, the city nearly fell to the Tsonga, who mobilized when colonial officials raised by 50 percent the "hut tax" on Africans living near Lourenço Marques on lands claimed by the state. Since the average Tsonga man maintained several grass-thatched huts for his extended family, it was an onerous increase. Tsonga chiefs, backed by three thousand soldiers, taunted panicked whites, calling them "chickens" and "women." In January 1895, António Enes, the newly appointed high commissioner for Portuguese East Africa (or Mozambique), arrived. A month later, two thousand Portuguese commanded by Enes and "armed with machine guns" defeated the Tsonga in a battle ten miles to the north of Lourenço Marques.[2]

FIGURE 24. Lourenço Marques, Mozambique. From Collection A2717-32, by permission of Historical Papers, William Cullen Library, University of the Witwatersrand, Johannesburg, South Africa.

By 1898, when the city became the capital, 4,902 people called it home. For its poorer residents, it continued to be "dirty, muddled [and] chaotic." Yet by 1904, the population had doubled again to 9,849. Another side of the city had emerged, clean and efficient, with a busy port whose wooden wharf had been replaced by one of concrete and with paved roads served by taxis and trams. As elsewhere in Portuguese Africa, foreign investors had initially funded the public projects, but by 1905, Portugal had paid off the loans and claimed full ownership of the port and the railroad. Visitors could stay at good hotels with rooms screened to keep out mosquitoes, and they could enjoy an evening stroll along the beachfront. It was this modern city that Joseph Burtt encountered when he arrived in Lourenço Marques in February 1907.[3]

The transformation of the city and the development of its infrastructure were intimately linked to the gold rush in South Africa, which had begun with the discovery of rich deposits on the Witwatersrand (or Rand) in 1886. The surrounding city of Johannesburg emerged almost overnight to service the mines and their laborers. In 1890, fourteen thousand miners were working on the Rand in what was then the South African Republic (or Transvaal), an independent state governed by Afrikaners. Foreign interests, mainly British, controlled the gold mines. By the time Britain defeated the South African Republic in the 1899–1902 war and claimed the territory as the Transvaal Colony, as many as sixty thousand Africans had migrated to Johannesburg's mines from Mozambique.[4]

Workers had long been among Mozambique's major exports. In the mid-nineteenth century, they had begun traveling to the farms of Madagascar, the large island off Mozambique's east coast claimed as a colony by the French, and to the sugar plantations of British Natal in the south. By the end of the century, they were also laboring on the farms and in the gold mines of British Southern Rhodesia on Mozambique's long eastern frontier.[5]

Competing with foreign farms and mines for labor were Mozambique's *prazos*, roughly equivalent to the roças of São Tomé and Príncipe and the fazendas of Angola. The *prazeros* (estate managers), many of whom were Afro-Portuguese, traded in gold and ivory beginning in the sixteenth century. A good part of their revenue came from taxes on resident peasant farmers, who usually paid in maize, wheat, millet, rice, and peanut oil. Repeated attempts by the Portuguese Crown to assert its authority over a massive territory that would eventually extend more than 2,800 miles along the coast from Lourenço Marques in the south to Rovuma Bay in the north—and, at points, 500 miles west into the interior—met with limited success.[6]

Following Britain's 1890 Ultimatum, which had dispelled Portugal's vision of a transcontinental empire linking Angola in the west to Mozambique in the east, Portuguese officials set out to establish effective control of the colony. In Lisbon, Enes, then serving as colonial minister, began by reforming the prazos with the goal of encouraging their economic development. Prazos had long been passed down as inherited property; in an effort to curtail prazeros' rights and redefine the prazo system, a new law granted leaseholders leases ranging from ten to twenty-five years. As Afro-Portuguese prazeros had long done, the new leaseholders retained the right to collect taxes from peasant farmers. In the new leaseholds on the south bank of the Zambezi River, half of a peasant's yearly taxes were assessed as labor, with the goal of encouraging cultivation. Not surprisingly, peasant farmers responded to the new regulations by migrating away from prazos where large-scale agriculture demanded more of their labor.[7]

Also competing for African laborers were three large companies, all intent on exploiting the colony's forests and mineral resources and developing its agricultural potential. Though they leased their land from the colonial state, the companies in many ways functioned independently of it. As elsewhere in Portuguese Africa, Mozambique's colonial administration was understaffed. In the south, the Companhia de Moçambique (Mozambique Company)—founded in 1888— occupied territory between the Zambezi and Save Rivers. The Companhia da Zambezia (Zambezia Company) leased land in the middle of the colony around the Zambezi River. In the far north, the

Companhia do Nyassa (Nyassa Company) acquired the territory between the Rovuma and Lurio Rivers in 1894. Sugar was an early success for the Companhia de Moçambique. The Companhia da Zambezia traded in copra—the dried coconut from which coconut oil was extracted—and in sisal, used to make rope. The companies also experimented with tobacco, coffee, peanuts, and cotton. Many laborers were forced to work, and they were whipped if they refused. Wages were often paid in alcohol, with the same devastating effects that Burtt had witnessed in São Tomé and Príncipe and in Angola. As elsewhere in its African empire, Portugal exported wine to Mozambique but attempted to exclude Africans from the commercial production of liquor. It also tried to prevent Africans from selling home-brewed alcohol distilled from the sap of the cocoa-palm. Ironically, Africans often used homemade cocoa-palm alcohol to pay part of their taxes, only to have it handed back to them as wages. District governors in the small sections of territory directly controlled by the colonial state resented that the companies accumulated much more revenue in the form of taxes on peasant farmers and laborers than they paid to the state for their leases.[8]

The seemingly endless demand for labor on the Witwatersrand's mines offered colonial Mozambique a new stream of tax revenue, adding to the existing preferences already granted by mine owners to the colony's railways and port. During the second South African War (or Anglo-Boer War), the Portuguese allowed Britain to move soldiers and supplies through Lourenço Marques and blocked Afrikaner access to the port. In 1900, British soldiers occupied Johannesburg. At the end of 1901, Britain signed a trade agreement (called the Modus Vivendi) with Portugal that guaranteed one-third of all the traffic from Johannesburg's mines would travel on Mozambican rail lines to Lourenço Marques. The Portuguese port, about 250 miles east of Johannesburg, was closest to the Transvaal's mines and offered direct access to the Indian Ocean. Ships sailed from there northward along the coast, through the Suez Canal, and into the Mediterranean. The port, however, was in competition with Durban in the nearby British Natal Colony and Cape Town in the more distant British Cape Colony. The 1901 Modus Vivendi thus protected a key source of Portuguese colonial revenue as the war drew to an end, and the ports at Durban and Cape Town again became fully accessible.[9]

The end of the war in 1902 brought a new opportunity. The Companhia da Zambezia, which had struggled to make a profit on its leases, agreed to allow the Witwatersrand Native Labour Association (WNLA) to recruit workers from its leaseholds. For each worker, the company received a fee of 5,040 reis, more than four times the average annual tax it could collect from a peasant farmer. In 1903, the colonial government also opened its northern territories, between the Lurio River and the Companhia da Zambezia concession, and its southern territories, south of the Sabi River, to licensed WNLA recruiters. Colonial officials charged recruiters and workers for issuing contracts and registering them, and they added extra fees for passports. For each laborer who signed a one-year renewable contract, Mozambique's government received 13 shillings, a substantial sum when multiplied by sixty thousand migrant workers per year. The Portuguese government also insisted on having a resident curador in Johannesburg, who would guarantee that Mozambican miners were well treated. As Burtt had discovered in São Tomé, the curador's responsibilities could be contradictory: he was also responsible for preventing "clandestine" workers from sneaking across the border without paying their taxes and fees. If a miner did not finish his contract and pay his taxes, the curador also made sure that he completed ninety days of forced labor for the colonial government when he returned home to Mozambique.[10]

Henry Nevinson insisted that Mozambican miners had been forced to cross the border; Joseph Burtt hoped that they had crossed voluntarily. So did the British government in its official pronouncements. The reality, from the African perspective, was open to interpretation. In the late 1880s, still-independent Gaza chiefs in the southern part of Mozambique taxed workers returning from the Transvaal a minimum of £1 and sometimes as much as £15. Young men who tried to avoid military service could be fined £10, a coercive tax that worked only if a man wanted to return home to marry, a contract for which he needed his chief's approval. In late 1895, however, Enes launched a successful military campaign that crushed the Gaza kingdom. When its leaders rebelled in 1897, they were again defeated, further limiting the authority of Gaza chiefs over their subjects. In 1899, however, neither the leaseholding companies nor Mozambique's colonial officials exercised complete control over the territories each claimed. The Afro-Portuguese prazeros who remained in the Zambezi River valley continued to tax their peasants directly. Ever adaptable, the prazeros abandoned slave trading in favor of labor recruiting for farms and mines. In Lourenço Marques, officials facing chronic labor shortages tried to force Africans to labor on public works. In a sense, Nevinson was right: the harsh conditions of the prazos, the strictures imposed by local chiefs, and the unpaid labor demanded by colonial officials all "forced" Mozambican workers across the border into the Transvaal. Yet by the first decade of the twentieth century, some Africans did cross voluntarily, in order to earn cash to pay their taxes and to contract marriages. Many also indulged an increasing attraction to European clothing, foodstuffs such as tea and coffee, and other consumer goods. For those who favored this second, rosier explanation of Mozambican labor migration, there was also "the incalculable benefit that Africans would be educated, taught the value of money, and, most important, taught how to work."[11]

The brevity of Joseph Burtt's visit to Lourenço Marques—he stayed only two weeks—led him to adopt the latter view. He found the contrast with labor recruiting for São Tomé and Príncipe striking: "Not only were the natives eager to volunteer for work in the Transvaal mines, but I saw them returning to their homes when the period of work for which they had been indentured had expired. From all sides," he reported to Cadbury, "I heard of the free and contented lot of the native in that colony."[12]

Burtt's sources included J. G. Baldwin, the British consul at Lourenço Marques, and Alfredo Augusto Freire de Andrade, the governor-general of Mozambique. Their pleasant public agreement masked the heated negotiations over labor recruiting in mid-1906. Competition for labor among mine owners on the Witwatersrand was intense, and one large company, the J. B. Robinson Group, set out to create its own recruiting organization in Mozambique. In London, the Colonial Office initially favored competition over the virtual monopoly on recruiting that the Witwatersrand Native Labour Association (WNLA) had enjoyed in Mozambique since 1895. In the Transvaal, the British high commissioner, Lord Selborne, worried that opening Mozambique to the "crowd of ruffians" who had dominated in pre-WNLA days would harm both African workers and mine owners. In Lourenço Marques, Andrade—backed in Lisbon by the colonial minister, Ornellas—suggested that all foreign recruiting agents be replaced by Portuguese colonial officials. The proposal would position Mozambique's governor-general to negotiate further preferences for his colony's railroads and port. Selborne was convinced it would also lead to forced rather than voluntary migration. In the end, the J. B. Robinson Group rejoined the WNLA. For his part, Andrade had demonstrated his talent for hard-edged diplomacy, as well as his loyalty to Lisbon.[13]

Burtt was so charmed by Andrade when he met him in February 1907 that he wrote a poem praising the "Soldier and Statesman, in whose toil-worn face / I read the trace of charging savage hordes, / And travel through drear deserts and swift fords, / O hero son of Lusitania's race." Written very much in the romantic style of Burtt's earlier odes to Príncipe and Angola, the poem urged Mozambique's governor-general to:

FIGURE 25. Alfredo Augusto Freire de Andrade, c. 1910. Photograph in Francisco Mantero, *Manual Labour in S. Thomé and Principe* (Lisbon, 1910), facing p. 38. By permission of Mantero's great-grandson, Francisco Mantero.

Pause for a moment in laborious days
Of governance and ruling of the land,
And lend thine ear to the glad song of praise
Of one who sees the mercy of thy hand,
And like a flower upon a rugged stone,
Thy love of the dark children of this zone.

Despite his "toil-worn face," Andrade was Burtt's senior by just three years. Commissioned a second lieutenant in the Engineering Corps in 1883 at the age of twenty-four, he had studied mining engineering in Paris on a state scholarship, completing the course in 1888. By age thirty, he had been appointed commissioner-general of mines in Mozambique—part of a plan, in light of the Transvaal gold strikes, to revive the gold mines north of Lourenço Marques at Manica, which had been known to Portuguese traders since the sixteenth century. Andrade visited Johannesburg for the first time in 1889, and three years later, he served on the commission to delineate the border between the South African Republic and Mozambique. In 1895, the bureaucrat became a soldier, joining Enes first in the relief of Lourenço Marques against the Tsonga and then in the conquest of Gaza, supervising the building of the fortifications and portable bridges that facilitated Portugal's effective occupation of the colony.[14]

As a young civil servant and soldier, Andrade evinced great loyalty to the Portuguese Crown but little "love of the dark children of this zone." Once appointed governor-general in October 1906, however, he formulated ambitious plans to develop the territory—plans that, when realized, would gain him instant fame and wide respect. He built hospitals and schools and affordable housing for state employees, established the Department of Agriculture and Veterinary Science, extended the railroad into Gaza, and constructed roads into the interior to transport agricultural exports to the coast. He accomplished all this with limited financial support from Lisbon and documented it carefully in a series of reports that by 1907 comprised more than eleven hundred pages in three volumes. These reports demonstrated Andrade's essential pragmatism in dealing with his African subjects. Regarding the still-troublesome Gaza chiefs, he advocated demobilizing their remaining soldiers and completely suspending what remained of the African kingdom, thereby essentially eliminating chiefly power. Peasants, he conceded, migrated to the Transvaal's mines to earn money to pay their taxes. To keep them in Mozambique and encourage agricultural development, he proposed limiting African emigration from certain districts, and more significantly, he suggested reconsidering the hut tax rate. He also sought to address corruption in the labor-recruiting system "undertaken by many individuals who profit from it at the expense of Africans whom they frequently do not pay." In Andrade's opinion, the 1901 Modus Vivendi with the Transvaal Colony, which linked the supply of labor with the usage of Mozambique's railroads and port, also had to be renegotiated. That prospect worried some in the British Transvaal Colony, but such policy decisions were ultimately approved in London and Lisbon, not in Johannesburg and Lourenço Marques.[15]

Writing to Cadbury about his meeting with Andrade, Burtt noted the governor-general thought "that the methods adopted in Angola were detrimental to the best interests of the colony, and this seems to be the opinion of many other Portuguese." In his own report to Ornellas in Lisbon, Andrade was rather more circumspect. He related that Burtt had arrived with a letter of introduction from Baldwin, the British consul, and that they had had a long chat about the conditions of African workers in Mozambique and about emigration to the Transvaal. Burtt described his experiences in Angola and recommended that Mozambique's labor practices be applied in Portugal's West African colonies. He left and shortly afterward sent a thank-you note to the governor-general praising the labor system he had found in Mozambique. Andrade was pleased to accept Burtt's comments on Mozambique, but—ever the loyal civil servant—he denied in his letter to Ornellas that he had agreed with any of Burtt's criticisms of labor practices in Angola.[16]

Burtt, meanwhile, had made the day-long journey by train from Lourenço Marques to Johannesburg, arriving on February 17. He began his investigation with a review of the "blue books," so named for the color of their covers. These official government reports surprised Burtt by revealing "a very different state of things from what I had anticipated." During his brief sojourn in Lourenço Marques, he had not realized the extent of the Transvaal mines' dependence on migrants from Mozambique. In 1902, the Transvaal Chamber of Mines had even proposed importing miners directly from Portugal, at a monthly wage of £5. The Cape Colony had recruited farm labor in Europe. Natal had imported indentured Indian labor to cut sugarcane. British Bechuanaland sent its small contingent of African migrants to the diamond mines at Kimberley. In the British-occupied Orange River Colony, Afrikaner farmers jealously guarded their African labor force.[17]

Among the blue books was the 1903 Transvaal Labour Commission report. Britain's postwar high commissioner to South Africa, Lord Alfred

Milner, had appointed the commission with advice from Rand mine owners. To Burtt, the most callous aspect of the report was the suggestion that Africans living in British colonies be denied access to land in order to force them into the wage-labor market. Milner was not a disinterested party. He envisioned a unified British South Africa with expansive agricultural, industrial, and mining sectors. The 1903 report asserted, not surprisingly, that the existing African labor supply did not meet the needs of the Transvaal's mines. Mine owners, Burtt informed Cadbury, were dependent on Mozambique, "a foreign power, who may at any time, for its own benefit, forbid the natives to cross its borders." Yet Burtt acknowledged that this was unlikely to happen, even though the conditions for Mozambican miners in the Transvaal were hardly ideal. Separated from their wives and children, the men lived in the ramshackle housing provided by the mines and spent their days underground exposed to the fine dust that left many suffering from the debilitating lung disease known as miner's phthisis.[18]

At first glance, it seemed Nevinson had a point: on São Tomé and Príncipe, Angolans were exploited by wealthy Portuguese planters; in the Transvaal, Mozambicans made mainly British mine owners rich. In Birmingham in late January 1907, William Cadbury labored over the first, limited-circulation proof of Burtt's exposé of slavery on the chocolate islands. Similar accusations made by Nevinson in 1906 had infuriated Portuguese commentators. Yet Portugal did not loudly protest the suffering experienced by African miners on the Rand at the hands of British mine owners. Francisco Mantero's efforts to redirect Mozambican labor to Portuguese planters on São Tomé and Príncipe found little support in Lisbon, despite the wealth generated by the islands. The revenue that flowed from the Transvaal's mines to Britain and, in the form of fees and taxes, to Portugal and Mozambique trumped all other concerns.[19]

On a visit to a Consolidated Gold Fields property, Burtt collected statistics. The company's records indicated that Mozambicans who had migrated from the regions closest to the Transvaal, south of latitude 22°, experienced the lowest mortality rate from accident and disease, 35.8 deaths per 1,000 miners per year. Among Africans from tropical regions, the death rate reached as high as 99 per 1,000. Overall, the annual death rate for African miners was 42 per 1,000, less than half the average rate for cocoa workers. Miners' diets, per government regulation, included a daily allowance of two pounds of cornmeal and a weekly allowance of two pounds of meat or fish, a pound of "soup meat," a pound of vegetables, a pound of sugar, and a half ounce of salt. The average length of a miner's contract was nine months, and the average wage was just under £3 per month, or five times that of a cocoa worker. At an estimated £3 per worker, the cost of recruiting Mozambicans for the Transvaal was less than half the cost of recruiting Angolans for São Tomé. The apparently generous salaries paid to Mozambicans masked the consistent efforts of mine owners to depress wages. In 1895, the average wage for an African miner was 63 shillings per month (or just over £3, at 20 shillings to the pound). It fell to 50 shillings in 1898 and recovered to 57 shillings per month in 1904. The Portuguese curador based in Johannesburg also took his cut. On top of passport and registration fees, a miner had to pay a fee of half a shilling (6 pence) if he wanted to extend his contract.[20]

African miners found their earning capacity further constrained by labor practices that dated to the 1890s, when blasting was defined as a skilled task and reserved for white miners. This "color bar" became law in 1904 as part of Milner's Labour Importation Ordinance. British colonial authorities, under pressure to provide jobs for unemployed Afrikaners, codified the list of jobs that could be performed by white skilled workers and by "colored" unskilled workers. The latter category included not just Africans but also Chinese indentured laborers, whom mine owners had begun contracting in May 1904.[21]

FIGURE 26. African miners, Witwatersrand, Transvaal Colony. From Collection AG2738-Fa13-12-16f, by permission of Historical Papers, William Cullen Library, University of the Witwatersrand, Johannesburg, South Africa.

By December 1906, there were 52,917 Chinese working in the mines, along with 117,163 Africans and 18,932 whites. The presence of the Chinese was hotly debated during the campaign for the election of the new colonial legislature. The election took place on February 20, 1907, just days after Burtt arrived in Johannesburg. The Progressive Party, backed by mine owners, favored the continued importation of Chinese labor but also counted on the support of white miners, most of whom were British. The Progressives argued that the prosperity of the mines was essential to the stability of a white-ruled South Africa. The party assured English-speaking miners that Chinese workers would be restricted to unskilled jobs and repatriated to China at the end of their contracts. Despite these promises, many white skilled miners were drawn to the Transvaal National Association and to the English-speaking labor activist F. H. P. Creswell, who argued that the mines could be effectively run using only white workers, both skilled and unskilled. Colonial authorities had also approved the creation of a third party, Het Volk, which represented Afrikaner interests. In 1905, Het Volk had tried to persuade the Transvaal Chamber of Mines to hire a thousand poor-white Afrikaners as unskilled laborers at 5 shillings a day, or a little over twice the daily wage for unskilled black African miners. To the surprise of British authorities in London and Johannesburg, the Transvaal National Association aligned with Het Volk and won a slim majority in the legislature in February 1907. Five years after being defeated in the South African War, Afrikaners reemerged as a political force in the now self-governing British Transvaal Colony.[22]

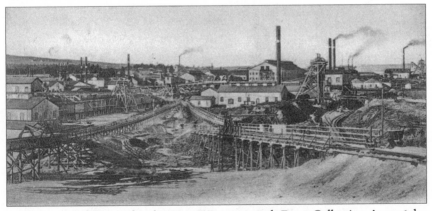

FIGURE 27. Simmer and Jack Mine, Witwatersrand. From Collection A2717-6, by permission of Historical Papers, William Cullen Library, University of the Witwatersrand, Johannesburg, South Africa.

Writing to Cadbury, Burtt failed to grasp that many white workers saw lower-paid Chinese miners as unwelcome competition. He thought the Transvaal National Association's opposition to Chinese labor was shortsighted and its assertion that there was enough African labor available to staff the mines disingenuous at best and delusional at worst. At the Simmer and Jack Mine, which employed 4,000 Chinese miners, the cleanliness of the compound and the general good health of the men impressed Burtt. The Chinese miners seemed much better suited to the Rand than did most Africans. The Chinese were used to hard work and cold weather, and they suffered a death rate of only 12.5 per 1,000 workers at the Simmer and Jack Mine and 19 per 1,000 overall. Burtt calculated that replacing 50,000 African miners with Chinese workers would save 1,500 lives per year, given the much lower mortality rates among the Chinese. The 1905 Coloured Labour Compound Commission, appointed to assess overcrowding by measuring—as the full title of the report indicated—"the cubic amount of air-space in the compounds of the mines of the Witwatersrand," had reached the same conclusion. The commissioners attributed the much higher death rate among Africans in part to their propensity, regardless of how roomy the available sleeping quarters were, "to congregate in one end or one corner of the room and sleep all huddled up together, just as they have been accustomed to do in their own kraals." The Chinese, by contrast, were so orderly "that it would be quite impossible to get 2,000 people of the labouring class from any town in Europe to occupy a compound and be more cleanly in their habits than the Chinese."[23]

The members of the 1905 labor commission, like their predecessors in 1903, wanted to keep importing Chinese labor. They were thus also propagandists, though they did call for improvements in the sanitation standards in compounds. Burtt saw some of these changes in February 1907, but he still found the Chinese compounds cleaner and less crowded than those of Africans. The 1905 report, the various blue books, and the publications of the Transvaal Chamber of Mines also reflected long-standing beliefs in white superiority and black inferiority, prejudices that Burtt shared. In his opinion, African miners were "boys," best suited for farming and family life and too easily seduced by alcohol and the female prostitutes in overwhelmingly male Johannesburg. Burtt's suggestion to allow African women to migrate to the Rand and set up households with their husbands was not, however, favored by the mine owners, who were reluctant to pay wages sufficient to support families in the city. Owners did try, with limited success, to control Africans' access to alcohol when its consumption threatened productivity. But the

FIGURE 28. Living quarters for Chinese miners. From Collection A2794-18D-6, by permission of Historical Papers, William Cullen Library, University of the Witwatersrand, Johannesburg, South Africa.

primary consideration for mine owners remained the cost of labor. Owners sought to replace high-cost skilled white miners with low-cost unskilled miners; to redefine tasks as unskilled; and, whenever possible, to depress the wages of all workers.[24]

Burtt knew his pro-Chinese labor stance was controversial, not only among the Transvaal's white workers but also in Britain. "Chinese slavery" had become a political issue in Britain as early as 1902. The ruling Conservative Party had argued that winning the South African War would create industrial and mining jobs for British workers in the new Transvaal Colony. When Conservatives then advocated contracting Chinese miners, the opposition Liberal Party attacked. Trade unions entered the fray, and at a rally in London in March 1904 that drew an estimated eighty thousand protesters, the prospect of Chinese slavery was condemned. As he had done during the South African War, George Cadbury again used the *Daily News* to criticize Conservative policies, this time, on Chinese labor.[25]

Arguing that indentured Chinese miners on the Rand were slaves was nonetheless problematic. By the standards of the day, they were freely recruited, decently paid, well fed, and well housed, and they had the option

FIGURE 29. Informal housing for African miners, Johannesburg. From Collection AG2738-Fa13-12-16b, by permission of Historical Papers, William Cullen Library, University of the Witwatersrand, Johannesburg, South Africa.

of returning home at the end of their contracts. In other words, they had, in Burtt's opinion, a great deal in common with Mozambican miners in the Transvaal, whose labor the British Foreign Office was keen to represent as voluntary. For Edmund Morel, who wanted to focus public attention on the atrocities in the Congo Free State documented by his Congo Reform Association (which was funded generously by William Cadbury), the so-called Chinese slavery controversy was an unwelcome distraction. In London, Cadbury's old nemesis, H. R. Fox Bourne of the Aborigines' Protection Society, joined the protest, asserting that competition from Chinese workers depressed wages for black as well as white miners. Further, Fox Bourne insisted, the unsanitary living conditions in Chinese compounds could trigger epidemics in Johannesburg, a claim that at least helped explain the mine owners' defensive public pronouncements stressing the cleanliness of Chinese workers.[26]

The Chinese slavery camp gained ground after a series of riots on the Rand over wages and news reports in May 1905 that Chinese miners were being whipped. In Britain, the Conservative Party's attempts to suppress the accusations and its defense of indentured Chinese labor contributed to the victory of the Liberal Party and its Labour Party allies in the January 1906 election. The new government quickly abandoned use of the term *slavery* to describe the situation of the Chinese miners, but then it offended mine owners by offering to subsidize Chinese who wished to return home. To the great relief of mine owners on the Rand, a mere 766 miners (less than 1.5 percent of the total) had taken up the British offer to return to China by January 1907. When the Afrikaner party Het Volk gained control of the Transvaal legislature in February 1907, it prohibited the importation of any more Chinese laborers, but in deference to the financial significance of the mines, it allowed Chinese already resident on the Rand to complete their contracts. In the end, the Chinese slavery debate was about protecting and creating jobs for white Britons and about British politics, including the anti–Conservative Party leanings of George Cadbury.[27]

Portuguese commentators watched the controversy unfold with a mixture of cynicism, concern, and relief. In their opinion, encouraging British workers to immigrate to the Rand had everything to do with decreasing the influence of Afrikaners, who made up the majority of the white population in the Transvaal Colony. The Chinese propensity to protest their wages and food rations, to desert, and to turn to robbery amply demonstrated their unsuitability for mine work. Most significantly, their presence threatened the labor clause of the 1901 Modus Vivendi and restricted Mozambique's revenue stream by replacing free Africans with indentured Chinese. Ultimately, it was the Transvaal's new Het Volk government that reassured the Portuguese of the importance of Mozambican migrants, who made up 63 percent of the Rand's labor force.[28]

Even Burtt had to concede that a Chinese miner, "however well treated, is an alien and a drudge," whereas an African "working for shorter periods returns to his wife and family from time to time and gets the benefit of rest and change." The question remaining was whether that mobility made Mozambican miners on the Rand "free." Burtt's answer was a qualified yes. He remained concerned about the comparatively high mortality rates for African miners and the living conditions that produced them. His visit to Portuguese East Africa and British southern Africa had been all too brief. After six months on São Tomé and Príncipe and a year in Angola, two weeks in Lourenço Marques followed by two weeks in Johannesburg had felt almost like a holiday. A brief side trip to Pretoria to see the high commissioner, Lord Selborne, nevertheless underscored the complexity of the issues surrounding the cocoa controversy that had taken Burtt to Africa. Selborne thought that publicity, along with pressure from the British government, might persuade Portugal to change its labor policies in Angola. What had become clear to Burtt, however, was that "one thing works into another, and that it is quite within the range of possibility that stopping the slave trade in Angola, might affect the mining interests" in the Transvaal, thereby destabilizing the British colony. Demanding that Portugal stop forcibly exporting Angolans to São Tomé and Príncipe's roças might prompt the Portuguese to do what still seemed unlikely in early 1907: close Mozambique's southern border and attempt to starve the Rand's mines of labor.[29]

In March 1907, Burtt could report that workers from Mozambique appeared to be freely contracted and that even though conditions in the mines could be improved, the workers were also free—unlike São Tomé's serviçais—to leave at the end of their contracts. There was no "new slavery" being practiced in the Rand's mines, as Nevinson had alleged and Cadbury had feared. With his investigation finally complete twenty-one months after it had begun, Burtt returned to Lourenço Marques and from there sailed for England and into a growing storm of controversy over cocoa and slavery.

Seven

CADBURY, BURTT, AND PORTUGUESE AFRICA

IN MID-MARCH 1907, William Cadbury sent proof copies of Joseph Burtt's report to his fellow Quaker chocolate makers Fry and Rowntree and to the German firm Stollwerck in Cologne, accompanied by a bill for just under £705, or one-quarter of the cost of Burtt's African sojourn. The secretary of state, Sir Edward Grey, also received a copy, along with the assurance that nothing would be published without his approval. The Foreign Office was Burtt's first stop when he returned to England a month later. On April 25, he spent forty-five minutes with Edward Clarke and Charles Lyell, who praised the "very moderate" tone of the report. Nevertheless, Grey's undersecretary, Eric Barrington, wrote to Cadbury Brothers Limited asking the firm to edit sections that might offend the Portuguese government and requesting that Burtt delay publication until Portugal had the opportunity to address the issues the report raised.[1]

Joseph Fry also equivocated when Burtt met with him in Bristol on April 29. Though Fry conceded that "the main point of the question is not how the serviçal is treated, but whether or no, he is a slave," he also noted that the quality of São Tomé's cocoa made it "very difficult to decline to buy it." Arnold Rowntree was more receptive, observing that the "painful" revelations about "the conditions of coloured labour in Portuguese West Africa" demanded that "some action must be taken." About the value of Burtt's impressions of Mozambique and the Transvaal, given his very short visit, Rowntree was rather more skeptical.[2]

At dinner with Henry Nevinson in London, Burtt passed on William Cadbury's appreciation of the journalist's work and mentioned Cadbury's "desire to support the solid part of it." Cadbury may have been stroking Nevinson's ego to encourage his discretion, but Travers Buxton of the Anti-Slavery Society was also willing to wait patiently for Burtt's report to be published. The wild card, not surprisingly, was H. R. Fox Bourne of the

Aborigines' Protection Society (APS), who wrote to Cadbury after meeting with Burtt to protest the "inexpedience, as it seems to me," of letting Grey and the Foreign Office determine when Burtt's work would be released to the public. "Ten years of apathy over Congo affairs" made Fox Bourne doubt the government's sincerity, and he urged Cadbury to "push the matter to the front before the evidence (much of which *you* have collected at great outlay and with such zeal) can be thrown aside as 'ancient history.'" Cadbury replied the next day, sympathizing with Fox Bourne's suspicions about the motives of the Foreign Office but noting that the four chocolate makers who had sponsored Burtt were willing to let Grey contact the Portuguese government. "It would be absurd," Cadbury thought, to ask Grey "to make the representation and then before he has had time to do so to cut the ground from under his feet."[3]

Burtt also had misgivings about the dissemination of his report. He did not trust the Portuguese government and regarded the plan of the British Foreign Office to forward a copy of his report through official channels as an effort to "shirk the responsibility of the matter and pacify us at the same time." What really worried him was what would happen to the missionaries in Angola who could be identified even if they were not named: "It does not seem right to expose such people brave as they are to the chance of persecution without their most definite consent." His experiences in São Tomé and Angola had demonstrated that even well-intentioned officials had little power to change policy. By May 1907, Lisbon appeared even less amenable to change: João Franco, appointed as prime minister by King Carlos I the previous year, had evolved into a dictator, and a Republican-led revolution to overthrow the monarchy seemed increasingly possible.[4]

On the question of the missionaries, Cadbury's reply appeared almost callous, and it was clearly influenced by his long association with Edmund Morel's Congo Reform Association. "Nothing was a greater hindrance to Congo reform," Cadbury asserted, "than the fact that the Baptist missionaries for years would not breathe a word of these abuses because they feared to lose their influence—nothing gave a bigger lift to the cause than when they bravely exposed the whole thing and it was made too hot for one or two of them to ever return." Further, Cadbury argued, publishing the report in the English press without first giving the Portuguese the opportunity to respond—which Burtt favored doing—would give them "every right to say, as they have done with Nevinson's report, that they consider that the whole attitude has been unfriendly and unfair." It was, ironically, the same claim that Grey had made when he argued he could not present Nevinson's popular articles written for *Harper's Magazine* as evidence of colonial misconduct to the Portuguese government. What Grey would do, Cadbury assured Burtt (and, separately, Nevinson), was append an official Foreign Office statement to his report and give the Portuguese a time frame within which to respond. Burtt persisted, sending Cadbury a list of edits that obscured place-names and individuals' identities. Fry and Rowntree agreed to the changes, though Rowntree thought they would "weaken the report."[5]

The flurry of letters continued through June and into July as the final form of Burtt's report was negotiated. Cadbury had his own reasons for attempting to pacify Burtt. Grey's desire to use the report as part of an official presentation to the Portuguese government and the delays that resulted from editing it to meet Foreign Office standards benefited Cadbury Brothers Limited. Edward Thackray, one of the firm's cocoa buyers, had begun looking for other potential suppliers as early as 1901, shortly after Cadbury had heard the rumors of slave labor on São Tomé while visiting Trinidad and read the sales catalog from the Traz-os-Montes roça equating serviçais with cattle. In 1907, as Burtt's report wound its way through official channels, Thackray intensified his search.[6]

Burtt added to the delays by pushing, in addition, for a "personal and private appeal to the planters" to ensure they understood "that the whole question has been taken up from a desire for decent conditions of coloured labour and not from English" self-righteousness and hypocrisy. Henrique Mendonça, who had made Boa Entrada into a model roça, and planters like him should be treated as allies, Burtt argued, not enemies.[7]

In late June, an increasingly impatient Fox Bourne insisted that if the chocolate makers did not forthwith issue Burtt's report, the APS would print its own assessment of conditions in São Tomé and Príncipe and Angola. Cadbury drafted a three-page reply and sent it to Fry and Rowntree for review. The letter all but called Fox Bourne an idiot: "It should at least be clear to you that you make it practically impossible for the Government to take any action short of armed force, or for us at any time again to approach the Lisbon cocoa planters by whose courtesy it has been possible to obtain Joseph Burtt's report." Roderick Fry offered qualified support for Cadbury's letter but noted, "We are anxious not to commit ourselves as to future actions." Arnold Rowntree's response was more surprising. He reread Burtt's report, decided it was poorly written, and suggested that the firms hire someone to help Burtt rewrite it. Cadbury rejected the idea but did let Rowntree's lawyer, Richard Cross, edit the report. In a further heated exchange of letters between Cadbury and Fox Bourne in early July, each accused the other of hypocrisy and Cadbury made the remarkable assertion that Burtt had not gone to Africa to convince the chocolate firms "that the condition of labour was slavery" but rather "for the purpose of convincing the Portuguese," a claim that Fox Bourne rejected. Ultimately, each man apologized in the interest of their shared goal of ending forced labor.[8]

The report that finally emerged in mid-July 1907 was several pages shorter than the December 1906 original. More than a few of Burtt's lengthy descriptive passages had been excised: gone, for example, were the Afrikaner farmers of Humpata whom he had visited when he first arrived in Angola in early 1906. The tone was also more official; a list of the British and Portuguese colonial officials Burtt had met in São Tomé and Príncipe, Angola, Mozambique, and South Africa appeared on page two, and the January 29, 1903, Portuguese decree on contract labor was explained in detail.[9]

The most striking difference between the two reports was the careful language in the 1907 version. As Burtt acknowledged, great care was taken to avoid "referring to the serviçaes as slaves or to the serviçal system as slavery, because, approaching the matter as I did with an open mind, I have wished to avoid question-begging epithets." His December 1906 draft had reflected no such worries. On the islands, he had been struck by "the mental distress and hopelessness of a man separated from his family, and doomed to perpetual slavery—a condition often accelerating death." Six months later, this became: "The mental distress and hopelessness of a man separated from his family, and placed in a strange environment have a highly prejudicial effect upon him." In both versions, he described as "slaves" the children his servant George had encountered being abused by his landlord in Luanda, but in the 1907 report, Burtt added this line: "The Portuguese law, of course, does not permit slavery, but this was only one of many instances I found on the mainland in which labour employed was not voluntary." Describing the beginning of his and Horton's journey into Angola's interior along the old slaving route at the end of July 1906, Burtt had written: "It was not long before we found evidence of the disregard of humanity and freedom, as in a few hours we saw skeletons and shackles." The 1907 version read: "It was not long before we found skeletons and shackles."[10]

Though the tone of the final report was more moderate than that of the 1906 draft, Burtt still pointed to the complicity of Portuguese colonial officers who ignored the African and Portuguese traders openly dealing in captive laborers. His conclusion also remained forceful: "I am satisfied that under the serviçal system as it exists at present thousands of black men and women are, against their will, and often under circumstances of great cruelty, taken away every year from their homes and transported across the sea to work on unhealthy islands, from which they never return. If this is not slavery, I know of no word in the English language which correctly characterises it." All the interested parties who had a hand in revising the report had to realize that the Portuguese would be offended.[11]

At the beginning of August, Burtt headed back to Porto to arrange the translation of his report into Portuguese, confident that if he diligently avoided the "I'm an English Saint and you're a Portuguese sinner tone," the planters would prove responsive. He recommended again that he visit a few planters to elicit sympathy for Cadbury before he arrived in Lisbon, explaining, "I could talk to them quite differently if I was alone; an unimportant person like myself doesn't rouse the opposition that important people like yourself with your wealth and influence might." Cadbury consulted the British Foreign Office; still concerned about political instability in Portugal, it turned down Burtt's suggestion. In Lisbon in late August to visit the British legation, Burtt learned its representatives planned to present his Portuguese translation, along with the English original, to the Portuguese foreign secretary in September.[12]

While Burtt complained about baking in Lisbon's late summer sun, Cadbury faced several small fires at home. Nevinson, disappointed by the muted response to his *Harper's* articles and by the news that the Foreign Office "complained they could not use my report," had decided to write an article for the *Fortnightly Review.* Rowntree's lawyer, Cross, tried to dissuade him and gave Nevinson a copy of Burtt's report, which the journalist dismissed "as an abstract of my book and no more." Nevinson's article appeared on September 1, 1907. He commended the Quaker chocolate firms for their investigation into labor conditions in Portuguese West Africa, criticized the British Foreign Office for its caution, and advocated a boycott of São Tomé's cocoa.[13]

At the end of September, Nevinson addressed the African section of the Liverpool Chamber of Commerce, again arguing in favor of a cocoa boycott and urging the British government to do everything in its power to end slavery in Portuguese Africa. On October 21, Cadbury responded with his own address at the invitation of the chamber. In essence, he presented a synopsis of Burtt's report. He rejected the idea of a boycott, since it would rob the chocolate makers of the leverage they enjoyed as major buyers of São Toméan cocoa. What British firms declined to buy, he said, would be "very readily absorbed by other nations, who do not concern themselves with the method of production." It was a weak defense, and Cadbury knew it. Nonetheless, he found allies in his audience. John Holt, whose shipping company traded in West Africa, criticized the chamber's president, Albert Jones, for attacking the chocolate makers while serving as a representative of King Leopold's Congo Free State. Labor abuses there had been exposed by the Congo Reform Association, which Cadbury supported financially. In Holt's view, if the chocolate manufacturers wanted to protect themselves from charges of hypocrisy as businesspeople and as philanthropists, they needed to seek out cocoa that had been indisputably produced by free labor. That Thackray, the Cadbury Brothers cocoa buyer, was in fact following Holt's suggestion remained, in October 1907, confidential.[14]

From Porto, Burtt wrote to encourage Cadbury to ignore another accuser, the Afrikaner general P. Joubert Pienaar. Pienaar had fought in the South African War (on the losing side), had lived in Angola, and opposed slavery. In 1907, he sought backing from the British Foreign Office for an expedition to invade Angola from the east via British Barotseland. Fox Bourne embraced Pienaar's antislavery stance, thinking it little different from Nevinson's or Burtt's. Travers Buxton, however, distanced himself from Pienaar, as did the British Foreign Office and—not surprisingly—the Portuguese government. The general's claim "that out of 500 natives landed in Principe only a dozen were alive after an interval of ten months" was false, Burtt assured Cadbury, though "quite in keeping with the loose statements [he had] made on other occasions." But Pienaar's allegations, though irritating, were also useful, since Burtt's report would likely appear all the more moderate in comparison.[15]

The translation of Burtt's report was quietly presented to Ornellas, the Portuguese colonial minister, by Francis Villiers, the British consul in Lisbon, in the third week of October. Villiers had read the English version and thought it weak and unimpressive; Ornellas had probably also read it. He had already publicly advocated introducing a recruiting system for São Tomé analogous to that which supplied miners to the Transvaal and guaranteed their repatriation to Mozambique at the end of their contracts. The colonial minister's diplomacy nevertheless contained a barb: "I say an analogous system because it is evident that a repatriation which we have enforced in a foreign colony, in our own colonies and among colonists of the same nation is not always necessary." Not only had the Portuguese done the work of repatriation for British officials in the Transvaal Colony but African subjects—Ornellas implied—were at home everywhere in the Portuguese Empire.[16]

By early November 1907, Burtt had distributed copies of his report to the major cocoa planters, including Mendonça and Mantero. The response was less favorable than he had hoped. Vale Flôr, who had impressed Cadbury when he met him in Lisbon in 1903, was so angry that he accused Carl de Merck of intentionally misleading him in order to arrange introductions for Burtt in São Tomé. Vale Flôr tried to persuade Mantero to rescind the invitation to the chocolate makers to visit Lisbon, and when he failed to do so, he left for Paris.[17]

Another critic was Jerónimo Paiva de Carvalho, whose 1907 pamphlet defended Portuguese labor practices on the islands. Carvalho worked in the curador's office in Príncipe, though Burtt appears not to have met him when he visited the island in 1905. Carvalho's defense was thoughtful, careful, and familiar. Portugal had traded in slaves and practiced slavery in its colonies through 1875. Subsequent laws had compelled African subjects to work but also recognized their freedom. Laborers on São Tomé and Príncipe enjoyed working conditions superior to those of crews who served on British ships, and they were also treated better than most rural workers in Europe. As in all civilized nations, Portuguese laws were intended to protect servants as "individuals of limited capacity" and to protect their employers against theft and disorder. On the Porto Real and Esperança roças on Príncipe, both of which Burtt had visited, great attention was paid to worker's housing, clothing, labor assignments, salaries, and health care. (Here, a reader might have thought Carvalho was drawing a direct analogy to George Cadbury's model workers' village in Bournville.) "If this is slavery," Carvalho concluded, "then we are completely in the dark about the problem of manual labor in the colonies."[18]

A similar image of contented workers emerged from Henrique Mendonça's *The Boa Entrada Plantation*, whose appearance in English translation in November struck Cadbury as hardly coincidental. Other Portuguese responses to the increasingly negative attention paid to São Tomé and Príncipe in the English newspapers and the British Parliament were more subtle. After hosting Crown Prince Luís Felipe during his 1907 visit to the islands, the Count of Vale Flôr was elevated to marquis. Mendonça received the Grand Cross of the Conception, and General Faro, manager of Mantero's Água Izé plantation, was also recognized for his service to Portugal.[19]

In late November, Cadbury arrived in Lisbon to meet with the planters on behalf of the English cocoa makers. Neither Fry nor Rowntree sent delegates. The British Foreign Office had suggested that Burtt meet informally with the planters to discuss his report, but Cadbury felt this was his duty rather than that of his representative. Real affection had grown between the two men—Burtt had signed two letters from Porto "with love to you and yours"—but he nonetheless remained a salaried employee. In Lisbon, he continued as Cadbury's translator and helped him arrange the meeting at the Centro Colonial

FIGURE 30. Francisco Mantero in an undated photograph. Photograph in Francisco Mantero, *A Mão de Obra em S. Tomé e Príncipe*, vol. 1, *Obras Completas* (Lisbon, 1954), frontispiece. By permission of Mantero's great-grandson, Francisco Mantero.

(Colonial Center) on November 28 with the committee representing the planters: Alfredo Mendes da Silva, Henrique Mendonça, Joaquim de Ornellas e Mattos, José Paulo Cancella, Nicolau McNicoll, and Francisco Mantero.[20]

Cadbury thanked the planters for their invitation and for the hospitality they had shown Burtt. He praised the quality of São Tomé's cocoa and said that his firm wanted to keep buying it. Despite the allegations in the Portuguese press, he continued, the English chocolate firms had no hidden plans to purchase roças on the islands. He conceded that workers enjoyed excellent treatment on many estates but insisted that their death rates were too high, that the recruiting methods in Angola bordered on slave trading, and that no contract laborers had ever been repatriated. If Cadbury Brothers Limited was to continue buying cocoa from the islands, the firm had to be sure "that in the future it is to be produced by free labour." Cadbury had chosen his words carefully. Some days earlier, writing privately to Fry and Rowntree, he had acknowledged that none of the workers presently on the islands could ever leave: "They have left their homes forever, & if put down in Loanda tomorrow, would die of starvation or be recaptured because there is no machinery to take them back on the long cruel road to the place where the home once was."[21]

The meeting lasted eight hours, with Burtt translating for Cadbury and Alfredo Mendes da Silva translating for his fellow planters. On December 4, the planters sent Cadbury a lengthy summary of the discussion, noting eleven mistakes about the islands that the chocolate maker and his representative had made in response to questioning. The errors ranged from the technical—rates of sickness and death on tropical islands should not be compared to those in the British Isles—to, in the planters' view, the indefensible. Burtt admitted that he had never witnessed corporal punishment, but he claimed that it had taken place based on testimony he had collected from informants he declined to name. Concerning Angola, the planters embraced Ornella's careful diplomatic argument. The abuses Burtt had encountered in the interior would be solved once Portugal had completed its military occupation of the hinterland. The planters also chided Burtt for his overly enthusiastic depiction of labor migration to the Transvaal. Not every worker returned to Mozambique: "Some go back with money, others take nothing, and not a few return crippled by hard work or accidents in the mines."[22]

The planters concluded by assuring Cadbury that they shared his "liberal and humane sentiment." They too wished to see São Toméan workers return home and "carry back to their country the accounts of the treatment they have received in the islands." To date, the planters had contributed £100,000 to the repatriation fund. The first workers contracted under the January 1903 law would begin returning home in 1908, taking with them severance payments of £18 each. Workers who decided to renew their contracts would receive an automatic raise of 10 percent. The colonial minister, Ornellas, planned to send one of his senior officials (Francisco de Paula Cid) to investigate conditions in Angola in January 1908, with the explicit "intention of replacing the present irresponsible recruiting agents by a proper government system," modeled—despite the planters' criticisms of Burtt—"on the lines employed with success in Mozambique."[23]

The planters' statement was very much a compromise; indeed, Cadbury thought its tone too apologetic. "I drafted half of it for them to suit the needs in England," he explained to his fellow directors in Birmingham, "and then they watered down my statements where we could possibly allow them to do so." They worried, however, that their fellow planters "would think they had granted far too much, when nothing short of 'Mr. Cadbury's head'" on a platter "would really satisfy them!" Writing to Mantero on December 19, Cadbury reported that the "reply of the planters" had been printed in "hundreds of papers" to universal acclaim for the Portuguese government and "the hearty support rendered by the estate proprietors."[24]

Cadbury's relief proved short-lived. On February 1, 1908, King Carlos and his heir Luís Felipe were assassinated in Lisbon, and Franco was ousted as prime minister. The succession of the king's eighteen-year-old second son to the throne as Manuel II did not restore stability. Ornellas left his post as colonial minister. Cadbury wrote to thank him for all his help and to express the hope that his successor would "carry out the reforms put in hand by your administration." Enclosed with Cadbury's letter were photographs of new wooden shackles from Angola, which he promised not to release. The photos might have been an implied threat, but Ornellas replied cordially, assuring Cadbury that he and his successor, Augusto Castilho, would continue to pursue the serviçais question.[25]

In London, Morel's Congo Reform Association was winning the battle to expose Leopold's abuses. In Lisbon, Villiers was convinced that British attention would turn again to Portugal once the Congo crisis was resolved. Cadbury agreed, especially since Nevinson and Fox Bourne were "feeling very sore at the success of Congo Reform" given that they and the Aborigines' Protection Society had been "left out in the cold" by Morel. In February 1908, Fox Bourne had fallen ill, though "unfortunately . . . not too ill," as Cadbury observed to Burtt, "to go on writing and making mischief." To Cadbury's amusement, Burtt thought his employer did not understand Fox Bourne. "I sat for two days . . . last autumn trying to get him to see the other side of the case," Cadbury protested, "and he ended exactly where he began—that the only right and proper action" was to boycott any "case connected with slavery." Fox Bourne's actions, Cadbury insisted, had almost rendered "futile our visit to Lisbon." Though worried about having to restart negotiations with a new Portuguese government, Cadbury was not willing to consider a boycott of São Toméan cocoa until "everything else has failed."[26]

In late March 1908, the new Portuguese government sent Cid, the former governor-general of São Tomé, to investigate labor recruiting in Angola. On April 23, a new resolution mandated that government agents supervise the export of laborers from Angola's ports. In Luanda, *A Voz d'Angola* (The Voice of Angola) noted that Cid had made no effort to end what the newspaper considered a slave trade in serviçais while serving as governor of Angola's Benguela District in the 1890s. There was no reason to think that his current mission would do anything except continue to "enrich half a dozen ambitious men at the expense of shaming Portugal." Mackie, the British consul in Luanda, shared the newspaper's cynicism and suggested appointing a commission that would interview contract laborers and thereby expose the abuses in the recruiting system.[27]

In April and May, Cadbury Brothers sought and secured apologies for articles in the *Manchester Guardian*, the *Standard*, and the *Evening Standard* that had questioned why the firm was still buying São Toméan cocoa. William Cadbury again made peace with Fox Bourne, whose pamphlet *Slave Traffic in Portuguese Africa* was favorably reviewed in George Cadbury's *Daily News*. The reviewer stressed the long history of Portuguese inaction on the labor issue. By June, William had resolved to visit the islands and Angola himself. To his fellow directors at Cadbury Brothers, he proposed a trip of eight to ten weeks. If Burtt was willing, he would serve as translator. "A first hand insight into the exact conditions," Cadbury explained, "might possibly help in the final solution of the matter." He was particularly keen "to inspect the actual system of signing on for contract in the courts," something neither Nevinson nor Burtt had succeeded in doing. Nor did either man speak any African languages, a flaw Cadbury proposed to remedy by inviting the missionary Charles Swan to accompany him.[28]

In early July, having secured the firm's approval, Cadbury wrote to Mantero, who sent a pointed reply. Planters on São Tomé and Príncipe, he said, "will receive you and your companion . . . with that frank and hearty hospitality that it is our custom to extend to strangers . . . with the perfect confidence of those who have nothing bad to hide in their private life." Mantero hoped this visit would allow him and his fellow planters to "forget the annoying and unjust manner in which the Burtt pamphlet and the English press referred to the voluntary continuance of residence of Portuguese labourers from Angola in the Portuguese colony of S. Thomé . . . as slavery."[29]

Swan, who had spent twenty-three years as a missionary in Angola before settling in Lisbon, proved harder to persuade. "If you send another expedition to Angola," he told Cadbury, "I am of the opinion that it ought to be a *secret* one, i.e. nobody should know that it is being done or the traders and everybody else will be on their guard." He did agree that someone who spoke the local African languages would have no trouble collecting information, but he declined to join Cadbury's party, citing his obligations to his wife and children. Cadbury replied that his own visit had to be public; he felt an obligation to the Portuguese to tell them what he was doing, in the "hope it may have the effect of really influencing their action, for I think they must be realising that the matter is not going to be dropped in England." Swan's trip could be private, but its results had to be made public: "I believe you know that I feel that some missionary should make a bold stand and *openly publish over his own name* a series of up-to-date facts and evidence on the subject." He offered Swan £500 to cover the costs of the journey and also offered to educate his children in England. In early August, after "much prayer about the matter," Swan finally agreed. His motivation was the "very real desire to do all I can for Africa and the Africans." He turned down the offer to pay for his children's schooling. Cadbury wired him money for a ticket for the October 1 Lisbon steamer to Angola and asked him, ironically, not to reveal the source of his funding or the goal of his mission.[30]

Meanwhile, Cadbury planned his own public trip. The Foreign Office would provide introductions to the British consuls in São Tomé and Príncipe and Angola; Cadbury and Burtt would have to arrange their own meetings with the Portuguese colonial governors. Arnold Rowntree encouraged Cadbury to consult with the Anti-Slavery Society and the Aborigines' Protection Society in the interest of maintaining a "friendly association with these two bodies, difficult though they are at times." Despite their recent rapprochement, Cadbury was unwilling to cater to Fox Bourne or the APS. His loyalties lay with Morel, who planned to turn his attention from the Congo to Angola with Cadbury's support. With the Anti-Slavery Society, he remained on better terms. The more open-minded Travers Buxton understood the chocolate maker's desire to travel to Africa "as a business man and not a philanthropist."[31]

In an editorial on September 26, 1908, just days before Cadbury planned to depart for São Tomé, the *Standard* called attention to the inherent contradictions of his business and philanthropic interests. Editor H. A. Gwynne's tone was satirical. He praised the concern Cadbury Brothers expressed for the welfare of its workers at its model factory yet wondered why the solicitude for the "white hands of the Bournville chocolate makers" seemed not to extend to the "African hands, whose toil also is so essential to the beneficent and lucrative operations." The attack was political. The imperialist Gwynne, who supported the Conservative Party, had favored the use of Chinese miners in South Africa's mines. George Cadbury's Liberal-leaning, anti-imperialist *Daily News* had opposed the policy as Chinese slavery. In an unexpected turn of events, Nevinson wrote to the *Standard* to defend the efforts by William Cadbury to expose abusive labor practices in Africa, and he noted that an editorial in the *Daily News* had condemned the practices in São Tomé in May 1908. This time, no apology was forthcoming. Cadbury Brothers Limited sued the *Standard* for libel.[32]

William Cadbury arrived in Príncipe on October 22, 1908, for a two-day visit. Burtt served again as his translator. Their first stop was Porto Real, where they found the manager, Augusto Rocha, constructing a new mechanized cocoa dryer. The number of workers dying from sleeping sickness had declined since Burtt's visit in 1905, but Cadbury had to wonder why the government did not prohibit cocoa cultivation in those districts still affected.[33]

On October 24, the two men arrived in São Tomé, where they were greeted by the new British consular agent, Francisco Marin. A nephew of Mantero's, he arranged a visit to the Ponta Furada roça, which he managed. Cadbury and Burtt also enjoyed the hospitality of Monte Café, Água Izé, and Boa Entrada, as Mantero had promised. Cadbury inspected the estates' buildings and machinery; he walked through the cocoa groves and observed the harvesting, fermenting, and drying processes. He inquired about workers' hours, wages, and opportunities for recreation, and he visited their living quarters. The cost of producing cocoa on São Tomé, he concluded, was quite high: "Few estates made above average profits, most were mortgaged to the hilt, and many were losing money hand over fist."[34]

Portuguese officials proved more evasive. The acting governor-general, Vítor Chaves Lemos e Melo, had arrived on the island at the beginning of October. He pleaded ignorance about labor conditions and referred Cadbury and Burtt to the curador and to the repatriation office. In December 1905, the curador, Emeríco Cabral, had willingly shared his statistics with Burtt. But now the acting curador, Arnaldo Vidal, offered "little in the way of concrete facts and definite figures" to Cadbury. Instead, he defended the planters and condemned Burtt's report and the British chocolate makers for "arousing the bad feeling of the British public." In Lisbon, commentators also decried the ongoing "campaign of defamation" and questioned Cadbury's motives. Was he a spy or, as he claimed, a defender of São Toméan cocoa?[35]

At the repatriation office, Luís F. da Saúde opened his books to Cadbury, who discovered that £62,200 had been contributed to the repatriation fund by estate owners and that each worker had been "credited with his share of the fund." Saúde had little cause to be defensive, since the fund proved that the planters were obeying the directive of the January 1903 law to repatriate workers to Angola at the end of their five-year contracts. Vidal, however, insisted that none of the three hundred serviçais whose contracts he had recently renewed on a large estate showed any interest in being repatriated. The curador also ignored Cadbury's repeated requests to witness the recontracting process.[36]

Cadbury left for Angola, arriving in Luanda on November 16. With a letter of introduction from Augusto Castilho, the new colonial minister, he requested a meeting with the governor-general, Henrique Paiva Couceiro. Burtt had dealt with Eduardo Costa at the end of 1906; Couceiro had begun his two-year appointment the following July. A monarchist and an imperialist, he had set out to occupy the colony's hinterland but was frustrated by a lack of financial and military support from Lisbon. That absence of effective occupation helped, in Couceiro's view, to explain the irregularities in the recruiting of serviçais for São Tomé.[37]

The governor-general proved no more welcoming than Vidal had been. He insisted that Mackie, the British consul in Luanda, attend their meeting on November 19. Couceiro gave Cadbury and Burtt permission to "visit the courts where the serviçaes were contracted." If they found any evidence of slavery, he would ensure that the malefactors were punished. Recruiting and contracting for São Tomé, however, was the responsibility of that colony. The government of Angola exercised no control over the process. As private citizens, Cadbury and Burtt had access to all published statistics, and they could move freely about the colony. Cadbury had traveled four thousand miles to carry out a "straightforward investigation." Not surprisingly, Couceiro's snub offended him.[38]

With no official support for their visit, Cadbury and Burtt spent six weeks steaming up and down the coast. Cadbury took photographs and collected postcards. He wrote letters to his wife, Emmeline, describing what he saw, asking after their children, and complaining about the heat. At Moçâmedes, Burtt bought a wooden stool for Cadbury's five-year-old son, John, and explained in a letter, "It came from the interior of Africa near where father is now and had to be carried for a very long way on the top of black men's heads. . . . I don't think the little black boys ever used it, because they like to sit on the ground without any clothes on." Grown men sat on stools. Burtt illustrated his charming note with a drawing of an axe and a knife.[39]

Cadbury had not, however, gone to Africa to play tourist. He called on the governor of Moçâmedes, who told him that contract workers no longer passed through the district's port. On December 5, he met with Francisco de Paula Cid, who was in Benguela conducting his officially sanctioned investigation of labor recruiting. Cadbury found him "quite pleasant and reasonable" but wondered if a man who had served as governor of both Angola's Benguela District and São Tomé would produce "impartial evidence." During a second visit to Benguela on December 21, Cadbury spoke with the district governor, who insisted that he had nothing to do with the trade in serviçais, who came "from the interior, away from his district." His curador, however, identified the two main agents exporting workers through Benguela. A visit to the courts to witness the contracting process proved impossible because the trade had been temporarily suspended. Cadbury found it "difficult to believe that one of the most profitable trades of the Colony was altogether suspended because of the presence in the city of two extra Englishmen" in a district where many worked for the Benguela railroad. Three visits to Novo Redondo did not yield a meeting with its district governor, though the curador told Cadbury that the "first ten men ever repatriated" from São Tomé had landed at the port on December 4. Cadbury and Burtt also saw "three shipments of Novo Redondo serviçaes." On December 26, they shared the Portuguese steamer *Ambaca* with eighty women and numerous young children. All were "well clothed with a bright cotton cloth and good blanket, and appeared to have sufficient accommodation." Cadbury spoke no African languages and could not interview the serviçais. It was the reason he had asked Swan to return to Angola's interior and why—as he explained to his fellow Cadbury directors—he considered the missionary's "enquiry . . . of infinitely more value than mine—he will see things with comparative ease that I could never see." In the first week of January 1909, Cadbury Brothers wrote to Fry and Rowntree to recommend that all three firms "cease buying S. Thome cocoa."[40]

Cadbury and Burtt left Luanda on January 11, heading north for the Gold Coast (modern-day Ghana), where free African farmers had been growing cocoa for two decades, though not on a scale large enough to meet commercial demand. In early February, they visited two farms, along with William Leslie, a cocoa buyer for Cadbury Brothers. A six-hour hammock ride took them on to Mangoase, where a new railroad was under construction. When finished, Cadbury thought, it might hold "the key to a vast cocoa district" in which the firm could invest, and he authorized the purchase of fourteen acres for a factory site.[41]

Morel had told Cadbury in mid-1908 that if he went to Africa, he would end up boycotting São Toméan cocoa, and indeed, within a week of Cadbury's return to England on March 9, 1909, the firm had formally decided to stop buying cocoa from the chocolate islands and wrote to officials in the Foreign Office to inform them. A notice in the *Daily Mail* on March 17 announced the decision by Cadbury Brothers, Fry, and Rowntree. Stollwerck's name had been left off the advertisement in error, but it too joined the boycott. William Cadbury wrote personally to the Portuguese colonial minister and to Francisco Mantero, explaining that of the repatriated workers he had met at Novo Redondo, only one had "any money from the Repatriation Fund on arrival in Angola." As far as Cadbury had been able to determine, "no alteration had been made in the system of recruiting." A skeptical Portuguese press suggested that the boycott had less to do with the chocolate maker's conscience than with his desire to enhance the market standing of cocoa from the British West Indies. For his part, Mantero had been trying for years to recruit labor from Mozambique for his roças on São Tomé and Príncipe. In early 1909, new legislation cleared the way for cocoa planters to divert at least some labor away from the Transvaal's mines, where—as the journal *Portugal em Africa* (Portugal in Africa) noted—British owners ignored the working conditions of a hundred thousand African miners even as Quaker chocolate makers obsessed about twenty thousand well-treated laborers on São Tomé. But as planters welcomed a solution to the chronic labor shortage, they faced a threat to their livelihood far greater than intrusive British philanthropists: cryptogamica, or swollen shoot disease, had invaded the cocoa plantations.[42]

In London, Travers Buxton and Henry Nevinson welcomed the boycott. (Cadbury's nemesis, Fox Bourne, had died in February 1909. He was replaced by John Harris, whom Cadbury found equally irritating.) The journalist wrote privately to congratulate Cadbury on "a great piece of work accomplished" that "does you great honour in every way" and then followed up with a supportive article in the *Daily News*. Other British newspapers also congratulated Cadbury, though they chastised him for taking so long to acknowledge the widely reported reality of slavery in Portuguese West Africa.

Cadbury meanwhile decided not to publish the draft report of his trip to São Tomé and Príncipe and Angola until the firm's libel suit against the *Standard* had concluded, though he did send a copy of "Labour in Portuguese West Africa" to the British Foreign Office.[43]

British officials may have shared Cadbury's report with their counterparts in Lisbon. In April, Francisco de Paula Cid presented his findings on labor recruiting in Angola to the colonial minister in Lisbon. Cid recommended that recruiting be limited to specific districts (those Portugal had effectively occupied) and be directly supervised by "specially appointed officials . . . responsible to the Governor General of the Province." The repatriation of workers from São Tomé and Príncipe should be made mandatory, and once they were in Angola, steps should be taken to allow them to return home. Finally, the process of recruiting labor from Mozambique for the islands should continue. The official decree issued on July 17, 1909, limited contracts to three years for workers from Angola and set out further guidelines on recruiting, wages, working conditions, and health care, but it did not make repatriation compulsory. At the end of July, the colonial minister, Manuel da Terra Viana, suspended the recruitment of contract workers in Angola for three months.[44]

The following month, Charles Swan's *Slavery of To-Day* was published in London and New York. As passionate as Nevinson's *Modern Slavery* and more graphic in its descriptions, it was also more sympathetic to the Portuguese position. Portugal, Swan noted, had outlawed slavery and understandably viewed the accusations about its colonies as an attempt by Britain "to concoct a case against Portugal with a view to deprive her of her lawful possessions." (Such sensitivity did not reassure Portuguese officials, who expected the book to turn its readers against Portugal and its policies in Africa.) The time had long passed, Swan argued, to free the slaves and condemn the slave traders. He had asked his fellow Protestant missionaries to sign a statement confirming that slave trading continued in the interior; he had identified the dealers by name, and he had interviewed many of their captives. He sent all the information to the British Foreign Office, although, as Burtt had done in his report, Swan declined to identify anyone by name in his book. Cadbury, worried that his association with the missionary would be more ammunition for the *Standard*, asked Swan to destroy their correspondence. It was a curious tactic for a man who had insisted on transparency regarding Burtt's and his own investigations of Portuguese Africa. It also failed—Swan was approached by the *Standard*'s lawyers as a potential witness.[45]

In late September 1909, the Anti-Slavery Society sent the newly married Burtt and his wife (also named Emmeline) to the United States. As Cadbury had predicted and Stollwerck had feared, the European boycott of São Tomé had flooded the American market with cheap cocoa. In public lectures in Boston, New York, Philadelphia, Baltimore, Washington, and Chicago, Burtt tried to persuade American chocolate manufacturers to join the boycott. He showed his audiences photographs of serviçais and wooden shackles and regaled them with a story of the horrors of slave trading drawn from his original December 1906 report. Walter Baker, the largest of the U.S. firms, had already stopped buying Portuguese cocoa. Burtt also wrote an article for the October issue of the illustrated *Leslie's Weekly*, provocatively titled "How America Can Free the Portuguese Cocoa Slave." In addition, he tried to convince the U.S. government to join the pressure campaign against Portugal.[46]

Portuguese diplomats in the United States followed Burtt's tour closely. His talks and his articles, they reported, did acknowledge that workers on São Tomé and Príncipe were well treated, well fed, and well housed. Officials took issue, however, with his description of contracted workers as slaves and his assertion that most had only limited access to the curador, the colonial official assigned to protect their interests. So bewildering were the inconsistencies in Burtt's attacks on the cocoa planters that the Portuguese consul in Washington, writing to Lisbon, asked: "Is it surprising to find that the planters can only with the greatest difficulty be brought to believe that the motives of their detractors are purely humanitarian?" In early October, diplomats sketched out a series of "notes that could be used discretely in conversations and communications" with American journalists. All were familiar to English audiences. Angola's hinterland had yet to be effectively occupied, a situation the extension of railroads promised to remedy. Recruiting from the interior had been temporarily suspended. As to the islands, numerous British visitors over the years—including Burtt—had attested to the good treatment of workers. One line in the notes captured diplomatic frustration: "Is it not high time that some association were formed in order to protect the world from the immense amount of suffering inflicted on humanity through the misguided efforts of rabid humanitarians?" That particular message was released not by a Portuguese official but by a British sympathizer, John Wyllie. A retired army lieutenant colonel and a member of Britain's Royal Geographical Society, he had translated Mendonça's *Boa Entrada Plantations* in 1907. In mid-1909, he sparred with Nevinson in the English press over the condition of labor in Portuguese Africa. In November, he followed Burtt to the United States, where newspapers printed Wyllie's counterassertions that "laborers for planters receive good treatment."[47]

Despite the public interest and diplomatic angst generated by Burtt's visit, New York City remained a major market for São Toméan cocoa. For some in the Portuguese press, the ability of traders to export directly to New York was a great asset in what had become a "war to the death" against São Tomé's cocoa. Portugal's enemies in this regard, as the press saw it, included Protestant missionaries and, regrettably, Portugal's own colonial minister, who had shut down Angola's export market in labor, if only temporarily. The chief enemy propagandist was Burtt, whose tour of the United States had fortunately been cut short by his obligation to testify in Cadbury Brothers' suit against the *Standard*.[48]

The weeklong trial began in Birmingham on November 29, 1909. The political divide reflected in Gwynne's September 1908 editorial continued, with the Conservative lawyer Edward Carson defending the *Standard* and the Liberal Rufus Isaacs representing Cadbury Brothers. For the firm, the issue was not whether it knew it was buying slave-produced cocoa. William Cadbury could document the company's concern with labor practices in São Tomé and Príncipe from 1901. Beginning with his first visit to Lisbon in 1903, he had spent six years and thousands of pounds trying to improve labor conditions on the cocoa islands. For the firm, what was at issue was the newspaper's allegation that Cadbury Brothers had not tried to do anything to improve workers' lives on the islands.[49]

Carson grilled William Cadbury over the three days he spent as a witness. The lawyer returned repeatedly to the question of whether the company knew that it was buying cocoa harvested by slaves. He questioned Cadbury about recruiting methods in Angola and working conditions in São Tomé and Príncipe. He inquired how much profit the firm had made from the £1.3 million worth of cocoa it had purchased from the islands between 1901 and 1908. For the most part, Cadbury maintained his composure. But when Carson asked what the effect might have been on chocolate sales if the *Daily News* had covered the cocoa controversy as vigorously as it had reported alleged Chinese slavery in the Transvaal's mines, Cadbury was evasive. He insisted that he had no direct influence over George Cadbury's newspaper. Further, he remained confident that if consumers knew all the company had tried to do on behalf of São Tomé's workers, they would have continued buying Cadbury products. Finally, he stressed his own commitment to transparency. The only document the firm had held back was Burtt's report, and that had been done at the request of the Foreign Office.[50]

Burtt testified on December 3. To Isaacs, he confirmed the bare bones of his relationship with William Cadbury. They had been acquaintances for many years when Cadbury asked him to undertake his investigation of labor conditions in Portuguese West Africa. The instructions had been open-ended: "The understanding was that I was to go out there and make an absolutely fair, as far as I was able, enquiry, and do the thing as thoroughly and reliably as possible." At no point had Cadbury asked him to delay his investigation or the release of his report. When Carson, in cross-examination, pressed him to admit that he had learned about slavery on the islands while studying Portuguese in Porto in 1904 and 1905, Burtt replied, "Up at Oporto, hardly anybody knows anything about these things." He admitted that his journey through Angola in 1906 had convinced him that a slave trade from the interior continued to supply labor to São Tomé, and it had prompted his own recent foray into protest journalism. His articles, however, had appeared more in the American press than in the English.[51]

Where Burtt had proved a strong witness and his employer at least a composed one, George Cadbury fared less well. It took Isaacs several attempts to get the elder Cadbury to reject firmly the accusation that the company had in any way acted dishonestly. Carson, as he had done with William, exposed George's insincerity. When pressed on his thin coverage of slavery in Portuguese West Africa in the *Daily News*, George offered a weak defense: "I thought it was injudicious, because my nephew at the time was nobly risking his life, and I did not want to make it more difficult for him by causing antipathy on the part of the planters."[52]

In his closing argument, Isaacs noted that Carson "had not called a single witness" to explain "how the article came to be written, why it was written, or whether the writer believed it to be true at the time it was written." Carson had succeeded in refocusing the trial on slavery and away from the *Standard*'s libel of the chocolate makers. In instructing the jury, Judge William Pickford asked them to consider whether there had been "a dishonest plot to delay the matter being brought before the British public in order to enable the plaintiffs to go on buying slave-grown cocoa when they knew they ought to give it up." The jury returned its verdict within an hour, deciding in favor of Cadbury Brothers but awarding only one farthing (one-quarter of a penny) in damages. Pickford directed the newspaper to pay £3,000 of the firm's court costs.[53]

The paltry award implied strongly that even though the jury agreed that Cadbury Brothers had been libeled, it was not terribly sympathetic to the firm's position. In the immediate aftermath of the trial, many consumers mailed clippings of Cadbury advertisements to the company, often marked with a variety of highly critical comments. One consumer wrote "You pious

Frauds" and "You Anointed Hypocrites" and amended the Cadbury Brothers line "Absolutely Pure Therefore Best Cocoa" to read "Absolutely Slave Grown Cocoa." At the bottom of the page, Cadbury's "You can't go wrong" now read "You can't go wrong For Profits increased by 'One Farthing.'" For the firm, this was a public relations nightmare, even if letters of support, totaling 257, outnumbered the 86 negative letters the company received.[54]

In January 1910, William Cadbury tried to redirect the conversation again by publishing *Labour in Portuguese West Africa,* a revision of the report he had submitted to the Foreign Office (and also circulated privately) in 1909. The new edition included an extra chapter that outlined the Portuguese reforms of July 1909 but also noted that workers from Mozambique had rioted in São Tomé in August when their contracts were extended without their consent from one year to three. The focus of the report remained Portuguese West Africa. Cadbury drew on his own notes from 1908 and 1909 and also on the more than three hundred pages of letters Burtt had written from Africa between 1905 and 1907. Cadbury acknowledged that debt: "The heaviest part of the whole work has fallen upon my friend Joseph Burtt, who faithfully carried out his original enquiry in face of many difficulties, and to whose knowledge and ability as interpreter, any usefulness of our recent visit is due. His views and mine coincide in the general conclusions of this statement." The report was thoughtful and evenhanded in its analysis. Even its title was carefully chosen, referencing labor in Portuguese West Africa, not slavery. But any hope Cadbury might have had of positioning himself as an "author of protest" alongside Nevinson and Swan was dashed by the muted response to the report's publication. Reviews appeared only in the *African Mail,* edited by Cadbury's longtime friend and ally, Morel; in the *Bournville Works Magazine*; and in the *Daily News.*[55]

Nor had the broader issues that prompted Cadbury to begin investigating the conditions of labor in Portuguese Africa been resolved. Effective February 1, 1910, labor agents were once again permitted to operate in Angola. The British Foreign Office and its consul in Luanda were cautiously optimistic that real change had been achieved, both in the process of recruiting and in repatriation. Skeptical British humanitarians remained vigilant and, from the Portuguese perspective, intrusive. Cadbury had satisfied his own conscience by boycotting São Tomé's cocoa, but along with Burtt, he remained the target of Portuguese commentators determined to assert their nation's innocence of the lingering charges of slavery. The controversy over cocoa and slavery would prove never ending.[56]

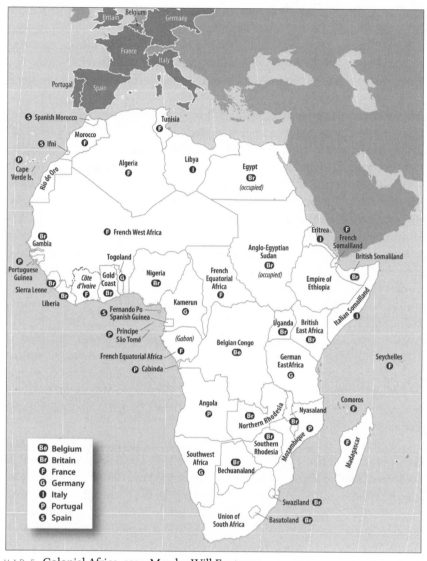

MAP 5. Colonial Africa, 1914. Map by Will Fontanez.

Epilogue

COCOA AND SLAVERY

THE PORTUGUESE translation of William Cadbury's report appeared in Lisbon and Porto in January 1910 under the title *Os Serviçaes de S. Thomé* (The Servants of S. Thomé). In his preface, Cadbury noted that the July 1909 labor reforms had done little to alleviate his concerns. His earnest presentation of the facts as he saw them was less well received than he might have hoped. The editors of *Portugal em Africa* chided him for his pomposity and wondered how he expected to give lessons in humanity to the Portuguese while British mine owners in the Transvaal continued to abuse Mozambican workers. In the same journal, the Marquis of Vale Flôr defended Portugal's humanitarian record. He also dismissed the photographs in the separate, limited-edition album Cadbury had circulated documenting his 1908–9 trip as fakes that could have been "taken in any part of the black Continent, even in London." The photographs—of plantations, workers, serviçais aboard ship in their standard-issue striped cotton clothing, and porters carrying their loads—strike the modern viewer as far less contentious than the shackles and skulls that illustrated Henry Nevinson's and Charles Swan's books, and Joseph Burtt's 1909 articles in *Leslie's Weekly*.[1]

In Lisbon, the colonial minister asked Francisco Mantero to write a report in response to Cadbury. *Manual Labour in S. Thomé and Príncipe* appeared in English translation in August 1910. In many ways, it mirrored Cadbury's book, with chapters devoted to working conditions on the islands and the recruitment of labor in Angola. A series of appendixes documented the planters' correspondence with Cadbury and his meeting with them in Lisbon in November 1907. Unlike Cadbury, Mantero included photographs—of buildings, workers' quarters, and hospital wards—meant to demonstrate the care afforded the islands' workers. Mantero's tone was strained but not hostile. The campaign against São Tomé cocoa, he acknowledged, predated the interference by the Quaker chocolate firms. Mantero claimed to admire Cadbury for visiting Lisbon;

traveling to the islands and to Angola; and attempting to harmonize the desires of the chocolate makers, the cocoa growers, and the Portuguese government. In his opinion, Cadbury had failed because he could not conciliate those interests in Britain that would only be satisfied by "the ruin of S. Thomé and also, perhaps the discredit of the English chocolate firms."[2]

In London, Mantero's attempt to redirect blame for the cocoa controversy away from Cadbury and thereby persuade him to abandon his boycott of São Toméan cocoa was met with skepticism. *Manual Labour* had been translated by John Wyllie, who had exchanged barbs with Henry Nevinson in the British press and followed Joseph Burtt to the United States in 1909 in an effort to discredit his speaking tour. Nevinson attacked the book, as did E. D. Morel as well as John Harris of the newly combined Anti-Slavery Society and Aborigines' Protection Society. Their venom and their refusal to believe that any positive changes had been made in Portuguese Africa seemed to prove Mantero's point. Their criticism also worried Edward Grey in the Foreign Office. He preferred to give the new Republican government in Lisbon, inaugurated in October, a chance to clear away the remnants of monarchical policies in the colonies.[3]

In November, at the invitation of a Portuguese government keen to set a new tone, Harris, Nevinson, and Charles Swan visited Lisbon, where they met with representatives of the new Portuguese Anti-Slavery Society. They were hosted by Alfredo da Silva, the reformer and antislavery activist who had translated Cadbury's book into Portuguese. To Harris's dismay, Silva portrayed the visit to Portuguese officials as an occasion to congratulate the government for its labor reforms in Africa, rather than as an investigation. When Harris wrote to Cadbury to protest Silva's "double-dealing," an angry Cadbury accused Harris of undermining, "in a flying visit of two days," the dedicated Silva. Cadbury also refused to support Harris's planned tour of Portuguese Africa.[4]

Burtt had accompanied Harris to Lisbon, but his loyalty to his former employer and friend was stronger than any affiliation to the British Anti-Slavery Society. In July 1911, he dedicated *The Voice of the Forest* to Cadbury "in memory of his enduring work for freedom in West Africa." In this romantic, fictionalized account of Burtt's journey to São Tomé and Príncipe and Angola, the heroes are the missionaries and the villains are the slave traders along the eastern border Angola shared with the Congo Free State. In the novel, Britain's foreign secretary, renamed Lord Cradley, commissions the central character, a railroad engineer named Russell, to investigate rumors of slave trading. Russell persuades his friend James Fletcher Beale to accompany him to Africa, and together, they march across the continent much as Burtt and Claude Horton did in 1906. Burtt borrowed liberally from his own letters; in the novel, Beale writes the poem that Burtt had sent to Cadbury portraying Africa as "a wanton woman enticing men to her, and then killing them." Russell falls in love with a missionary's daughter, and he and Beale help the missionary defeat the Batatela slave traders in a climactic battle. Nevinson wrote a positive review, and the novel sold well enough to go through a second printing in September 1911.[5]

While Burtt reimagined history, Britain's Foreign Office struggled with continued Portuguese intransigence. In May 1911, Portugal passed a law limiting contracts on São Tomé and Príncipe to two years but reaffirming the legal obligation of Africans to work and the right of colonial officials to force them to work. The repatriation of workers remained voluntary. Disappointed British officials responded by issuing, in 1912, the first in a series of "white books" on "Contract Labor in Portuguese West Africa." This report confirmed that although working conditions on the islands were good, laborers who had completed their contracts were not returning home to Angola. Harris, who had returned from a month-long tour of the Congo and Angola in 1911 and 1912 that had included a two-day visit to São Tomé and Príncipe, continued to press Grey, insisting that slavery persisted and that repatriation funds were being misappropriated. Cadbury joined his friend Morel in writing what was—for the chocolate maker—an intemperate article in the *Nineteenth Century and After* alleging that "slavery is as rampant throughout Angola to-day as it was in the fifteenth century."[6]

In Lisbon, the new colonial minister, Alfredo Augusto Freire de Andrade, who had so impressed Burtt in 1907 as governor-general of Mozambique, registered his protest—in English. Writing to Grey about the 1912 white book, he admitted that abuses still occurred in Angola (as they did in all European colonies), despite the best efforts of its police force. Repatriation remained a complicated issue, he said, impossible to achieve for those workers who had long resided in the islands but under way for those who were "engaged according to modern laws, have contracts and a repatriation fund." He was pleased that the white book recognized the good treatment of serviçais on São Tomé and Príncipe; what disturbed him was the insistence of critics that corporal punishment continued on the islands, even though the report acknowledged that there was no evidence to that effect. Why, Andrade asked, did the British government not recognize both the good intentions and the remedial measures of Portugal in Africa?[7]

Though Morel had coauthored the *Nineteenth Century* article, Cadbury was the sole target of Andrade's anger. Particularly offensive to him was Cadbury's assertion that slavery in Angola's interior was unchanged from the fifteenth century. The Englishman had to know this was false, Andrade thought; it was an outright lie designed to serve those interests in Germany and Britain that wished to take over Portugal's colonies. Cadbury's reliance in the article on Harris's testimony, given the brevity of his visit to the islands, was disingenuous. So too was Cadbury's observation that labor from Mozambique was recruited under "virtually free conditions." There was nothing "virtual" about it, as demonstrated by Burtt's 1907 thank-you letter to Andrade praising the "good government" and free labor he had found in Mozambique. Further, every time Grey had praised the progress that Portugal had made, Cadbury and his coauthor had dismissed it as ignorance on the foreign secretary's part. Cadbury was a hypocrite, and Andrade made no apologies for the admittedly uncivil tone of his own reply.[8]

In late 1912 and early 1913, Cadbury got caught up in the controversy surrounding the publication of Jerónimo Paiva de Carvalho's pamphlet *Alma Negra* (Black Soul). Carvalho's 1907 pamphlet had defended labor practices on Príncipe; in 1912, he appeared to reverse his position, asserting that "the existence of slavery on the islands is a fact." *Alma Negra* caused a sensation in Portugal, and in February 1913, Carvalho wrote to the newspaper *O Mundo* (The World) to deny that he was the author. Alfredo da Silva of the Portuguese Anti-Slavery Society had arranged the publication of two thousand copies of the pamphlet, subsidized by Cadbury. By March, the British Anti-Slavery Society had issued Burtt's translation of sections of *Alma Negra*. In mid-April, Silva published *O Monstro da Escravatura* (The Monster of Slavery), in which he asserted that Carvalho had indeed written *Alma Negra*. Silva claimed that his own motive in publishing the pamphlet had been to end the scourge of slavery and restore the honor of the Portuguese republic in Britain. Also in April, Cadbury published a copy of a July 1911 letter in which Carvalho offered to sell him the manuscript of *Alma Negra* for £200.[9]

For Andrade, this was yet more evidence of Cadbury's poor judgment and the malice of his campaign against Portugal. At the end of April 1913, he asked the Colonial Office to investigate Carvalho. The subsequent report, if accurate (and Carvalho protested loudly that it was not), revealed a checkered employment history in Príncipe that included a suspension for incompetence in 1904; a demotion for allegedly mistreating serviçais in 1907; and, while Carvalho was serving as a judge in 1910 and 1911, a charge of embezzlement.

The Carvalho controversy figured prominently in Andrade's reply to Harris's *Portuguese Slavery: Britain's Dilemma,* which had been published in June 1913. Writing that August, Andrade accused Carvalho of trying to extort money from Príncipe's planters. Carvalho had threatened that if they refused to pay him, he would "write against them and in favor of Cadbury's campaign." When the planters ignored him, Carvalho had tried to sell his manuscript to Cadbury. Though Andrade's report was formally a response to Harris, Cadbury, "one of our most tenacious accusers," remained the focus of Andrade's wrath. Portugal, he declared, had done everything asked of it—including working to end abuses in Angola's hinterland and improving the conditions of labor in São Tomé and Príncipe—by an international community whose own hands were hardly clean. If the corporations and philanthropists (including Cadbury) who had long attacked Portuguese policies were sincere in their concern for Africans' welfare and their desire to introduce "civilization" to the continent, they would join the campaign to end the sale of alcohol and gunpowder to Africans, as Portugal had recently done.[10]

It had taken Portugal twenty years to embrace the antialcohol stance Britain had favored at the 1889–90 Brussels Conference. Andrade's assertion that relieving Africans of their guns benefited them more than their colonial masters also opened him to a countercharge of insincerity. Still, he did seek to end slavery in Portuguese Africa. In 1913, Angola's governor-general, José Norton de Matos, sent colonial officers to every fazenda. Serviçais were given the right to choose their employers, and issued new contracts limited to two years, at the end of which they could return home. One loophole remained: vagrancy was illegal, and vagrants could be compelled to work (as was the case in most European colonies). Nevertheless, slavery in Angola's hinterland had formally ended. Workers for the islands were recruited by the Sociedade de Emigração para São Tomé and Príncipe (the Emigration Society for São Tomé and Príncipe). A consortium of planters that included Mantero and Vale Flôr, the society was subject to government regulation, published a yearly statistical report, and was patterned on the Witwatersrand Native Labour Association that funneled laborers from Mozambique to the Transvaal's mines.[11]

In its 1914 white book, the British Foreign Office acknowledged the improvements. Cadbury was generally pleased by this report, and Burtt considered it "an official vindication of ten long years of work for freedom in Portuguese West Africa." In 1916, the British consul H. Hall Hall confirmed from Luanda that workers were returning regularly to Angola carrying their severance payments from the repatriation fund. Those who stayed on the islands appeared to be doing so by choice. The cocoa controversy faded into obscurity, replaced by news of the Great War that had begun in August 1914.[12]

Cadbury and Burtt continued to pay attention to cocoa and slavery. In 1917, Burtt wrote a review of the final white book for the *Bournville Works Magazine*. He lauded the reforms Portugal had introduced on the islands but noted that "serious flaws" remained, including ambiguities in the recontracting process, delays in repatriation, and persistently high death rates. The Portuguese response to Burtt's 5-page article (which included a page and a half of photographs) arrived in the form of a 460-page study of labor conditions on the islands by São Tomé's curador, António Corrêa Aguiar. This report included a history of the cocoa controversy, a point-by-point refutation of Burtt's article, and over 100 pages of statistical tables meant in part to demonstrate Burtt's misreading of morbidity and mortality rates on the islands and among Mozambican miners working in the Transvaal. Even as Portuguese soldiers were dying bravely in Flanders Fields on the British side in the Great War, Aguiar charged, Cadbury and his agent Burtt continued to assault the honor of Portugal. All the evidence, including Hall Hall's 1916 report to the British government, demonstrated that Portugal had addressed every concern about the recruiting, recontracting, and repatriating of serviçais. The time had come, Aguiar concluded, for Cadbury and his fellow chocolate makers to end their boycott of São Toméan cocoa.[13]

Despite Aguiar's admonitions, Cadbury Brothers Limited continued to buy its cocoa from the Gold Coast. In September 1918, as Aguiar was completing his report, the swollen shoot disease that had first appeared on the islands a decade earlier threatened to destroy São Tomé's cocoa crop. In 1917, planters had exported 27,127 metric tonnes of cocoa. In 1918, exports declined by 56 percent to 12,074 tonnes. Planters flooded the market with 52,514 tonnes of stored cocoa in 1919, but exports dropped again the next year to 19,018 tonnes. In the end, swollen shoot disease proved a more devastating enemy for São Tomé's cocoa than the Cadbury Brothers boycott, as other importers also turned to the British colonies of the Gold Coast and Nigeria.[14]

The charge of slavery resurfaced in 1925 with the publication of Edward Ross's *Report on Employment of Native Labor in Portuguese Africa*. Ross, a sociologist at the University of Wisconsin, had visited Angola and Mozambique in 1924 at the invitation of the New York–based International Missionary Council, which hoped to present his findings to the Temporary Slavery Commission of the League of Nations. Ross described abusive white settlers forcing

DIRECTORS OF CADBURY BROS., LTD., 1921.

Standing—George Cadbury Junr., Dorothy A. Cadbury, William A. Cadbury, Walter Barrow, Paul S. Cadbury, Laurence J. Cadbury.

Sitting—Edward Cadbury, George Cadbury (Chairman), Barrow Cadbury.

FIGURE 31. Photograph in Iola A. Williams, *The Firm of Cadbury, 1831–1931* (London: Constable, 1931). By permission of the Cadbury Archives, Kraft Foods, Birmingham, UK.

Africans to work on plantations and build roads and government buildings for no pay. Commission members read the report but did not accept it as official evidence (much as the British Foreign Office had rejected Nevinson's report two decades earlier). The *New York Times,* however, reported on Ross's findings, making them international news and raising the question of whether Portugal should retain its colonies. For the Portuguese government, the parallel to the cocoa controversy and to the books by Nevinson, Swan, Cadbury, and Harris was painfully obvious. In June 1925, the *Boletim Oficial de S. Tomé e Príncipe* (Official Bulletin of S. Tomé and Príncipe) reprinted Andrade's condemnation of Carvalho's *Alma Negra* and Cadbury's support of it, with the goal of informing São Toméans—white and black—about the history of the "libelous campaigns undertaken by strangers against our country." The Portuguese delegation to the League of Nations responded with its own pamphlet, noting that Ross had spent just forty-five days in Angola and twenty-four days in Mozambique. Although he mentioned the British accusations made during the cocoa crisis, Ross had not visited São Tomé and Príncipe, nor had he read any of the literature defending Portuguese policies. He did not speak Portuguese and did not name his informants or verify his sources or his evidence. The Portuguese delegates were more worried about the threat of negative publicity posed by the *New York Times* than about any potential sanctions by the League of Nations. The hands of the members of the Temporary Slavery Commission—including Britain, France, and Belgium—were no cleaner than when Andrade had criticized Harris twelve years earlier. In 1925, slavery still existed in parts of British India, French Morocco, and the Belgian Congo. In the end, Portugal kept its African colonies, but the controversy sparked by the Ross report contributed to the coup d'état that overthrew the Republican government. As the new government declined into dictatorship, Portugal largely withdrew from the world stage.[15]

At the invitation of the Society of Friends, Burtt visited Greece and Smyrna in 1925, where he interviewed Armenian exiles. The next year, he published *The People of Ararat*, a history of Armenia and of the Turkish massacre of Armenians during World War I. His 1929 book of sonnets included two poems calling for British and international intervention to relieve Armenians' suffering. The volume also evoked the African experiences that had made Burtt an activist: one poem praised Andrade, and another was Burtt's ode to an Africa that had kissed him "with her warm and clinging lips." Burtt died in 1939, as Europe descended into a second world war.[16]

Cadbury served on Birmingham's city council and continued to support causes long associated with his family: public hospitals, housing, and libraries. When the *Friend* published an article in October 1949—forty years after the libel trial—urging readers to remember "Nevinson's difficulties in persuading Quaker cocoa firms to boycott the importation of slave-grown cocoa," Cadbury did not respond publicly. Instead, he wrote a "private inside history" for his family, in which he chastised the "brilliant journalist" Nevinson for trying to take the credit due to Burtt and Morel for helping end slavery in Portuguese Africa. In 1955, Cadbury made one last public statement—a short introduction in the *Anti-Slavery Reporter* to C. W. W. Greenridge's review of *The African Awakening,* a book written by another crusading journalist, Basil Davidson. This volume confirmed that labor recruiting in Angola continued to be supervised by government agents and that recruits traveled in relative comfort by train from the interior to the coast, rather than marching. Yet a system of forced labor still existed, alleged Davidson, and Cadbury called on the British government, via the United Nations, to act.[17]

FIGURE 32. Joseph Burtt in the late 1920s. Photograph in Joseph
Burtt, *Sonnets and Other Poems* (London: Oliphants, [1929?]).

In 1957, the year Cadbury died, the British government did act, though not on the issue of forced labor in Angola. Instead, Britain began the process of decolonization by granting independence to its own Gold Coast colony. The new African leaders renamed the country Ghana. Belgium granted its African colonies independence in 1960. France's African colonies, including Côte d'Ivoire (Ivory Coast), a major cocoa exporter, gained independence that same year. By the mid-1960s, most of Britain's other African colonies had also become independent. In 1975, a year after another coup d'état in Lisbon ended nearly fifty years of dictatorship, Portugal released its African colonies.[18]

São Tomé and Príncipe's African cocoa farmers failed to regain a foothold in the competitive international cocoa market. African farmers in Ghana and the Côte d'Ivoire became the major suppliers of cocoa to the world's chocolate manufacturers. Yet allegations of slavery persisted. In 2000 and 2001, newspaper editorials and a television documentary alleged that Cadbury and the French firm Nestlé were knowingly buying cocoa harvested by child laborers enslaved on Côte d'Ivoire's cocoa plantations. Cadbury representatives replied that the company purchased the bulk of its cocoa from Ghana, where there was no evidence of slavery. Cadbury referred critics to the World Cocoa Foundation, established in 2000 to encourage "sustainable, responsible cocoa growing" in Africa, Asia, and the Americas. Foundation initiatives included literacy and vocational-training programs for laborers. In Côte d'Ivoire, the world's largest exporter of cocoa, government officials agreed to cooperate with cocoa exporters and importers and the International Labor Organization to "eliminate child slave labour in the cocoa chain." In 2002, the London-based Anti-Slavery International (the successor to the British Anti-Slavery Society) estimated that approximately 284,000 children worked in the cocoa fields of West Africa. Of these, perhaps 15,000 (5.3 percent) were enslaved in Côte d'Ivoire. Less clear was whether the employers considered those young workers slaves, in societies where children commonly worked in extended family settings. Identifying the specific factors (including hunger and poverty at home) that force children to labor on Côte d'Ivoire's plantations has proved as difficult as it was for Burtt in São Tomé and Príncipe in 1905. Today, despite anecdotal evidence collected by a new generation of crusading journalists, African workers remain largely anonymous—and the meaning of slavery and freedom in an African context sometimes unfathomable—to the predominantly Western consumers of chocolate.[19]

In Côte d'Ivoire, which had been much envied in the rest of Africa for its prosperity and stability, the peace shattered in September 2002. Cocoa prices had fallen in the late 1990s; the accusations of child slavery soon followed. As the economy weakened, political, ethnic, and religious tensions increased. Treaties were negotiated and then broken. Yet truckers hauling cocoa through conflict zones made it safely to the coast, and cocoa beans found their way to chocolate manufacturers. Côte d'Ivoire's president, Laurent Gbagbo, used cocoa profits to buy guns, as did his opponents. In November 2010, Gbagbo was defeated in an election deemed fair by international observers. He refused to leave office. His opponent, the victorious president-elect Alassane Ouattara, called for a ban on cocoa exports in order to starve Gbagbo of the funds required to pay the army and run the government. World cocoa prices soared. Gbagbo finally conceded defeat in April 2011. The idea, one imagines, of a democratically elected leader advocating a boycott to overthrow a tyrant would have appealed to early twentieth-century antislavery activists, including Joseph Burtt—and to William Cadbury the philanthropist, if not William Cadbury the businessman.[20]

A NOTE ON CURRENCY

Number of Portuguese reis to one British pound, 1904–10

1904	5,410
1905	4,790
1906	4,580
1907	4,640
1908	5,200
1909	5,190
1910	4,900

Source: William Gervase Clarence-Smith, *The Third Portuguese Empire, 1825–1975: A Study in Economic Imperialism* (Manchester, UK: Manchester University Press, 1985), 227.

Number of U.S. dollars to one British pound, 1904–10

1904	4.87
1905	4.86
1906	4.85
1907	4.86
1908	4.87
1909	4.87
1910	4.86

Source: www.measuringworth.com.

A NOTE ON SOURCES

The letters Joseph Burtt wrote to William Cadbury from Africa between June 1905 and March 1907 (covering 311 typescript pages) form the core of this volume. They were collected by James Duffy in the late 1950s and early 1960s for his book *A Question of Slavery: Labour Policies in Portuguese Africa and the British Protest, 1850–1920* (1967). Some of the letters—but not all—appear in the court documents that Cadbury Brothers Limited submitted when the firm sued the *Standard* for libel in 1908. Cadbury Brothers subsequently donated its records about the trial and more broadly about its West African operations to the University of Birmingham Library's Special Collections (now housed in the Cadbury Research Library) in 1972. The collection of Burtt's letters apparently was misplaced in this transfer, but it reappeared when several boxes of Duffy's research notes were donated by his widow to the African Collection at Yale University in 2000. Comparing Burtt's official report of his trip to the letters he used to compose it, Duffy observed: "The report itself—in any version—is of much less value than the collection of Burtt's letters to Cadbury, which run to 400 pages." (One can hope that the missing 89 pages are in the Cadbury Papers [CP].) Cadbury Brothers Limited's commitment to transparency was evident in its 1972 gift to the University of Birmingham's Special Collections. In addition, the curator of Yale's African Collection donated a copy of the recovered Burtt-Cadbury correspondence to the University of Birmingham's Special Collections.[1]

In Portugal, the Sociedade de Geografia de Lisboa (the Geographical Society of Lisbon) boasts one of the richest collections of contemporary pamphlets and books documenting the Portuguese Empire in Africa in the late nineteenth and early twentieth centuries. At the Arquivo Histórico Diplomático (the Historical and Diplomatic Archive) in Lisbon, archival collection 3°P-A-3 "Serviçais em S. Tomé" includes—among other documents—the correspondence of the Portuguese consul in Washington, D.C., reporting on Joseph Burtt's 1909 visit to the United States. Scholars have remembered the cocoa controversy: in 1998, the noted Portuguese historian A. H. de Oliveira Marques would describe the scandal as a "more or less violent campaign" by Britain against Portugal. In 2003, Cadbury and Burtt's story became a subplot in Miguel Sousa Tavares's popular novel *Equador*. More recently, Miguel Bandeira Jerónimo's scholarly study *Livros Brancos, Almas Negras: A "Missão Civilizadora" do Colonialismo Português c. 1870–1930* (White Books, Black Souls: The "Civilizing Mission" of Portuguese Colonialism, c. 1870-1930 [2010]) set the confrontation within the evolving context of the Portuguese "civilizing mission" in Africa.[2]

Photographs also shaped the cocoa controversy, and in his preface to Jerónimo's *Livros Brancos,* Diogo Ramada Curto analyzed the competing interpretations of empire and labor suggested by the pictures of shackles and skulls that appeared in Henry Nevinson's and Charles Swan's books and the more formal illustrations chosen by Francisco Mantero. Readers may observe that many of the photographs I have chosen to illustrate *Chocolate Islands* belong in this latter group—that is, they are staged. For scholars who have studied these images of empire, including James R. Ryan, Wolfram Hartmann, Jeremy Silvester, Patricia Hayes, Paul S. Landau, and Deborah D. Kaspin, that was precisely the point. The photographs were meant to convey the "truth" of empire to their viewers, assert its legitimacy, and shape its consumption. Many of the photographs in *Chocolate Islands* come from the extensive selection of postcards collected by João Loureiro. They are a fitting representation of what Joseph Burtt encountered as he traveled through São Tomé and Príncipe and Angola, in part because his critics suggested that what he saw was being managed by his Portuguese hosts. Yet even in these images, not everything is hidden: the Angolan serviçal woman in figure 7 appears angry, the São Toméan women in figure 6 seem content, and some of the Angolare children in figure 12 look remarkably carefree.[3]

William Cadbury did not include photographs in *Labour in Portuguese West Africa.* Copy 49 of the 50-copy album he circulated in 1909 of the trip he took to West Africa with Burtt survives (in CP 242), but the quality of the photographs is poor. Few captions describe the shiny and faded images. The album was controversial, perhaps because the Portuguese officials and planters who received copies (including Vale Flôr) inferred a threat in this different presentation of the supposed truth of colonial Portuguese Africa. Yet even William Cadbury was not immune to the temptation to stage a photograph. The frontispiece (from CP 308) in *Chocolate Islands* is one of the few surviving photographs of Cadbury and Burtt together. They are posing with a bare-chested, unidentified African man wearing what Mary Kingsley might have described as "a highly ornamental table-cloth" around his waist. In the alternate version of this photograph—in which Burtt's face is blurred—the same African man is wearing Western-style trousers, an image that conveyed a very different meaning, both in 1909 and a century later.[4]

The cocoa controversy continues to engage writers and scholars. In English, an extensive secondary literature documents the attempts of Cadbury Brothers Limited to influence labor practices in São Tomé and Príncipe, to control newspaper reports, to defend its integrity as an antislavery Quaker firm, and finally, to protect the Cadbury brand. Two accounts by Cadbury company historians—A. G. Gardiner's *Life of George Cadbury* (1923) and Iola A. Williams's *The Firm of Cadbury, 1831–1931* (1931)—praise the attempts of William Cadbury, on behalf of the firm, to improve labor conditions in Portuguese West Africa. Scholars of Portuguese Africa, including James Duffy in *Portuguese Africa* (1959) and *A Question of Slavery* (1967) and William Gervase Clarence-Smith—in his 1990 and 1993 articles—have noted the contradiction inherent in the company's antislavery stance and its desire to secure the finest cocoa available, a theme also explored by Gillian Wagner in *The Chocolate Conscience* (1987). All nevertheless have applauded William Cadbury for his astute assessment of labor conditions in São Tomé and Príncipe and his attempts to improve them. More recent analyses include Lowell J. Satre, *Chocolate on Trial: Slavery, Politics, and the Ethics of Business* (2005), and Kevin Grant, *A Civilised Savagery: Britain and the New Slaveries in Africa, 1884–1926* (2005). Grant's is the more caustic work, noting that "an immediate boycott" of São Tomé's cocoa "would have had a detrimental effect on the works at Bournville, prompting the company to lay off several hundred employees on a temporary basis"; William Cadbury's cautious protests were thus all about preserving the flow of cocoa to the factory at Bournville. In a 2008 article, Marouf Hasian Jr. reconsiders the 1909 libel trial and Grant's and Satre's interpretations of it. Deborah Cadbury's popular study *Chocolate Wars: The 150-Year Rivalry between the World's Greatest Chocolate Makers* (2010), places the cocoa controversy in the context of the global competition between European and North American chocolate manufacturers, whereas Robert M. Burroughs revisits the impact of Henry Nevinson's *Modern Slavery* in *Travel Writing and Atrocities: Eyewitness Accounts of Colonialism in the Congo, Angola, and the Putumayo* (2011).[5] To this literature, *Chocolate Islands: Cocoa, Slavery, and Colonial Africa* adds the perspective of Joseph Burtt, erstwhile bank clerk, Quaker utopian, employee and friend of William Cadbury, and ultimately antislavery activist.

ABBREVIATIONS IN THE NOTES

ABCFM	American Board of Commissioners for Foreign Missions
AHD	Arquivo Histórico Diplomática, Lisbon, Portugal
AHSTP	Arquivo Histórico de São Tomé e Príncipe, São Tomé
AHU	Arquivo Histórico Ultramarino, Lisbon, Portugal
BOSTP	*Boletim Oficial de S. Tomé e Príncipe*
CB	Cadbury Brothers Ltd.
CP	Cadbury Papers, Cadbury Research Library, Special Collections, University of Birmingham, Birmingham, UK
FFM	Fundo Francisco Mantero, AHU
FO	British Foreign Office
JB	Joseph Burtt
JDC	James Duffy Collection, African Collection, Yale University Library, New Haven, Connecticut
Nevinson Diaries	Henry Woodd Nevinson Diaries, Bodleian Library, Oxford University, Oxford, UK
SEMU	Secretaria do Estado Marinha e Ultramor
WAC	William A. Cadbury
WAC Family Papers	William Adlington Cadbury Family Papers, Birmingham City Archives, Birmingham, UK

NOTES

PREFACE

1. On travel literature, see Mary Louise Pratt, *Imperial Eyes: Travel Writing and Transculturation* (London: Routledge, 1992), 5; Robert M. Burroughs, *Travel Writing and Atrocities: Eyewitness Accounts of Colonialism in the Congo, Angola, and the Putumayo* (New York: Routledge, 2011), 1–2, 4, 9, 17, 114, 117–19. On the impact of Burtt's report, see Lowell Satre, *Chocolate on Trial: Slavery, Politics, and the Ethics of Business* (Athens: Ohio University Press, 2005), 93–95. On slavery in the twenty-first century, see Kevin Bales, *Disposable People: New Slavery in the Global Economy*, rev. ed. (Berkeley: University of California Press, 2004); Henry Woodd Nevinson Diaries, June 18, 1905, MS. Eng. misc.e.613/1, Bodleian Library, University of Oxford, Oxford, UK (hereafter Nevinson Diaries) (quote).

PROLOGUE

1. William A. Cadbury (hereafter WAC) to Joseph Burtt (hereafter JB), July 21, 1904, in the Cadbury Papers (hereafter CP), Cadbury Research Library, Special Collections, University of Birmingham, Birmingham, United Kingdom, CP 4/96; WAC to JB, August 27, 1904, CP 4/97; WAC to H. R. Fox Bourne, May 20, 1903, CP 4/41; Cadbury Brothers Ltd. (hereafter CB) to H. H. Johnston, September 29, 1904, CP 4/100; "Plaintiffs' Board Minutes," CP 133: 12–13; William A. Cadbury, *Labour in Portuguese West Africa*, 2nd ed. (London: George Routledge and Sons, 1910), 141.

2. "Joseph Burtt," *Friend*, May 19, 1939, 408; JB to WAC, July 4, 1905, 26, "Copy of letters received from Joseph Burtt," in the James Duffy Collection, African Collection, Yale University Library, New Haven, Conn. (hereafter JDC).

3. John F. Crosfield, *A History of the Cadbury Family* (London: privately published, 1985), 2:385 (first quote); Charles Dellheim, "The Creation of a Company Culture: Cadburys, 1861–1931," *American Historical Review* 92, no. 1 (February 1987): 17 (second and third quotes).

4. Crosfield, *History of the Cadbury Family*, 2:385.

5. Dellheim, "Creation of a Company Culture," 14–17, 19–20, 21, 31 (quote); Eric Hopkins, *Birmingham: The Making of the Second City, 1850–1939* (Stroud, Gloucestershire, UK: Tempus Publishing, 2001), 98–102; Crosfield, *History of the Cadbury Family*, 2:385.

6. Crosfield, *History of the Cadbury Family*, 2:385 (quotes), 386; Dellheim, "Creation of a Company Culture," 21.

7. Ibid., 2:386; Peter Gay, *The Bourgeois Experience: Victoria to Freud*, vol. 1, *Education of the Senses* (New York: Oxford University Press, 1984), 103, and vol. 2, *The Tender Passion* (New York: Oxford University Press, 1986), 3–5.

8. Dellheim, "Creation of a Company Culture," 14–17, 19–20, 21.

9. By 1918, the Cadbury Brothers workforce was evenly divided between men and women; ibid., 14 (first quote), 21–23, 25, 34 (second quote); Gillian Wagner, *The Chocolate Conscience* (London: Chatto and Windus, 1987), 48.

10. Dellheim, "Creation of a Company Culture," 26, 29. See also Richard Price, *Labour in British Society: An Interpretative History* (London: Croom Helm, 1986), 99; Wagner, *Chocolate Conscience*, 51; Iolo A. Williams, *The Firm of Cadbury, 1831–1931* (London: Constable, 1931), 168–69, 216–37; Crosfield, *History of the Cadbury Family*, 2:385.

11. "Joseph Burtt," 408; Nellie Shaw, *Whiteway: A Colony on the Cotswolds* (London: C. W. Daniel, 1935), 38; Joseph Burtt, foreword to Shaw, *Whiteway*, 5 (quote); Hopkins, *Birmingham*, 82.

12. Dennis Hardy, *Alternative Communities in Nineteenth Century England* (London: Longman, 1979), xi, 1 (first quote); Ebenezer Howard, *Tomorrow: A Peaceful Path to Real Reform*, original edition with commentary by Peter Hall, Dennis Hardy, and Colin Ward (New York: Routledge, 2003), 130, 157 (second quote), 159, 217; Dellheim, "Creation of a Company Culture," 35.

13. Shaw, *Whiteway*, 20, 21 (quote); Dennis Hardy, *Utopian England: Community Experiments, 1900–1945* (London: E. and F. N. Spon, 2000), 175; Hardy, *Alternative Communities*, 11, 12, 175.

14. Hardy, *Alternative Communities*, 172–73; Hardy, *Utopian England*, 172, 173 (quote).

15. Shaw, *Whiteway*, 35, 37, 38–39, 40, 41, 43; Hardy, *Utopian England*, 175.

16. Shaw, *Whiteway*, 24 (second quote), 43–45, 48 (first quote), 68, 127, 128 (third quote); Hardy, *Utopian England*, 176 (fourth quote).

17. Burtt, foreword to Shaw, *Whiteway*, 5 (quotes).

18. Shaw, *Whiteway*, 56 (quote).

19. Ibid., 52 (quote), 53, 55–57, 64.

20. Ibid., 48 (first and second quotes), 49–50; Burtt, foreword, 6 (third through fifth quotes).

21. Shaw, *Whiteway*, 50 (first quote), 51–52, 67, 68, 69 (second quote; Shaw quoting the *Stroud Journal*, September 1, 1899), 70.

22. "Joseph Burtt," 408; WAC to JB, July 21, 1904, CP 4/96; Crosfield, *History of the Cadbury Family*, 2:386.

23. Suzanne Miers, *Britain and the Ending of the Slave Trade* (New York: Africana Publishing, 1975), 30, 31 (second quote); Lowell Satre, *Chocolate on Trial: Slavery, Politics, and the Ethics of Business* (Athens: Ohio University Press, 2005), 21; Dellheim, "Creation of a Company Culture," 15 (first quote).

24. Travers Buxton to WAC, November 11, 1903, CP 4/63; WAC to Buxton, November 12, 1903, CP 4/64; Satre, *Chocolate on Trial*, 30.

CHAPTER 1: COCOA CONTROVERSY

1. "Plaintiffs' Board Minutes," CP 133: 1–2; Geoffrey I. Nwaka, "Cadburys and the Dilemma of Colonial Trade in Africa, 1901–1910," *Bulletin de l'Institut Fondamental d'Afrique Noire* 42 (October 1980): 782 (quote), 783; Lowell Satre, *Chocolate on Trial: Slavery, Politics, and the Ethics of Business* (Athens: Ohio University Press, 2005), 18, 19, 234n17; Charles Dellheim, "The Creation of a Company Culture: *Cadburys, 1861–1931*," *American Historical*

Review 92, no. 1 (February 1987): 26–27, 34–35; William Gervase Clarence-Smith, *Cocoa and Chocolate, 1765–1914* (London: Routledge, 2000), 238–39.

2. David Birmingham, *A Concise History of Portugal* (Cambridge: Cambridge University Press, 1993), 1 (first quote), 86; Richard J. Hammond, *Portugal and Africa, 1815–1910: A Study in Uneconomic Imperialism* (Stanford, Calif.: Stanford University Press, 1966), 1 (second quote), 2–4; Gerald J. Bender, *Angola under the Portuguese: The Myth and the Reality* (Berkeley: University of California Press, 1978), xix; Douglas L. Wheeler, *Republican Portugal: A Political History, 1910–1926* (Madison: University of Wisconsin Press, 1978), 41; A. H. de Oliveira Marques, *História de Portugal*, vol. 3, *Das Revoluções Liberais aos Nossos Dias*, 13th ed. (Lisbon: Editorial Presença, 1998), 194–95. On British prejudices toward the Portuguese, see Rosa Williams, "Migration and Miscegenation," in *Creole Societies in the Portuguese Colonial Empire*, ed. Philip J. Havik and Malyn Newitt, Lusophone Studies 6 (Bristol, UK: University of Bristol, 2007), 16n2; Eugene E. Street, *A Philosopher in Portugal* (London: T. Fisher Unwin, 1903), 167–90; Malyn Newitt, "British Travellers' Accounts of Portuguese Africa in the Nineteenth Century," *Revista de Estudos Anglo-Portugueses* 11 (2002): 108–9, 117, 119, 122; and James Duffy, *A Question of Slavery: Labour Policies in Portuguese Africa and the British Protest, 1850–1920* (Cambridge, Mass.: Harvard University Press, 1967), 135.

3. Birmingham, *Concise History of Portugal*, 62–64, 96, 103; Nuno Severiano Teixeira, "Between Africa and Europe: Portuguese Foreign Policy, 1890–2000," in *Contemporary Portugal: Politics, Society and Culture*, ed. António Costa Pinto (Boulder, Colo.: Social Science Monographs, 2003), 86; João Pedro Marques, *The Sounds of Silence: Nineteenth-Century Portugal and the Abolition of the Slave Trade*, trans. Richard Wall (New York: Berghahn Books, 2005), x–xi, xiv, 99, 101–3, 183–86; Niall Ferguson, *Empire: How Britain Made the Modern World* (London: Penguin Books, 2003), 119.

4. Kevin Grant, *A Civilised Savagery: Britain and the New Slaveries in Africa, 1884–1926* (New York: Routledge, 2005), 27–29; Duffy, *Question of Slavery*, 126–28; Suzanne Miers, *Britain and the Ending of the Slave Trade* (New York: Africana Publishing, 1975), 22, 88–89, 94, 118, 171–72, 173 (quote), 241–45; Miers, "Slavery to Freedom in Sub-Saharan Africa: Expectations and Reality," in *After Slavery: Emancipation and Its Discontents*, ed. Howard Temperley (London: Frank Cass, 2000), 244–50; Teixeira, "Between Africa and Europe," 87; Henri Médard, "Introduction," in *Slavery in the Great Lakes Region of East Africa*, ed. Henri Médard and Shane Doyle (Oxford: James Currey, 2007), 7; Jan Georg Deutsch, *Emancipation without Abolition in German East Africa c. 1884–1914* (Oxford: James Currey, 2006), 97–101, 107–8.

5. Teixeira, "Between Africa and Europe," 86–88; Oliveira Marques, *História de Portugal*, 3:223. On the humiliation of the 1890 Ultimatum, see Alfredo Margarido, preface to *O Império Português entre o Real e o Imaginário* by Adelino Torres, Colecção Estudos sobre África 5 (Lisbon: Escher, 1991), 9; Malyn Newitt, *A History of Mozambique* (Bloomington: Indiana University Press, 1995), 341 (quotes); William Gervase Clarence-Smith, *The Third Portuguese Empire, 1825–1975: A Study in Economic Imperialism* (Manchester, UK: Manchester University Press, 1985), 81; Eric Axelson, *Portugal and the Scramble for Africa, 1875–1891* (Johannesburg, South Africa: University of the Witwatersrand Press, 1967), 223–33.

6. Teixeira, "Between Africa and Europe," 88; Oliveira Marques, *História de Portugal*, 3:188–89, 195, 284; Valetim Alexandre, *Velho Brasil, Novas Áfricas: Portugal e o Império (1808–1975)* (Porto, Portugal: Edições Afrontamento, 2000), 220, 237, and "The Colonial Empire," in *Contemporary Portugal: Politics, Society and Culture*, ed. António Costa Pinta

(Boulder, Colo.: Social Science Monographs, 2003), 64. Gerald Bender has suggested that the Portuguese were in a constant state of resentment: "It is difficult to find a single decade during the five centuries of Portugal's presence in Angola when a king or prime minister did not feel compelled to defend the country's colonial policies against foreign and domestic censure"; see Bender, *Angola under the Portuguese*, xix. On other "'imperial' imaginings," see Benedict Anderson, *Imagined Communities: Reflections on the Origin and Spread of Nationalism*, rev. ed. (London: Verso, 1991), 108–11.

7. Clarence-Smith, *Third Portuguese Empire*, 70, 76, 100; Duffy, *Question of Slavery*, 100 (quote), 101, 182; William Gervase Clarence-Smith, "The Hidden Costs of Labour on the Cocoa Plantations of São Tomé and Príncipe, 1875–1914," *Portuguese Studies* 6 (1990): 164 (citing Nogueira, *A Ilha de S. Thome*, 97); Clarence-Smith, "Labour Conditions in the Plantations of São Tomé and Príncipe, 1875–1914," *Slavery and Abolition* 14, no. 1 (1993): 149, 150; Marques, *Sounds of Silence*, x–xi, xiv, 99, 101–3, 183–86; Frederick Cooper, "Conditions Analogous to Slavery," in Frederick Cooper, Thomas C. Holt, and Rebecca J. Scott, *Beyond Slavery: Explorations of Race, Labor, and Citizenship in Post-emancipation Societies* (Chapel Hill: University of North Carolina Press, 2000), 119–21; Clarence-Smith, *Cocoa and Chocolate*, 213; Miers, *Britain and the Ending of the Slave Trade*, 257–61, 299; Tony Hodges and Malyn Newitt, *São Tomé and Príncipe: From Plantation Colony to Microstate* (Boulder, Colo.: Westview Press, 1988), 30.

8. Aida Faria Freudenthal, "Angola," in *O Império Africano 1890–1930*, ed. A. H. de Oliveira Marques, vol. ii of *Nova História da Expansão Portuguesa*, ed. Joel Serrão and A. H. de Oliveira Marques (Lisbon: Editorial Estampa, 2001), 451; Duffy, *Question of Slavery*, 178–79; "Projecto Bicker sobre trabalho indigena (Angola) (1898)," 1° Repartição, 1° Secção, Secretaria do Estado Marinha e Ultramar (SEMU), Gabineto do Ministro, Caixa 2546–49, Anos 1881–1911, Sala 12, Arquivo Histórico Ultramarino (hereafter AHU), Lisbon, Portugal; Joachim Pedro Vieira Júdice Biker, "Ilha de S. Thomé," *Revista Portugueza Colónial e Marítima* 1 (1897–98) 5: 307–10, 308 (quote), translated by and cited in James Duffy, *Portuguese Africa* (Cambridge, Mass.: Harvard University Press, 1959), 158, 159 (quote), who incorrectly dates Biker's article to 1903 (359n35).

9. Dellheim, "Creation of a Company Culture," 19; WAC to Joseph Sturge, May 1, 1901, CP 4/6 (quote); WAC to Sturge, April 27, 1901, CP 4/5; WAC to William Albright, May 2, 1901, CP 4/4; Satre, *Chocolate on Trial*, 18.

10. WAC to Joseph Sturge, May 1, 1901, CP 4/6; WAC to Sturge, April 27, 1901, CP 4/5; WAC to William Albright, May 2, 1901, CP 4/4 (quote); Satre, *Chocolate on Trial*, 16; Leonard Thompson, *History of South Africa*, 3rd ed. (New Haven, Conn.: Yale Nota Bene/Yale University Press, 2000), 138–43. See also WAC to Joseph Storrs Fry, February 17, 1903, CP 4/12.

11. Foreign Office, *Diplomatic and Consular Reports. Trade and Commerce of the Province of St. Thomé and Príncipe for the Year 1901*, No. 2922, Cd. 786-226 (December 1902), 4 (first and second quotes), 11; Duffy, *Question of Slavery*, 179–80 (third quote), 181; "Plaintiffs' Board Minutes," CP 133: 5; H. R. Fox Bourne to WAC, July 23, 1903, CP 4/49.

12. Duffy, *Question of Slavery*, 175–77, 184; William A. Cadbury, *Labour in Portuguese West Africa*, 2nd ed. (London: George Routledge and Sons, 1910), 38–41; Jeanne Marie Penvenne, *African Workers and Colonial Racism: Mozambican Strategies and Struggles in Lourenço Marques, 1877–1962* (Portsmouth, N.H.: Heinemann, 1995), xvi (quotes).

13. Soveral on behalf of Portuguese Legation, London, to British and Foreign Anti-Slavery Society, February 26, 1903, CP 4/14, 4/15 (first and fifth quotes); CB to H. H.

Johnston, July 9, 1904, CP 4/87; Satre, *Chocolate on Trial*, 50; Duffy, *Question of Slavery*, 24 (second and third quotes), 94–95, 121–23, 123n36; Dorothy Hammond and Alta Jablow, *The Africa That Never Was: Four Centuries of British Writing about Africa* (New York: Twayne Publishers, 1970), 100; Grant, *Civilised Savagery*, 120. See also H. H. Johnston, "Conferencia feita na Sociedade de Geographia de Londres," in *A Ilha de S. Thomé e o Trabalho Indigena*, Separata da *Revista Portugueza Colónial e Marítima* (Lisbon: Livraria Ferin, 1907), 93–96, 97 (fourth quote [see also CP 4/15]), 99. Although most of the articles in the collection include the original date of publication, Johnston's does not.

14. "Os serviças em S. Thomé são mais felizes do que os nossos camponezes," *O Século*, October 8, 1908, 1, col. 7 (quote); Carl de Merck to WAC, June 18, 1904, CP 4/78; WAC to Merck, June 25, 1904, CP 4/80; Francisco de Paula Cid to Francisco Mantero, November 25, 1904, in Fundo Francisco Mantero (hereafter FFM), AHU, FM 063 (D.m.); Augusto Nascimento, *Poderes e Quotidiano nas Roças de S. Tomé e Príncipe de Finais de Oitocentos a Meados de Novecentos* (Lisbon: by the author, 2002), 205n10.

15. WAC to Joseph Storrs Fry, February 17, 1903, CP 4/12; "Proof of W. A. Cadbury, 1909," synopsis of letter from WAC to JB, June 17, 1907, CP 3/53: 428; Satre, *Chocolate on Trial*, 18, 22–23; www.1911encyclopedia.org/Lisbon.

16. WAC to CB, March 17, 1903, CP 4/20; Clarence-Smith, *Third Portuguese Empire*, 95, 98; Satre, *Chocolate on Trial*, 30; *Grande Enciclopédia Portuguesa e Brasileira* (Lisbon: Editorial Enciclopédia, 1945), 5:210–11; Newitt, *History of Mozambique*, 372.

17. WAC to CB, March 17, 1903, CP 4/20 (quotes); Carl de Merck to WAC, June 18, 1904, CP 4/78; *Grande Enciclopédia*, 33:856.

18. See www.1911encyclopedia.org/Portugal; Maria Filomena Mónica, *Artesãos e Operários: Indústria, Capitalismo e Class Operária em Portugal (1870–1934)* (Lisbon: Edições do Instituto de Ciências Sociais da Universidade de Lisboa, 1986), 12, 16; Mónica, *A Formação da Classe Operária Portuguesa: Antologia da Imprensa Operária, 1850–1934* (Lisbon: Fundação Calouste Gulbenkian, 1982), 85–86, 90–91.

19. Wheeler, *Republican Portugal*, 40; José Cutileiro, *A Portuguese Rural Society* (Oxford: Clarendon Press, 1971), 1 (quote), 3–5, 7, 8; Caroline B. Brettell, *Men Who Migrate, Women Who Wait: Population and History in a Portuguese Parish* (Princeton, N.J.: Princeton University Press, 1986), 29.

20. Brettell, *Men Who Migrate*, 29, 77 (quote), 85–87, 90–97.

21. Hodges and Newitt, *São Tomé and Príncipe*, 56; David Birmingham, *Empire in Africa: Angola and Its Neighbors*, Africa Series no. 84 (Athens: Ohio University Press, 2006), 82; Augusto Nascimento, *Órfãos da Raça: Europeus entre a Fortuna e a Desventura no S. Tomé e Príncipe Colonial* (São Tomé: Instituto Camões, Centro Cultural Português em S. Tomé e Príncipe, 2002), 40–45, 82–83.

22. Clarence-Smith, *Cocoa and Chocolate*, 156; Clarence-Smith, *Third Portuguese Empire*, 104; WAC to CB, March 17, 1903, CP 4/20.

23. *Grande Enciclopédia*, 16:150; Clarence-Smith, *Third Portuguese Empire*, 104–5; Clarence-Smith, *Cocoa and Chocolate*, 111.

24. WAC to CB, March 17, 1903, CP 4/20 (quotes).

25. Clarence-Smith, *Third Portuguese Empire*, 105 (first quote); WAC to CB, March 17, 1903, CP 4/20 (second quote); CB to Conde [Count] Valle Flor, Jose Ferreira de Amaral and Francisco Mantero, March 31, 1903, CP 4/36.

26. WAC to CB, March 19, 1903, CP 4/21 (quotes); Linda Heywood, *Contested Power in Angola, 1840s to the Present* (Rochester, N.Y.: University of Rochester Press, 2000), 8, 12; Robert W. Harms, *River of Wealth, River of Sorrow: The Central Zaire Basin in the Era of the Slave and Ivory Trade, 1500–1891* (New Haven, Conn.: Yale University Press, 1981), 24–33; Duffy, *Question of Slavery,* 182–83.

27. WAC to CB, March 24, 1903, CP 4/24; Duffy, *Question of Slavery,* 143–44.

28. WAC to CB, March 24, 1903, CP 4/24 (first and second quotes); CB to W. A. Albright, March 31, 1903, CP 4/27; Travers Buxton to CB, April 6, 1903, CP 4/30; CB to Travers Buxton, April 7, 1903, CP 4/31; CB to H. R. Fox Bourne, May 12, 1903, CP 4/39; H. R. Fox Bourne to CB, May 16, 1903, CP 4/40; WAC to H. R. Fox Bourne, May 20, 1903, CP 4/41; CB to E. D. Morel, July 7, 1903, CP 4/48; H. R. Fox Bourne to WAC, July 23, 1903, CP 4/49; CB to H. R. Fox Bourne, July 25, 1903, CP 4/50.

29. Duffy, *Question of Slavery,* 159–60, 169–70, 182, 183 (quote); Satre, *Chocolate on Trial,* 21–22; Miers, *Britain and the Ending of the Slave Trade,* 31.

30. Duffy, *Question of Slavery,* 183nn27–30; Adam Hochschild, *King Leopold's Ghost: A Story of Greed, Terror, and Heroism in Colonial Africa* (Boston: Mariner Books, 1998), 1, 161–62, 164–66, 190–91. The African American writer George Washington Williams's pamphlet about abuses in the Congo was published in the *New York Herald* in 1890, but his stories were dismissed as fanciful; Hochschild, *King Leopold's Ghost,* 1–2, 108–12, 207–8, 213; see also Robert W. Harms, "The End of Red Rubber: A Reassessment," *Journal of African History* 16, no. 1 (1975): 73–88.

31. WAC to CB, June 4, 1903, CP 4/43; Hochschild, *King Leopold's Ghost,* 51–54; CB to E. D. Morel, July 7, 1903, CP 4/48; CB to H. R. Fox Bourne, July 25, 1903, CP 4/50; CB to Martin Gosselin, September 15, 1903, CP 4/58; WAC to George Whitla, November 2, 1903, CP 4/60; WAC to A. Arkell-Hardwick, November 6, 1903, CP 4/61; Travers Buxton to WAC, November 11, 1903, CP 4/63; WAC to Buxton, November 12, 1903, CP 4/64; Satre, *Chocolate on Trial,* 30. Ward's *My Life with Stanley's Rear-Guard* appeared in 1890. Tim Jeal does dispute some of the allegations of brutality against Stanley; see Jeal, *Stanley: The Impossible Life of Africa's Greatest Explorer* (New Haven, Conn.: Yale University Press, 2007), 228, 321, 325, 341, 410.

32. Carl de Merck to WAC, June 18, 1904, CP 4/78; WAC to Merck, June 23, 1904, CP 4/79 (quote).

33. WAC to JB, July 21, 1904, CP 4/96; WAC to H. I. Rowntree & Co., January 19, 1905, CP 4/145; WAC to JB, August 27, 1904, CP 4/97; Richard Wall to Catherine Higgs and CH to RW, October 29, 2004. Richard Wall is the great-grandson of Alfredo H. da Silva. "The Young People of an Old Country: Y.M.C.A. Work in Portugal," postcard [1909] from the Richard Wall Collection, Lisbon.

34. See www.1911encyclopedia.org/Oporto.

35. Travers Buxton to WAC, October 7, 1904, CP 4/104; Henry W. Nevinson to WAC, October 10, 1904, CP 4/105; WAC to Nevinson, October 13, 1904, CP 4/112. Hochschild, *King Leopold's Ghost,* 186, 207; Duffy, *Question of Slavery,* 186 (quote), 187; "Notes for cross-examination of Mr. Nevinson," CP 121; Satre, *Chocolate on Trial,* 28–29; Angela V. John, *War, Journalism and the Shaping of the Twentieth Century: The Life and Times of Henry W. Nevinson* (London: I. B. Tauris, 2006), 42.

36. Travers Buxton to WAC, October 7, 1904, CP 4/104; Henry W. Nevinson to WAC, October 10, 1904, CP 4/105; WAC to Board of Directors, October 10, 1904, CP 4/106; WAC to Nevinson, October 13, 1904, CP 4/112; WAC to H. R. Fox Bourne, February 13, 1905, CP 4/153 (quote); J. B. Monde, director, Rowntree & Co., Ltd., to CB, November 2, 1904, CP 4/124; Satre, *Chocolate on Trial*, 29.

37. JB to WAC, April 11, 1905, CP 4/161 (quote).

38. Carl de Merck to WAC, April 11, 1905 CP 4/157 (first through sixth quotes); WAC to Merck, April 17, 1905, CP 4/158.

39. Carl de Merck to WAC, April 11, 1905, CP 4/157; WAC to Merck, April 17, 1905, CP 4/158 (quotes).

40. The German firm Stollwerck also supported sending a representative, whereas the American firm Baker declined, noting that all the chocolate firms in the United States "had imported only 4 percent of São Tomé's production in 1901." Satre, *Chocolate on Trial*, 27, 28 (quote); see also J. B. Monde, director, Rowntree & Co., Ltd., to Cadbury Bros. Ltd., November 2, 1904, CP 4/124.

CHAPTER 2: CHOCOLATE ISLAND

1. JB to WAC, June 15, 1905, JDC, 5–6; JB to WAC, June 26, 1905, JDC, 15 (quotes).

2. JB to WAC, June 15, 1905, JDC, 5–6; JB to WAC, June 18, 1905, JDC, 7 (quote); JB to WAC, August 5, 1905, JDC, 72.

3. JB to WAC, July 27, 1905, JDC, 56 (first quote); Lowell Satre, *Chocolate on Trial: Slavery, Politics, and the Ethics of Business* (Athens: Ohio University Press, 2005), 32; Tony Hodges and Malyn Newitt, *São Tomé and Príncipe: From Plantation Colony to Microstate* (Boulder, Colo.: Westview Press, 1988), 30, 40–42; Augusto Nascimento, "S. Tomé and Príncipe," in *O Império Africano, 1890–1930*, ed. A. H. de Oliveira Marques, vol. 11 of *Nova História da Expansão Portuguesa*, ed. Joel Serrão and A. H. de Oliveira Marques (Lisbon: Editorial Estampa, 2001), 253; William Gervase Clarence-Smith, *The Third Portuguese Empire, 1825–1975: A Study in Economic Imperialism* (Manchester, UK: Manchester University Press, 1985), 87 (third quote).

4. WAC to CB, March 17, 1903, CP 4/20; Carl de Merck to WAC, June 18, 1904, CP 4/78; *Grande Enciclopédia Portuguesa e Brasileira* (Lisbon: Editorial Enciclopédia, 1945), 33:856; JB to WAC, June 18, 1905, JDC, 7 (quotes).

5. JB to WAC, June 18, 1905, JDC, 8 (quotes). Burtt arrived in São Tomé aboard the *Malange* on June 13, 1905. *Boletim Oficial de S. Tomé e Príncipe* (hereafter *BOSTP*), no. 27, July 8, 1905, 201; William Gervase Clarence-Smith, *Cocoa and Chocolate, 1765–1915* (London: Routledge, 2000), 121.

6. JB to WAC, June 18, 1905, JDC, 9–11; JB to WAC, September 11, 1905, JDC, 99.

7. JB to WAC, June 18, 1905, JDC, 9 (first quote), 10, 11 (second quote); JB to WAC, August 5, 1905, JDC, 61; Satre, *Chocolate on Trial*, 14; Hodges and Newitt, *São Tomé and Príncipe*, 15.

8. JB to WAC, June 26, 1905, JDC, 13 (first quote); Caroline Alexander, *One Dry Season: In the Footsteps of Mary Kingsley* (New York: Alfred A. Knopf, 1990), 5–6; Mary Kingsley, *Travels in West Africa: Congo Français, Corisco and Cameroons*, 3rd ed. (1897; repr., London: Frank Cass, 1965), 340 (second quote).

9. JB to WAC, June 26, 1905, JDC, 12; JB to WAC, September 11, 1905, JDC, 86; Clarence-Smith, *Third Portuguese Empire*, 48, 98, 103–4; Hodges and Newitt, *São Tomé and Príncipe*, 13–14, 17, 21, 29 (quote); Manuel Ferreira, "Gente do Mundo Português: O Barão de Água-Izé Figurado Império," *O Mundo Português* 9, no. 98 (1942): 83–87; *Grande Enciclopédia*, 1:629–30, 15:994.

10. JB to WAC, June 26, 1905, JDC, 18–19 (quotes); Clarence-Smith, *Third Portuguese Empire*, 4; Pablo B. Eyzaguirre, "Small Farmers and Estates in São Tomé, West Africa" (Ph.D. diss., Yale University, 1986), 169.

11. JB to WAC, June 26, 1905, JDC, 13 (quotes); JB to WAC, August 5, 1905, JDC, 69. Construction of the first four miles of public railways on São Tomé began in 1907 and was completed in 1911. Salomão Vieira, *Caminhos-de-Ferro em S. Tomé e Príncipe: O Caminho-de-Ferro do Estado e os Caminhos-de-Ferro das Roças* (São Tomé: IPAD, Intituto Camões-Centro Cultural Português em S. Tomé e Príncipe, Biblioteca Nacional de S. Tomé e Príncipe, 2005), 28, 67–69, 76–77; Ezequiel de Campos, *Obras Publicas em S. Tomé e Príncipe: Subsidios para a Elaboracão e Realisação d'um Plano* (n.p.: author's edition, [1914]), 48–50; Hodges and Newitt, *São Tomé and Príncipe*, 86.

12. JB to WAC, June 26, 1905, JDC, 14 (quotes); JB to WAC, October 21, 1905, 118; BOSTP, Apenso no. 43, October 24, 1908, 5; Francisco Mantero, *Manual Labour in S. Thomé and Principe*, trans. John Wyllie (Lisbon: Annuario Commercial, 1910), 38.

13. JB to WAC, June 26, 1905, JDC, 14; Nevinson Diaries, June 17, 1905.

14. Eyzaguirre, "Small Farmers," 145–46; Hodges and Newitt, *São Tomé and Príncipe*; xv, 56–57; Augusto Nascimento, *Poderes e Quotidiano nas Roças de S. Tomé e Príncipe de Finais de Oitocentos a Meados de Novecentos* (Lisbon: by the author, 2002), 509–10n2; JB to WAC, June 26, 1905, JDC, 17 (quote); Carlos Espírito Santo, *Enciclopédia Fundamental de São Tomé e Príncipe* (Lisbon: Cooperação, 2001), 164, 295; Gerald J. Bender, *Angola under the Portuguese: The Myth and the Reality* (Berkeley: University of California Press, 1978), 31–33; Augusto Nascimento, *Órfãos da Raça: Europeus entre a Fortuna e a Desventura no S. Tomé e Príncipe Colonial* (São Tomé: Instituto Camões, Centro Cultural Português em S. Tomé e Príncipe, 2002), 50; Francisco Tenreiro, *A Ilha de São Tomé*, Memórias da Junta de Investigações do Ultramar 24 ([Lisbon], 1961), 195–96, 198, 200–201.

15. JB to WAC, June 26, 1905, JDC, 16–17; Hodges and Newitt, *São Tomé and Príncipe*, 29–30, 34–35.

16. *Quaresma* translates as "Lent"; loosely rendered, the roçeiro's surname in English was "forty days of grace." The name also suggests that the family converted to Catholicism and may have claimed descent from two thousand Jewish children settled in São Tomé in the late fifteenth century. By the mid-twentieth century, São Toméans used *forro* and *filho da terra* interchangeably. Eyzaguirre, "Small Farmers," 145–47, 168, 170; Nascimento, *Poderes e Quotidiano*, 588n32; Hodges and Newitt, *São Tomé and Príncipe*, xv, 56.

17. JB to WAC, August 5, 1905, 66; Clarence-Smith, *Cocoa and Chocolate*, 121–22.

18. JB to WAC, July 4, 1905, JDC, 29 (quotes).

19. Ibid. (quotes); Hodges and Newitt, *São Tomé and Príncipe*, 57.

20. JB to WAC, July 4, 1905, JDC (first quote); Hodges and Newitt, *São Tomé and Príncipe*, 28, 29, 34, 57 (citing Francisco Mantero, *Obras Completas*, vol. 1, *A Mão-de-Obra em*

S. Tomé e Príncipe [Lisbon, (1954)], 243 [second quote]); JB to WAC, June 26, 1906, JDC, 19 (third and fourth quotes).

21. JB to WAC, September 11, 1905, JDC, 80 (quote); Dorothy Hammond and Alta Jablow, *The Africa That Never Was: Four Centuries of British Writing about Africa* (New York: Twayne Publishers, 1970), 109–10; Hodges and Newitt, *São Tomé and Príncipe*, 28, 29, 34; Nascimento, *Poderes e Quotidiano*, 512n13, 536n10; Mantero, *Manual Labour*, 103n1. On the use of *nativo*, see Josué dos Santos Aguiar, "Os Nativos d'esta Ilha" and "As Eleições e a Educação dos Nativos," in *Torre de Razão*, vol. 1, ed. Carlos Espírito Santo (Lisbon: Cooperação, 2000), 92–93; Benedict Anderson, *Imagined Communities: Reflections on the Origin and Spread of Nationalism*, rev. ed. (London: Verso, 1991), 122–23, 149–50.

22. *Grande Enciclopédia*,16:905; Henrique José Monteiro de Mendonça, *The Boa Entrada Plantations, S. Thomé, Portuguese West Africa, "La Perle des Colonies Portuguaises,"* trans. J. A. Wyllie (Edinburgh: Oliphant Anderson and Ferrier, 1907), 14.

23. JB to WAC, July 4, 1905, JDC, 21 (first quote), 22 (second and third quotes), 33; Mendonça, *Boa Entrada Plantations*, 17.

24. Mendonça, *Boa Entrada Plantations*, 22; Nascimento, *Poderes e Quotidiano*, 364.

25. JB to WAC, June 26, 1905, JDC, 19–20 (fourth and fifth quotes); Satre, *Chocolate on Trial*, 2, 12, 32; BOSTP, no. 27, July 8, 1905, 201; BOSTP, no. 30, July 29, 1905, 222–23; JB to WAC, July 4, 1905, JDC, 21, 23; Nevinson Diaries, June 19, 1905 (first, second, and third quotes), June 26, 1905 (sixth through tenth quotes), June 29, 1905 (eleventh quote), and July 1, 1905; Angela V. John, *War, Journalism and the Shaping of the Twentieth Century: The Life and Times of Henry W. Nevinson* (London: I. B. Tauris, 2006), xvi, 48–50; Robert M. Burroughs, *Travel Writing and Atrocities: Eyewitness Accounts of Colonialism in the Congo, Angola, and the Putumayo* (New York: Routledge, 2011), 109–10, 117–18.

26. JB to WAC, July 4, 1905, JDC, 23 (first quote); Nevinson Diaries, June 29, 1905 (second and third quotes).

27. Mendonça, *Boa Entrada Plantations*, 25, 31 (fourth quote), 41, 42 (first, second, third, and fifth quotes). It is interesting to note that in this translated version of Mendoça's work, J. A. Wyllie refers to white employees as servants (42)—the literal translation of the Portuguese *serviçais*—whereas the Portuguese original uses *empregados*, (employees) to describe the white staff; see Henrique José Monteiro de Mendonça, *A Roça Boa Entrada, S. Thomé, Africa Occidental Portugueza, La Perle des colonies portuguaises* (Lisbon: A Editora, 1906), 44. Wyllie was a sympathetic supporter of the Portuguese and may have intended to imply equality among black and white workers by describing them all as servants. See also Nascimento, *Órfãos da Raça*, 51; JB to WAC, July 4, 1905, JDC, 23; Nevinson Diaries, June 29, 1905.

28. José Cutileiro, *A Portuguese Rural Society* (Oxford: Clarendon Press, 1971), 63 (quote); Hodges and Newitt, *São Tomé and Príncipe*, 56; Nascimento, *Órfãos da Raça*, 48–50, 56–57, 59, 64–65; Nascimento, *Poderes e Quotidiano*, 306–7.

29. Mendonça, *Boa Entrada Plantations*, 41 (third quote), 42, 43 (first and second quotes), 44; Nevinson Diaries, June 29, 1905.

30. Mendonça, *Boa Entrada Plantations*, 26, 43 (first quote), 44 (third quote); Hodges and Newitt, *São Tomé and Príncipe*, 54, 73–74; Clarence-Smith, *Third Portuguese Empire*, 92–93; William Gervase Clarence-Smith, "The Hidden Costs of Labour on the Cocoa Plantations of São Tomé and Príncipe, 1875–1914," *Portuguese Studies* 6 (1990) 164; David

Birmingham, *Empire in Africa: Angola and Its Neighbors,* Africa Series no. 84 (Athens: Ohio University Press, 2006), 14–17; Nascimento, *Poderes e Quotidiano,* 412–13, 412n71, 413n73; JB to WAC, May 30, 1905, JDC, 2; JB to WAC, July 4, 1905, JDC, 22, 30 (second quote).

31. William Gervase Clarence-Smith, "Labour Conditions in the Plantations of São Tomé and Príncipe, 1875–1914," *Slavery and Abolition* 14, no. 1 (1993): 154; Clarence-Smith, "Hidden Costs of Labour," 164–65; Mendonça, *Boa Entrada Plantations,* 45 (quote); JB to WAC, August 23, 1905, JDC, 77.

32. Mendonça, *Boa Entrada Plantations,* 41; Clarence-Smith, "Hidden Costs of Labour," 164–65; Clarence-Smith, "Labour Conditions," 150–51; Nascimento, *Poderes e Quotidiano,* 416–18; JB to WAC, September 11, 1905, JDC, 89–90; *BOSTP,* no. 37, September 16, 1905, 286.

33. Clarence-Smith, "Hidden Costs of Labour," 165, 166 (first quote), see also 166n110 (quoting AHSTP); JB to WAC, January 3, 1906, CP 5/1; JB to WAC, July 4, 1905, JDC, 26 (third quote), 27 (second quote); William Gervase Clarence-Smith, *Slaves, Peasants and Capitalists in Southern Angola, 1840–1926* (Cambridge: Cambridge University Press, 1979), 64.

34. JB to WAC, August 5, 1905, JDC, 63 (quote); JB to WAC, August 14, 1905, JDC, 68; William A. Cadbury, *Labour in Portuguese West Africa,* 2nd ed. (London: George Routledge and Sons, 1910), 47–48; Hodges and Newitt, *São Tomé and Príncipe,* 67–69; Clarence-Smith, "Labour Conditions," 156–57; Nascimento, *Poderes e Quotidiano,* 272, 275.

35. JB to WAC, July 4, 1905, JDC, 27 (quote); Clarence-Smith, "Hidden Costs of Labour," 168; Clarence-Smith, "Labour Conditions," 155; Nascimento, *Poderes e Quotidiano,* 228–32; Eyzaguirre, "Small Farmers," 252; Hodges and Newitt, *São Tomé and Príncipe,* 70–71.

36. *Trade and Commerce of the Province of St. Thomé and Príncipe for the Year 1901,* No. 2922, Cd. 786-226: 4, 11, 12; JB to WAC, July 27, 1905, JDC, 53 (first quote), 54 (second through fourth quotes); JB to WAC, August 5, 1905, JDC, 69; Nascimento, *Poderes e Quotidiano,* 233, 236; Eyzaguirre, "Small Farmers," 252, 255–56. On abortion as a form of resistance, see Claude Meillassoux, "Female Slavery," in *Problems in African History: The Precolonial Centuries,* ed. Robert O. Collins, James McDonald Burns, and Erik Kristofer Ching (New York: Markus Wiener Publishing, 1993), 195–96, and Robert W. Harms, *River of Wealth, River of Sorrow: The Central Zaire Basin in the Era of the Slave and Ivory Trade, 1500–1891* (New Haven, Conn.: Yale University Press, 1981), 182–83. JB to WAC, September 11, 1905, JDC, 98 (fifth quote); Hodges and Newitt, *São Tomé and Príncipe,* 62.

37. Hodges and Newitt, *São Tomé and Príncipe,* 71; Nascimento, *Poderes e Quotidiano,* 233, 233–34n97.

38. JB to WAC, July 18, 1905, JDC, 39 (first and second quotes), 42 (third quote).

39. JB to WAC, September 11, 1905, JDC, 84 (first quote), 85 (second quote). By the mid-twentieth century, many Portuguese had lost this linguistic flexibility and dismissed African languages as those "of dogs or of monkeys." Bender, *Angola under the Portuguese,* 219n35.

40. JB to WAC, July 18, 1905, JDC, 41; JB to WAC, August 5, 1905, JDC, 61; Nevinson Diaries, June 25, 1905; António Carreira, *Cabo Verde (Aspectos Sociais, Secas e Fomes do Século XX),* 2nd ed. (Lisbon: Biblioteca Ulmeiro, 1984), 29, 65; Manuel dos Santos Abreu to Francisco Mantero, March 4, 1905, FFM, AHU, FM 060 (D.o.); Nascimento, *Poderes e Quotidiano,* 454n24.

41. Hodges and Newitt, *São Tomé and Príncipe,* 64, 70–71; Nascimento, *Poderes e Quotidiano,* 231, 233–34n97, 237; Eyzaguirre, "Small Farmers," 252, 253, 256; JB to WAC, July 18, 1905, JDC, 41 (quotes).

42. JB to WAC, August 5, 1905, JDC, 60 (first and second quotes), 62 (third quote); Hodges and Newitt, *São Tomé and Príncipe*, xv; Joseph Burtt, *The Voice of the Forest* (London: T. Fisher Unwin, 1911), 24.

43. Augusto Nascimento, "A Passagem de *Coolies* por S. Tomé e Príncipe," *Arquipélago-História*, 2e série, 8 (2004): 79–81, 85–90, 104–5; Clarence-Smith, "Hidden Costs of Labour," 167–68; Nascimento, *Poderes e Quotidiano*, 357–59, 379n21, 380n22; Hodges and Newitt, *São Tomé and Príncipe*, 37, 63; JB to WAC, August 5, 1905, JDC, 67 (quotes). See, for example, Report of the Curador, dated October 11, 1904, Caixa no. 332, Pasta no. 3, Curadoria Geral dos Serviçais e Colonos (1904), and Report of the Curador, dated November 13, 1905, Caixa no. 348, Pasta no. 1, Curadoria Geral dos Serviçais e Colonos (1905), Arquivo Histórico de São Tomé e Príncipe (hereafter AHSTP); Clarence-Smith, *Third Portuguese Empire*, 63, 76–77, 86–88, 111–12; Patrick Harries, *Work, Culture, and Identity: Migrant Laborers in Mozambique and South Africa, c. 1860–1910* (Portsmouth, N.H.: Heinemann, 1994), 82, 108; Bender, *Angola under the Portuguese*, 69. Portugal's school to train colonial officials, the Escola Colónial, opened in 1906. Andrew Roberts, "Portuguese Africa," in *The Cambridge History of Africa*, ed. John D. Fage, A. D. Roberts, and Roland A. Oliver (Cambridge: Cambridge University Press, 1986), 7:498; Albino Lapa, *O Conselheiro Ramada Curto*, Colecção Pelo Império (no. 62), vol. 2 (Lisbon: Agência Geral das Colónias, 1940), 44.

44. JB to WAC, August 5, 1905, JDC, 67 (first and second quotes); JB to WAC, October 6, 1905, JDC, 112 (third quote); JB to WAC, September 11, 1905, JDC, 86 (fourth quote), 87 (fifth quote).

45. JB to WAC, July 4, 1905, JDC, 35 (quotes); Satre, *Chocolate on Trial*, 30.

46. JB to WAC, July 4, 1905, JDC, 34 (quote).

47. Henry W. Nevinson, "The New Slave Trade: Introductory—Down the West Coast" *Harper's Monthly Magazine* 111, no. 663–43 (August 1905): 350 (quotes).

48. Satre, *Chocolate on Trial*, 12; Nevinson to WAC, July 25, 1905, CP 4/170 (first quote); WAC to JB, July 29, 1905, JDC (second through fourth quotes).

49. JB to WAC, September 11, 1905, JDC, 100 (quotes); *BOSTP*, no. 30, July 29, 1905, 222.

50. JB to WAC, August 23, 1905, JDC, 76 (first quote); JB to WAC, August 25, 1905, JDC, 79; JB to WAC, August 5, 1905, JDC, 71; JB to WAC, September 11, 1905, JDC, 80, 95 (second through fourth quotes), 100.

51. JB to WAC, September 11, 1905, JDC, 96 (quote); Hodges and Newitt, *São Tomé and Príncipe*, 60; Gerhard Seibert, *Comrades, Clients and Cousins: Colonialism, Socialism and Democratization in São Tomé and Príncipe* (Leiden, The Netherlands: Brill, 2006), 42–43; Seibert, "Castaways, Autochthons, or Maroons? The Debate on the *Angolares* of São Tomé Island," in *Creole Societies in the Portuguese Colonial Empire*, ed. Philip J. Havik and Malyn Newitt, Lusophone Studies 6 (Bristol, UK: University of Bristol, 2007), 119–24.

52. JB to WAC, September 11, 1905, JDC, 95 (second through fourth quotes), 96, 97 (first quote), 98–99.

53. JB to WAC, September 11, 1905, JDC, 99 (first quote), 100–101 (second quote).

54. JB to WAC, September 11, 1905, JDC, 100 (first quote); WAC to Nevinson, August 31, 1905, CP 4/171; Nevinson to WAC, September 1, 1905, CP 4/172 (second and third quotes); John, *War, Journalism and the Shaping of the Twentieth Century*, 50.

1. Joseph Burtt, *The Voice of the Forest* (London: T. Fisher Unwin, 1911), 48–49 (first quote); Burtt misspells *Papagaio* as *Papaguia*. JB to WAC, October 7, 1905, JDC, 116 (second quote); JB to WAC, September 23, 1905, JDC, 104 (third quote); Peter Gay, *The Cultivation of Hatred*, vol. 3 of *The Bourgeois Experience: Victoria to Freud* (New York: W. W. Norton, 1993), 87, 90–91.

2. JB to WAC, September 23, 1905, JDC, 104 (first quote); JB to WAC, October 6, 1905, JDC, 106 (second quote); Pablo B. Eyzaguirre, "Small Farmers and Estates in São Tomé, West Africa" (Ph.D. diss., Yale University, 1986), 131–32, 133 (third quote), 159–60.

3. Bernardo F. Bruto da Costa, *Sleeping Sickness in the Island of Principe: Sanitation Statistics, Hospital Services, and Work of the Official Conservancy Brigade*, trans. J. A. Wyllie (Lisbon: Centro Colonial, 1913), 1–2 (first quote), 5–6, 44, 77, 78 (second quote); Tony Hodges and Malyn Newitt, *São Tomé and Príncipe: From Plantation Colony to Microstate* (Boulder, Colo.: Westview Press, 1988), 54; Eyzaguirre, "Small Farmers," 258–59; JB to WAC, October 6, 1905, JDC, 110; JB to WAC, October 21, 1905, 121; JB to WAC, January 3, 1906, JDC, 155. See also JB to WAC, January 3, 1906, CP 5/1.

4. JB to WAC, October 6, 1905, JDC, 107 (first quote), 108 (third and fourth quotes); JB to WAC, September 23, 1905, JDC, 104 (second quote); Augusto Nascimento, *Poderes e Quotidiano nas Roças de S. Tomé e Príncipe de Finais de Oitocentos a Meados de Novecentos* (Lisbon: by the author, 2002), 254, 254n47.

5. JB to WAC, October 6, 1905, JDC, 107 (quotes); Rudyard Kipling quoted in Gay, *Cultivation of Hatred*, 85; JB to WAC, July 4, 1905, JDC, 34.

6. JB to WAC, October 6, 1905, JDC, 106–7 (first quote); JB to WAC, October 7, 1905, JDC, 114 (second quote); Costa, *Sleeping Sickness*, 27, 28 (third quote), 80.

7. Costa, *Sleeping Sickness*, 45, 79 (first, second, and fourth quotes), 77 (third quote), 72; JB to WAC, October 21, 1905, JDC, 121.

8. JB to WAC, October 6, 1905, JDC, 109 (quotes), 110, 113.

9. JB to WAC, October 6, 1905, JDC, 110 (first quote), 111 (second and fourth quotes), 112–113; Henry W. Nevinson, "The New Slave Trade: Introductory II.—West-African Plantation Live To-day," *Harper's Monthly Magazine* 111, no. 664–67 (September 1905): 539 (third quote).

10. JB to WAC, October 6, 1905, JDC, 111 (first and second quotes), 112 (third and fourth quotes), 113 (fifth quote); J. D. Y. Peel, ed., *Herbert Spencer on Social Evolution: Selected Writings* (Chicago: University of Chicago Press, 1972), xxxviii; Andreas M. Kazamias, ed., *Herbert Spencer on Education* (New York: Teacher's College Press, Columbia University, 1966), 8–10.

11. JB to WAC, October 7, 1905, JDC, 113, 114 (first through third quotes), 115 (fourth quote). Nicolau McNicoll is identified as Nicolau Mac. Nicoll in William A. Cadbury, *Os Serviçaes de S. Thomé: Relatorio d'uma Visita ás Ilhas de S. Thomé e Príncipe e a Angola, Feita em 1908, para Observar as Condições da Mão d'Obra Empregada nas Roças de Cacao da Africa Portugueza*, trans. Alfredo da Silva (Lisbon: Livraria Bertrand, 1910), 119.

12. James Duffy, *A Question of Slavery: Labour Policies in Portuguese Africa and the British Protest, 1850–1920* (Cambridge, Mass.: Harvard University Press, 1967), 176–77; Angela V. John, *War, Journalism and the Shaping of the Twentieth Century: The Life and Times of Henry W. Nevinson* (London: I. B. Tauris, 2006), 47 (fourth and fifth quotes); Nevinson, "New Slave

Trade," 539, 541 (sixth quote), and Nevinson, "The Slave Trade of Today: pt. 3," *Harper's Monthly Magazine* 111, no. 665–84 (October 1905): 672 (first through third quotes), 670; JB to WAC, October 7, 1905, JDC, 115 (seventh quote). On the reaction to Nevinson, see "compara os serviçaes contractados com os carneiros indo para o talho" (compared contracted workers with sheep sent to the butcher's shop) in *A Ilha de S. Thomé e o Trabalho Indigena* (Lisbon: Livraria Ferin, 1907), vi.

13. JB to WAC, October 25, 1905, JDC, 123, 125 (quotes).

14. JB to WAC, October 21, 1905, JDC, 121 (fourth quote); JB to WAC, October 25, 1905, JDC, 123 (first through third quotes), 124 (fifth through seventh quotes).

15. JB to WAC, October 25, 1905, JDC, 126 (first quote), 129, 130 (second through fourth quotes); JB to WAC, November 15, 1905, 132, 134 (fifth and sixth quotes); William Gervase Clarence-Smith, "Labour Conditions in the Plantations of São Tomé and Príncipe, 1875–1914," *Slavery and Abolition* 14, no. 1 (1993): 150; João Maria da Silva to Francisco Mantero, October 4, 1904, FFM, AHU, FM 063 (D.k.); Nascimento, *Poderes e Quotidiano*, 434n162.

16. JB to WAC, October 25, 1905, JDC, 131 (quotes).

17. WAC to JB, October 11, 1905, CP 4/183 (first, second, third, fifth, and sixth quotes); Nevinson, "Slave Trade of Today," 669–70; WAC to JB, November 7, 1905, CP4/184 (fourth quote); WAC to JB, November 20, 1905, CP 4/185; John, *War, Journalism and the Shaping of the Twentieth Century*, 42.

18. Nevinson, "Slave Trade of Today," 669–70; JB to WAC, November 15, 1905, JDC, 133 (first through third quotes); JB to WAC, December 8, 1905, JDC, 149.

19. JB to WAC, November 14, 1905, JDC, 134, 135 (first and second quotes); JB to WAC, August 23, 1905, JDC, 77; Augusto Chevalier, "A Ilha de S. Thomé," in *A Ilha de S. Thomé e o Trabalho Indigena*, 1111, 3, 6; JB to WAC, November 22, 1905, JDC, 139 (third through fifth quotes), 141.

20. JB to WAC, December 8, 1905, JDC, 149 (first through third quotes), 150 (fourth quote), 151 (fifth quote).

21. "Interim Report from Joseph Burtt received February 12, 1906," JDC, 158 (first quote), 159, 160 (second quote), 161, 162 (third through fifth quotes), 163 (sixth quote). A second version of the report, dated January 3, 1906, appears in CP 5/1.

22. WAC to JB, November 7, 1905, CP 4/184 (first quote); JB to WAC, December 23, 1905, JDC, 153; Nevinson, "New Slave Trade," 537 (second quote).

CHAPTER 4: LUANDA AND THE COAST

1. JB to WAC, December 23, 1905, JDC, 153; Henry W. Nevinson, "The New Slave Trade: Introductory II.—West-African Plantation Live To-day," *Harper's Monthly Magazine* 111, no. 664–67 (September 1905): 535, 536 (first through third quotes), 537 (fourth quote); David Birmingham, *Empire in Africa: Angola and Its Neighbors*, Africa Series no. 84 (Athens: Ohio University Press, 2006), 7; Aida Faria Freudenthal, "Angola," in *O Império Africano 1890–1930*, ed. A. H. de Oliveira Marques, vol. 11 of *Nova História da Expansão Portuguesa*, ed. Joel Serrão and A. H. de Oliveira Marques (Lisbon: Editorial Estampa, 2001), 320; Robert M. Burroughs, *Travel Writing and Atrocities: Eyewitness Accounts of Colonialism in the Congo, Angola, and the Putumayo* (New York: Routledge, 2011), 105, 117.

2. Nevinson, "New Slave Trade," 535, 536 (quote); Douglas L. Wheeler and René Pélissier, *Angola* (New York: Praeger Publishers, 1971), 3; Malyn Newitt, "Angola in Historical

Context," in *Angola: The Weight of History*, ed. Patrick Chabal and Nuno Vidal (New York: Columbia University Press, 2008), 50; Linda Heywood, *Contested Power in Angola, 1840s to the Present* (Rochester, N.Y.: University of Rochester Press, 2000), 26–30. See also Douglas L. Wheeler and C. Diane Christensen, "'To Rise with One Mind: The Bailundo War of 1902," in *Social Change in Angola*, ed. Franz W. Heimer (Munich, Germany: Weltforum Verlag, 1973), 53–92, and Maria da Conceição Neto, "Hóspedes Incómodos: Portugueses e Americanos no Bailundo no Último Quartel do Século XIX," in *Actas do Seminário: Encontro de Povos e Culturas em Angola* (Luanda: Comissão Nacional para as Comemorações dos Descobrimentos Portugueses, 1995), 377–89. Joseph C. Miller questions the utility of the term *kingdom* to describe African polities and argues in favor of *composites*; Miller, "From Group Mobility to Individual Movement: The Colonial Effort to Turn Back History," in *Angola on the Move: Transport Routes, Communications and History/Angola em Movimento: Vias de Transporte, Communicação e História*, ed. Beatrix Heintze and Achim von Oppen (Frankfurt, Germany: Verlag Otto Lembek, 2008), 245.

3. JB to WAC, February 12, 1906, JDC, 168–69 (first and second quotes); see also JB to WAC, February 12, 1906, CP 5/18.

4. Newitt, "Angola," 22, 23 (first quote), 24–25, 26 (second quote), 27–28; David Birmingham, *Portugal and Africa* (Athens: Ohio University Press, 1999), 55–56; Joseph C. Miller, *Way of Death: Merchant Capitalism and the Angolan Slave Trade, 1730–1830* (Madison: University of Wisconsin Press, 1988), 246–51. (Miller describes this new group as "Luso-Africans" [247]; Newitt, writing twenty years later in "Angola," uses "Afro-Portuguese" [24].)

5. Heywood, *Contested Power,* 12; Miller, *Way of Death,* 28, 256–57, 260–62, 264; Newitt, "Angola," 28–30, 32; Birmingham, *Portugal and Africa,* 94, 97–98.

6. Miller, *Way of Death,* 106–8, 115–22; Heywood, *Contested Power,* 7–8; John Thornton, "Sexual Demography," in *Problems in African History: The Precolonial Centuries,* ed. Robert O. Collins, James McDonald Burns, and Erik Kristofer Ching (New York: Markus Wiener Publishing, 1993), 187–90. On resistance by female slaves, see Claude Meillassoux, "Female Slavery," in *Problems in African History,* 194–98; Newitt, "Angola," 30–31, 37–38; Marianna P. Candido, "'Trade, Slavery, and Migration in the Interior of Benguela: The Case of Caconda, 1830–1870," in *Angola on the Move,* 70. On the Mbundu traders around Luanda, see Jill R. Dias, "Changing Patterns of Power in the Luanda Hinterland: The Impact of Trade and Colonization on the Mbundu, ca. 1845–1920," *Paideuma* 32 (1985): 285–318.

7. Ibrahim K. Sundiata, *From Slavery to Neoslavery: The Bight of Biafra and Fernando Po in the Era of Abolition, 1827–1930* (Madison: University of Wisconsin Press, 1996), 127 (first and second quotes), 128 (third quote); Henry Woodd Nevinson, *A Modern Slavery* (London: Harper and Brothers Publishers, 1906), 14, 15 (fourth quote), 16; Suzanne Miers and Igor Kopytoff, "Slavery in Africa," in *Problems in African History,* 268–69.

8. Newitt, "Angola," 45; Heywood, *Contested Power,* 39 (first quote); Wheeler and Pélissier, *Angola,* 110; *Boletim Oficial da Província de Angola,* no. 6 (10 de Fevereiro de 1900): 66, 68–73; Foreign Office, *Diplomatic and Consular Reports: Trade and Commerce of Angola for the Year 1899,* No. 2555, Cd. 429-13 (London: February 1901), 7 (second and third quotes).

9. Birmingham, *Portugal and Africa,* 94; Miller, *Way of Death,* 21, 30; Heywood, *Contested Power,* 37; Freudenthal, "Angola," 309, 317n154; Foreign Office, *Diplomatic and Consular*

Reports: *Trade and Commerce of Angola for the Year 1899*, 6; Francisco de Paula Cid, *Relatorio do Governador do Districto de Benguella, 1892*, Relatorios dos Governadores das Províncias Ultramarinas (Lisbon: Ministerio da Marinha e Ultramar, 1894), 25.

10. Wheeler and Pélissier, *Angola*, 110; James Duffy, *A Question of Slavery: Labour Policies in Portuguese Africa and the British Protest, 1850–1920* (Cambridge, Mass.: Harvard University Press, 1967), 168, 169 (quote); Birmingham, *Portugal and Africa*, 101–2; JB to WAC, April 14, 1906, JDC, 196.

11. JB to WAC, April 14, 1906, JDC, 195 (quotes).

12. JB to WAC, April 14, 1906, JDC, 195; Wheeler and Pélissier, *Angola*, 94–96, and on the decline of the African *assimilado* (assimilated) class, see 106–7, citing *Voz d'Angola Clamando no Deserto: Offerecida aos Amigos da Verdade pelos Naturaes* (The Voice of Angola Crying in the Wilderness: Offered to the Friends of Truth by the Natives) (1901; repr., Lisbon: Edições 70, 1984).

13. Wheeler and Pélissier, *Angola*, 97–98; Valetim Alexandre, *Velho Brasil, Novas Áfricas: Portugal e o Império (1808–1975)* (Porto, Portugal: Edições Afrontamento, 2000), 222–23; José Maria Gaspar, "A Colonização Branca em Angola e Moçambique," *Estudos de Ciências Politicas e Sociáis*, 7 (1958): 34–36; Cid, *Relatório do Governador do Districto de Benguella*, 7; Visconde de Giraúl, *Idéas Geraes sobre a Colonização Europeia da Provincia de Angola* (Lisbon: Imprensa Nacional, 1901), 4, 16–18; J. Pereira do Nascimento and A. Alexandre de Mattos, *A Colonisação de Angola* (Lisbon, 1912), 38; J. A. Alves Roçadas, *La main d'oeuvre indigène à Angola*, IIIe Congrès International d'Agriculture Tropicale (Lisbon: Editora Limitada, 1914), 40.

14. Newitt, "Angola," 50; Rosa Williams, "Migration and Miscegenation," in *Creole Societies in the Portuguese Colonial Empire*, ed. Philip J. Havik and Malyn Newitt, Lusophone Studies 6 (Bristol, UK: University of Bristol, 2007), 162, cited in Newitt, "Angola," 51–52 (quote); Freudenthal, "Angola," 372–80. On the complexity of Angola's Afro-Portuguese communities, see Jacopo Corrado, "The Fall of a Creole Elite? Angola at the Turn of the Twentieth Century: The Decline of the Euro-African Urban Community," *Luso-Brazilian Review* 47, no. 2 (2010): 100–119.

15. JB to WAC, December 23, 1905, JDC, 153–154; JB to WAC, February 12, 1906, JDC, 164 (quote). See also JB to WAC, February 12, 1906, CP 5/18; Lowell Satre, *Chocolate on Trial: Slavery, Politics, and the Ethics of Business* (Athens: Ohio University Press, 2005), 50–51.

16. JB to WAC, February 12, 1906, JDC, 165 (first through fifth quotes), 166 (sixth and seventh quotes). See also JB to WAC, February 12, 1906, CP 5/18; William Gervase Clarence-Smith, *The Third Portuguese Empire, 1825–1975: A Study in Economic Imperialism* (Manchester, UK: Manchester University Press, 1985), 100; Henry W. Nevinson, "The Slave Trade of Today," pt. 6, "The Slaves at Sea," *Harper's Monthly Magazine*, 112, no. 688–30 (January 1906): 242, 246; Nevinson, *Modern Slavery*, 45; Malyn Newitt, "British Travellers' Accounts of Portuguese Africa in the Nineteenth Century," *Revista de Estudos Anglo-Portugueses* 11 (2002): 104–6, 127–29.

17. Joseph Burtt, *The Voice of the Forest* (London: T. Fisher Unwin, 1911), 57, 58–59. On Robert Shields and the Methodist Mission, see W. C. Bell to James L. Barton, December 31, 1909, American Board of Commissioners for Foreign Missions (hereafter ABCFM), ABC 15.1, Microfilm Reel 164, Houghton Library, Harvard University, Cambridge, Mass.; Heywood, *Contested Power*, 38.

18. JB to WAC, December 23, 1905, JDC, 153–154; JB to WAC, February 12, 1906, JDC, 167 (first through fourth quotes). See also JB to WAC, February 12, 1906, CP 5/18; JB to WAC, June 6, 1906, JDC, 212; JB to WAC, October 13, 1906, JDC, map of Burtt's route from Benguela to Kavungu, following p. 273; Jelmer Vos, "The Economics of the Kwango Rubber Trade, c. 1900," in *Angola on the Move*, 86.

19. JB to WAC, February 12, 1906, JDC, 169–70 (quotes). Burtt estimated Benguela's population at 6,000; the 1900 census counted 3,312 residents. Freudenthal, "Angola," 320. See also Nevinson, *Modern Slavery*, 43.

20. Cid, *Relatório do Governador do Districto de Benguella*, 5–6. On Cid's record, see *A Famosa e Histórico Benguela: Catálogo dos Governadores (1779 a 1940)*, Edição do Govêrno da Província (Lisbon: Edições Cosmos, [1940]), 280–96.

21. Nevinson, "New Slave Trade," 537; JB to WAC, February 12, 1906, JDC, 165, 171 (quotes), 172. See also JB to WAC, February 12, 1906, CP 5/18; JB to WAC, December 23, 1905, JDC, 153; JB to WAC, January 3, 1906, JDC, 155; JB to WAC, January 3, 1906, CP 5/1; Burtt, *Voice of the Forest*, 67–68; JB to WAC, February 24, 1906, JDC, 171, 173–74; JB to WAC, February 9, 1906, CP 5/17.

22. JB to WAC, February 12, 1906, JDC, 171. See also JB to WAC, February 12, 1906, CP 5/18; JB to WAC, February 24, 1906, JDC, 174; Burtt, *Voice of the Forest*, 19, 20; John Kerr Lawson, "John Norton-Griffiths," in *Oxford Dictionary of National Biography*, available at www.oxforddab.com; Emmanuel Esteves, "As Vias de Communicação e Meios de Transporte como Factores de Globalização, de Estabilidade Política e de Transformação Económica e Social: Caso do Caminho-de-ferro de Bengela (Benguela) (1889–1950)," in *Angola on the Move*, 103; Clarence-Smith, *Third Portuguese Empire*, 99–100, 105; *Ao País* (Lisbon: Typograhia, 1903), 3, 4, 6–7; Foreign Office, *Diplomatic and Consular Reports. Trade and Commerce of Angola for the Year 1899*, 4, 5.

23. William Gervase Clarence-Smith, *Slaves, Peasants and Capitalists in Southern Angola, 1840–1926* (Cambridge: Cambridge University Press, 1979), 26–27, 52, 83; Nicásia Casimiro Matias, "Os Boers Portugueses da Humpata: Um Fracasso da Política de Assimilação Portuguesa?" in *Actas do Seminário*, 284–85, 288–89, 292–94; Manuel Viegas Guerreiro, *Boers de Angola*, separata de *Garcia de Orta*, Revista da Junta das Missões Geográficas e de Investigações do Ultramar, vol. 6, no. 1 (Lisbon, 1958): 2–5; Nevinson, *Modern Slavery*, 59–69; Esteves, "As Vias de Communicação e Meios de Transporte," 102; Birmingham, *Empire in Africa*, 46; David Birmingham, "Wagon Technology, Transport and Long-Distance Communication in Angola, 1885–1908," in *Angola on the Move*, 17, 18, 28.

24. Clarence-Smith, *Slaves, Peasants and Capitalists*, 16; Nevinson, *Modern Slavery*, 67, 68 (quotes); Birmingham, "Wagon Technology," 60–61.

25. JB to WAC, May 8, 1906, JDC, 198 (first quote), 199 (second and third quotes); JB to WAC, March 26, 1906, JDC, 186; JB to WAC, March 30, 1906, JDC, 188, 189 (fourth and fifth quotes).

26. Leonard Thompson, *History of South Africa*, 3rd ed. (New Haven, Conn.: Yale Nota Bene/Yale University Press, 2000), 114–15, 139; JB to WAC, February 12, 1906, JDC, 170 (quote), 171. See also JB to WAC, February 12, 1906, CP 5/18; "John Norton-Griffiths," available at www.oxforddab.org.

27. JB to WAC, February 12, 1906, JDC, 170 (third and fourth quotes), 171 (first, second, fifth, and sixth quotes). See also JB to WAC, February 12, 1906, CP 5/18.

28. JB to WAC, March 9, 1906, JDC, 177 (quotes), 178; Birmingham, "Wagon Technology," 59.

29. JB to WAC, March 17, 1906, JDC, 179 (quotes); Nevinson, *Modern Slavery*, 42; Freudenthal, "Angola," 320, 324–25; Clarence-Smith, *Third Portuguese Empire*, 91–92; Cid, *Relatório do Governador do Districto de Benguella*, 7, 29; Wheeler and Pélissier, *Angola*, 110.

30. JB to WAC, March 9, 1906, JDC, 177; JB to WAC, March 17, 1906, JDC, 180; Nevinson, *Modern Slavery*, 42 (first quote), 43 (second quote); Miller, *Way of Death*, 208; JB to WAC, March 19, 1906, JDC, 182 (third quote), 183 (fourth quote); see also JB to WAC, March 19, 1906, CP 5/19.

31. JB to WAC, March 17, 1906, JDC, 180 (first quote); JB to WAC, March 19, 1906, JDC, 182 (second and third quotes). See also JB to WAC, March 19, 1906, CP 5/19.

32. Douglas L. Wheeler, *Republican Portugal: A Political History, 1910–1926* (Madison: University of Wisconsin Press, 1978), 24, 25 (quote), 26–29, 32–35, 37–38, 52; Freudenthal, "Angola," 279. Among the royalists in the Angolan civil service was Henrique Paiva Couceiro, who fought in the 1889 campaign to pacify Angola, served as governor-general of the province from June 1907 through June 1909, and fought unsuccessfully to restore the monarchy after the Republican coup of October 1910. See Vasco Pulido Valente, *Um Herói Português: Henrique Paiva Couceiro (1861–1944)*, 2nd ed. (Lisbon: Alêtheia Editores, 2006), 17–25, 47–48, 71–80, and Henrique Paiva Couceiro, *Angola (Dous Annos de Governo, Junho 1907–Junho 1909): Historia e Commentarios* (Lisbon: Editora a Nacional, 1910).

33. Concelho da Catumbela, "Resposta ao Questionario de que Trata a Circular da Repartição do Gabinete, de 23 de Junho de 1906," Caixa 3660, Catumbela, Arquivo Histórico Nacional de Angola (hereafter AHNA).

34. Ibid.; Thomas Collelo, ed., *Angola: A Country Study*, 3rd ed. (Washington, D.C.: Federal Research Division, Library of Congress, 1991), 71; Wheeler and Pélissier, *Angola*, 96; Harry Hamilton Johnston, *A Comparative Study of the Bantu and Semi-Bantu Languages* (Oxford: Clarendon Press, 1919), 1:801. See J. Pereira do Nascimento, *Grammatica do Umbundu, ou Lingua de Benguella* (Lisbon: Imprensa Nacional, 1894); Sociedade de Geographia, *Boletim*, 13° serie, no. 102; and Ernesto Lecomte, *Methodo Pratico da Lingua Mbundu, Fallada no Districto de Benguella* (Lisbon: Imprensa Nacional, 1897).

35. JB to WAC, February 12, 1906, JDC, 172 (first through third quotes). See also JB to WAC, February 12, 1906, CP 5/18; JB to WAC, August 30, 1906, JDC, 247; JB to WAC, January 3, 1907, 284; JB to WAC, March 17, 1906, JDC, 181 (fourth quote).

36. JB to WAC, March 17, 1906, JDC, 181, poem follows p. 181 (second and fifth quotes); Kipling quoted in Peter Gay, *The Cultivation of Hatred*, vol. 3 of *The Bourgeois Experience: Victoria to Freud* (New York: W. W. Norton, 1993), 85 (first quote); JB to WAC, July 6, 1906, JDC, 229; JB to WAC, June 6, 1906, JDC, 210 (third and fourth quotes); JB to WAC, February 9, 1906, CP 5/17; Burtt, *Voice of the Forest*, 66. See also Joseph Burtt, *Sonnets and Other Poems* (London: Oliphants, n.d. [1929?]), 45–47, and Ann Laura Stoler, *Carnal Knowledge and Imperial Power: Race and the Intimate in Colonial Rule* (Berkeley: University of California Press, 2002), 75–78.

37. JB to WAC, March 18, 1906, JDC, 181 (first quote); JB to WAC, March 25, 1906, JDC, 184a (second, third, and fifth quotes); Henry W. Nevinson, "The Slave Trade of Today: Conclusion—The Islands of Doom," *Harper's Monthly Magazine*, 112, no. 669 (February 1906): 328 (fourth quote).

38. JB to WAC, March 25, 1906, JDC, 184a–184b (quotes); Nevinson, "Slave Trade of Today: Conclusion," 330, 333, 335.

39. Nevinson, "Slave Trade of Today: Conclusion," 337 (quote); Burroughs, *Travel Writing and Atrocities*, 107–10; John W. Cell, *The Highest Stage of White Supremacy: The Origins of Segregation in South Africa and the American South* (Cambridge: Cambridge University Press, 1982), 82–102; Satre, *Chocolate on Trial*, 28; JB to WAC, March 25, 1906, JDC, 184b.

40. JB to WAC, March 26, 1906, JDC, 185; JB to WAC, April 7, 1906, 192 (first and second quotes); JB to WAC, July 22, 1906, 233; JB to WAC, May 17, 1906, JDC, 206, 207 (third quote); Clarence-Smith, *Slaves, Peasants and Capitalists*, 51.

41. Clarence-Smith, *Slaves, Peasants and Capitalists*, 14–16, 64; Horst Dreschsler, "Germany and S. Angola, 1898–1903," in *Actas do Congresso Internacional dos Descobrimentos*, vol. 6 (Lisbon: Commissão Executiva do V Centário do Morte do Infante D. Henrique, 1961), 73–74.

42. Freudenthal, "Angola," 320; Clarence-Smith, *Slaves, Peasants and Capitalists*, 24–25, 51, 64.

43. Clarence-Smith, *Slaves, Peasants and Capitalists*, 65; JB to WAC, June 6, 1906, JDC, 210, 211 (quote).

44. JB to WAC, May 31, 1906, JDC, 208 (first quote); JB to WAC, July 18, 1905, JDC, 43; JB to WAC, February 12, 1906, 170. See also JB to WAC, February 12, 1906, CP 5/18; JB to WAC, December 23, 1905, JDC, 153; JB to WAC, May 8, 1906, JDC, 197, 198 (second quote), 199–200, 206 (third and fourth quotes); JB to WAC, June 12, 1906, 208; Clarence-Smith, *Slaves, Peasants and Capitalists*, 52–53.

45. JB to WAC, June 6, 1906, JDC, 209 (quote); JB to WAC, June 12, 1906, JDC, 208; John T. Tucker, *Angola: The Land of the Blacksmith Prince* (London: World Dominion Press, 1933), 66; Thomas Masaji Okuma, *Angola in Ferment: The Background and Prospects of Angolan Nationalism* (1962; repr., Westport, Conn.: Greenwood Press, 1974), 125; Roland A. Oliver, *Sir Harry Johnston and the Scramble for Africa* (London: Chatto and Windus, 1957), 31; Duffy, *Question of Slavery*, 174; JB to WAC, July 18, 1906, JDC, 44.

46. Duffy, *Question of Slavery*, 171–75; Joseph C. Hartzell, *The African Mission of the Methodist Episcopal Church* (New York: Board of the Foreign Missions of the Methodist Episcopal Church, 1909), 35 (first quote); Heywood, *Contested Power*, 22; JB to WAC, June 6, 1906, JDC, 211 (second and third quotes); M. Stober to WAC, February 22, 1906, CP 5/12; JB to WAC, July 6, 1906, JDC, 228.

47. Henry Woodd Nevinson and Ellis Roberts, *Fire of Life* (London: James Nisbet, 1935), 161 (first quote); Synopsis of letter from WAC to JB, June 17, 1907, CP 3/53: 428 (second quote); M. Stober to WAC, February 22, 1906, CP 5/12 (third through fifth quotes); WAC to Stober, April 2, 1906, CP 5/12 (sixth quote); Cadbury Brothers Ltd. to Rowntree & Co. Ltd., August 20, 1906, CP 5/27.

48. "A Ilha de S. Thomé: Relatorio do Dr. Strunck," in *A Ilha de S. Thomé e o Trabalho Indigena* (Lisbon: Livraria Ferin, 1907), 25; "A Ilha de S. Thomé: Relatorio do Dr. Strunck," *Revista Portugueza Colonial e Maritima* 18, no. 109 (September 1906), 255–56; "A Ilha de S. Thomé: Relatorio do Dr. Strunck," *Revista Portugueza Colonial e Maritima*, 19, no. 109 (October 1906), 1–8; Henrique José Monteiro de Mendonça, *The Boa Entrada Plantations, S. Thomé, Portuguese West Africa, "La Perle des Colonies Portuguaises,"* trans. J. A. Wyllie (Edinburgh: Oliphant Anderson and Ferrier, 1907), 21–22; Newitt, "Angola," 38.

49. Jan Georg Deutsch, *Emancipation without Abolition in German East Africa c. 1884–1914* (Oxford: James Currey, 2006), 97–99.

50. Newitt, "Angola," 38–39; JB to WAC, June 26, 1906, JDC, 217 (first, second, third, and fifth quotes), 218 (fourth quote); Augusto Nascimento, "Cabindas em São Tomé," *Revista Internacional de Estudos Africanos* 14–15 (1991): 183–85, 188, 196.

51. JB to WAC, June 28, 1906, JDC, 220–22.

52. JB to WAC, July 8, 1906, JDC, 224 (quote), 225; JB to WAC, June 28, 1906, JDC, 219; Albino Lapa, *O Conselheiro Ramada Curto,* Colecção Pelo Império (no. 62), vol. 2 (Lisbon: Agência Geral das Colónias, 1940), 44; Freudenthal, "Angola," 11:451.

53. JB to WAC, July 18, 1905, JDC, 44; JB to WAC, April 7, 1906, JDC, 193 (quote); JB to WAC, July 8, 1906, JDC, 223; Claude Horton to WAC, May 15, 1906, CP 5/20; Horton to WAC, June 5, 1906, CP 5/21; Horton to WAC, July 7, 1906, CP 5/22.

54. JB to WAC, July 6, 1906, JDC, 228, 229 (quotes).

55. JB to WAC, July 6, 1906, JDC, 229 (first through third quotes), 230 (fourth and fifth quotes); Nevinson, *Modern Slavery,* 159.

56. Claude Horton to WAC, July 7, 1906, CP 5/22; Horton to WAC, September 17, 1906, CP 5/29 (quote).

57. JB to WAC, July 6, 1906, JDC, 228; *The Mission of the American Board to West Central Africa: Pioneer Work, 1881* (Boston: American Board of Commissioners for Foreign Missions, 1882), 4; *Papers of the American Board of Commissioners for Foreign Missions: Documents Administered by the Houghton Library of Harvard University—Guide to the Microfilm Collection* (Woodbridge, Conn.: Research Publications International, 1994); Johnston, *Comparative Study of the Bantu and Semi-Bantu Languages,* 1:801; W. H. Sanders and W. E. Fay, *Vocabulary of the Umbundu Language, Comprising Umbundu-English and English-Umbundu* (Boston: Beacon Press, 1885); Nevinson, *Modern Slavery,* 158–59; "Report of Bailundu Station," June 1902, "Report of Sakanjimba Station," June 1902, "Report of Sakanjimba Station," June 1903, "Report of the Committee on Memorial to the Portuguese Government, 1903, "Report of Ocileso Station," June 1905, in ABCFM Microfilm, Unit 2, ABC 15.1, Reel 163.

58. JB to WAC, July 6, 1906, JDC, 228 (quotes).

59. JB to WAC, July 6, 1906, JDC, 227, 230 (quote).

CHAPTER 5: THE SLAVE ROUTE

1. Beatrix Heintze and Achim von Oppen, "Introduction," in *Angola on the Move: Transport Routes, Communications and History/Angola em Movimento: Vias de Transporte, Communicação e História,* ed. Beatrix Heintze and Achim von Oppen (Frankfurt: Verlag Otto Lembeck, 2008), 7, 9–10; Joseph C. Miller, *Way of Death: Merchant Capitalism and the Angolan Slave Trade, 1730–1830* (Madison: University of Wisconsin Press, 1988), 180, 220, 223; JB to WAC, July 8, 1906, JDC, 224; Maria Emília Madeira Santos, "Em Busca dos Sítios do Poder na África Centro Ocidental: Homens e Caminhos, Exércitos e Estradas (1483–1915)," in *Angola on the Move,* 28, 29; JB to WAC, July 22, 1906, JDC, 233; JB to WAC, July 28, 1906, JDC, 236 (first and second quotes). On cloth as currency, see Gladwyn Murray Childs, *Kinship and Character of the Ovimbundu* (Oxford: Oxford University Press, 1949; repr., London: Dawsons of Pall Mall, 1969), 215.

2. JB to WAC, July 31, 1906, JDC, 238; JB to WAC, August 6, 1906, JDC, 241 (first quote), 240 (second and third quotes); Pauline Summerton, *Fishers of Men: The Missionary*

Influence of an Extended Family in Central Africa (n.p.: Brethren Archivists and Historians Network, 2003), 19; Alexandre Malheiro, Chrónicas do Bihé (Lisbon: Livraria Ferreira, 1903), map following p. 176.

3. JB to WAC, August 29, 1906, JDC, 249 (first through sixth quotes); JB to WAC, March 17, 1906, JDC, 179.

4. Adrian C. Edwards, The Ovimbundu under Two Sovereignties: A Study of Social Control and Social Change among a People of Angola (London: Oxford University Press, 1962), 13–14. On the rituals followed when burying a chief, see Malheiro, Chrónicas do Bihé, 187–89; Henry Woodd Nevinson, A Modern Slavery (London: Harper and Brothers Publishers, 1906), 114–15 (first quote); Nevinson, "The Slavery of Today," pt. 4, "The Hungry Country," Harper's Monthly Magazine 111, no. 666–106 (November 1905): 853–54 (first quote); JB to WAC, July 31, 1906, JDC, 239 (second through fourth quotes); CB to Rowntree & Co., August 20, 1906, CP 5/27; Douglas L. Wheeler and C. Diane Christensen, "To Rise with One Mind: The Bailundo War of 1902," in Social Change in Angola, ed. Franz W. Heimer (Munich, Germany: Weltforum Verlag, 1973), 60.

5. Malheiro, Chrónicas do Bihé, 25; John T. Tucker, Angola: The Land of the Blacksmith Prince (London: World Dominion Press, 1933), 44; JB to WAC, August 8, 1906, JDC, 240; JB to WAC, August 17, 1906, JDC, 243; Nevinson, Modern Slavery, 45; Wheeler and Christensen, "To Rise with One Mind," 54–55, 56; Joseph C. Miller, "From Group Mobility to Individual Movement: The Colonial Effort to Turn Back History," in Angola on the Move, 255–56.

6. Wheeler and Christensen, "To Rise with One Mind," 54–55, 60–61, 62 (second quote), 63, 68; Maria da Conceição Neto, "Hóspedes Incómodos: Portugueses e Americanos no Bailundo no Último Quartel do Século XIX," in Actas do Seminário: Encontro de Povos e Culturas em Angola (Luanda: Comissão Nacional para as Comemorações dos Descobrimentos Portugueses, 1995), 381 (quote ["onde os Africanos pensam aliançam entendem os Europeus sujeição"]). Wheeler and Christensen suggest (61) that the Portuguese saw Bailundo as a rival rather than a subjugated state.

7. JB to WAC, August 29, 1906, JDC, 251–52; Wheeler and Christensen, "To Rise with One Mind," 68, 78. A preliminary version of Burtt's report on his trip dated "Rec'd FEB 1 1908" appears in ABCFM Microfilm, Unit 2, ABC 15.1, Reel 163; JB to WAC, July 6, 1906, JDC, 232; JB to WAC, October 4, 1906, JDC, 255.

8. Wheeler and Christensen, "To Rise with One Mind," 65, 73, 79; Fola Soremekun, "A History of the American Board Missions in Angola, 1880–1940" (Ph.D. diss., Northwestern University, 1965), 126–28; Malheiro, Chrónicas do Bihé, 133–34, 18–20, map following p. 240; Neto, "Hóspedes Incómodos," 388.

9. Wheeler and Christensen, "To Rise with One Mind," 66–68, 70, 71–72 (third quote), 73 (first quote), 77; Neto, "Hóspedes Incómodos," 378, 379 (second quote: "seu principal rival comercial"). For a competing interpretation of the impact of the war on the Ovimbundu, see Linda Heywood, Contested Power in Angola, 1840s to the Present (Rochester, N.Y.: University of Rochester Press, 2000), 29–30. The Brethren missionary Frederick Arnot witnessed the Portuguese conquest of Bihé in 1890; see Fred S. Arnot, Bihé and Garenganze; or, Four Years Further Work and Travel in Central Africa (London: J. E. Hawkins, 1893), 19–23.

10. Marquez do Lavradio, Pedro Francisco Massano de Amorim (Lisbon: Editorial Ática, 1941), 9–10, 11–12; Adam Hochschild, King Leopold's Ghost: A Story of Greed, Terror, and

Heroism in Colonial Africa (Boston: Mariner Books, 1998), 123–24; Nevinson, *Modern Slavery,* 45 (first quote), 46 (second quote), 119; Wheeler and Christensen, "To Rise with One Mind," 77 (third quote); Soremekun, "History of the American Board Missions," 132; JB to WAC, October 13, 1906, JDC, 263–64. In his letters to Cadbury, Burtt anglicized Moxico as "Moshico," which better conveys the sound of the Portuguese *x.* JB to WAC, September 16, 1906, JDC, 257.

11. Wheeler and Christensen, "To Rise with One Mind," 78, 79; JB to WAC, October 13, 1906, JDC, 263; JB to WAC, August 30, 1906, JDC, 245; Nevinson, *Modern Slavery,* 119, 120 (first and second quotes); JB to WAC, August 29, 1906, JDC, 251, 252 (third and fourth quotes), 253 (fifth quote).

12. JB to WAC, August 17, 1906, JDC, 244 (first and second quotes); JB to WAC, August 30, 1906, JDC, 245 (third quote), 247. On the struggles of the journey to Bihé, see Summerton, *Fishers of Men,* 19; Malheiro, *Chrónicas do Bihé,* 160, 216; Nevinson, *Modern Slavery,* 150, 83 (fourth and fifth quotes); JB to WAC, December 15, 1906, JDC, map following p. 273; Claude Horton to WAC, September 17, 1906, CP 5/29.

13. JB to WAC, August 30, 1906, JDC, 245; Malheiro, *Chrónicas do Bihé,* 106–7, map following p. 240. See also map following p. 150 in Arnot, *Bihé and Garenanze;* Summerton, *Fishers of Men,* 89; Soremekun, "History of the American Board Mission," 132–34, 137–38, 139; Tucker, *Angola,* 45, 48, 160; W. H. Sanders to J. Smith, April 19, 1906, ABCFM Microfilm, Unit 2, ABC 15.1, Reel 165; WAC to Rowntree & Co. Ltd., August 20, 1906 (quote), CP 5/27; Nevinson, *Modern Slavery,* 141; Horton to WAC, September 17, 1906, CP 5/29.

14. JB to WAC, October 13, 1906, JDC, 262–63, 268 (second and third quotes), 269–70 (first quote), 270 (fifth quote), 271 (fourth quote); Summerton, *Fishers of Men,* 19; Charles A. Swan, *The Slavery of To-day, or the Present Position of the Open Sore of Africa* (Glasgow, Scotland: Pickering and Inglis, 1909), 50–51; Paul E. Lovejoy, *Transformations in Slavery: A History of Slavery in Africa* (Cambridge: Cambridge University Press, 1983), 41; Joseph Burtt, *The Voice of the Forest* (London: T. Fisher Unwin, 1911), 92 (seventh quote), 98 (sixth quote). Neyambi was ultimately redeemed, though it is unclear where the money came from. See Joseph Burtt, "Report on the Condition of Coloured Labour Employed on the Coco Plantations of S. Thomé and Principe, and the Methods of Procuring it in Angola," December 24, 1906, FO 367/46, 22.

15. Summerton, *Fishers of Men,* 3 (first quote), 19–20, 27, 43, 73, 80, 81 (second and third quotes); Thomas Collelo, ed., *Angola: A Country Study,* 3rd ed. (Washington, D.C.: Federal Research Division, Library of Congress, 1991), 79; Soremekun, "History of the American Board Missions," 104, 105 (fourth quote), 106 (fifth quote), 107, 110, 121, 123.

16. Arnot, *Bihé and Garenganze,* 25 (first and second quote), 26 (third quote); Nevinson, *Modern Slavery,* 105 (fourth and fifth quotes), 111.

17. Nevinson, *Modern Slavery,* 111–12 (first quote); 113 (second quote); JB to WAC, October 13, 1906, JDC, 266; James Duffy, *A Question of Slavery: Labour Policies in Portuguese Africa and the British Protest, 1850–1920* (Cambridge, Mass.: Harvard University Press, 1967), 172–73. The British South Africa Company administered North Western Rhodesia from 1891, and combined it in 1911 with North Eastern Rhodesia to create Northern Rhodesia, which became a British protectorate in 1923. Lewis H. Gann, "History of Rhodesia and Nyasaland 1889–1953," *Handbook to the Federation of Rhodesia and Nyasaland,* ed. William Verson Brelsford (London: Cassell, 1960), 62, 74.

18. Nevinson, *Modern Slavery*, 106, 107 (first and second quotes), Nevinson identifies the Chokwe as Chibokwe, 107–8; Miller, *Way of Death*, 150–51.

19. Nevinson, *Modern Slavery*, 86, 126 (first quote), 127 (second quote), 128 (fifth quote), 128–29 (third quote), 129 (fourth quote), 130; Arnot, *Bihé and Garenganze*, 25, 28–31.

20. Nevinson, *Modern Slavery*, 123 (second and third quotes), 124 (first quote).

21. JB to WAC, September 16, 1906, JDC, 258 (first and second quotes); Nevinson, *Modern Slavery*, 85; Horton to WAC, September 17, 1906, CP 5/29 (third quote).

22. Henry W. Nevinson, *Fire of Life* (London: James Nisbet, 1935), 167–68; JB to WAC, September 17, 1906, JDC, 258 (first quote); Horton to WAC, September 17, 1906, CP 5/29 (second quote).

23. Lowell Satre, *Chocolate on Trial: Slavery, Politics, and the Ethics of Business* (Athens: Ohio University Press, 2005), 61; Augusto Ribeiro, "O Trabalho Indígena nas Colónias Portuguezas," *Boletim da Sociedade de Geographia de Lisboa*, 24.ª Série, N.° 9 (September 1906): 265n, 268–70, 271 ("não e uma chimera") (first and second quotes).

24. JB to WAC, October 4, 1906, JDC, 254 (first through third quotes), 256 (fourth through seventh quotes), and see also map following p. 273; J. C. B. Statham, *Through Angola: A Coming Colony* (Edinburgh: William Blackwood and Sons, 1922), 268. Arnot refers to the Kifumadji Flat in *Bihé and Garenganze*, 42 and 42n.

25. JB to WAC, October 4, 1906, JDC, 254 (first quote), 255 (second and third quotes); Arnot, *Bihé and Garenganze*, 37.

26. JB to WAC, October 14, 1906, JDC, 260 (first and second quotes); JB to WAC, October 13, 1906, JDC, 262–63; Duffy, *Question of Slavery*, 137; Richard J. Hammond, *Portugal and Africa, 1815–1910: A Study in Uneconomic Imperialism* (Stanford, Calif.: Stanford University Press, 1966), 140–41; Arnot, *Bihé to Garengaze*, 86 (third through sixth quotes).

27. Duffy, *Question of Slavery*, 135 (second quote), 137 (first quote); David Birmingham, *Empire in Africa: Angola and Its Neighbors*, Africa Series no. 84 (Athens: Ohio University Press, 2006), 41–42. In the 1890s, Chatelain also worked at Luanda as a commercial agent for the United States. Heli Chatelain, ed., *Folk-Tales of Angola: Fifty Tales, with Ki-Mbundu Text, Literal English Translation, Introduction, and Notes* (1894; repr., New York: Negro Universities Press, 1969), iii.

28. JB to WAC, October 13, 1906, JDC, 264–65; Lavradio, *Pedro Francisco Massano de Amorim*, 9–10.

29. JB to WAC, October 4, 1906, 255 (first and second quotes), 256; JB to WAC, October 14, 1906, JDC, 259 (third through eighth quotes), 260; Summerton, *Fishers of Men*, 31, 34, 38–39.

30. JB to WAC, October 13, 1906, JDC, 267; JB to WAC, December 18, 1906, JDC, 276 (quote), 277.

31. JB to WAC, October 13, 1906, JDC, 267 (second quote), 272 (first quote); Duffy, *Question of Slavery*, 196; Hochschild, *King Leopold's Ghost*, 123–25. See also Guy de Boeck, *Les révoltes de la force publique sous Léopold II: Congo, 1895–1908* (Anvers, Belgium: Editions EPO, 1987), 181–90.

32. Hochschild, *King Leopold's Ghost*, 166; JB to WAC, October 13, 1906, JDC, 267 (first and second quotes). See also William A. Cadbury, *Labour in Portuguese West Africa*, 2nd ed. (London: George Routledge and Sons, 1910), 123; Nevinson, *Modern Slavery*, 52 (third quote). On the extent of cannibalism in the Congo, see Robert W. Harms, *River of Wealth, River of Sorrow: The Central Zaire Basin in the Era of the Slave and Ivory Trade,*

1500–1891 (New Haven, Conn.: Yale University Press, 1981), 240n15. Angolans working on the Benguela railway apparently feared that the ground-up brains of murdered workers were used to lubricate European machinery. Emmanuel Esteves, "As Vias de Communicação e Meios de Transporte como Factores de Globalização, de Estabilidade Política e de Transformação Económica e Social: Caso do Caminho-de-ferro de Bengela (Benguela), 1889–1950," in *Angola on the Move*, 112.

33. JB to WAC, October 13, 1906, JDC, 272 (quote), 273.

34. JB to WAC, September 17, 1906, JDC, 258; JB to WAC, October 14, 1906, JDC, 259 (first quote); WAC to JB, October 19, 1906, CP 5/30 (second through fourth quotes).

35. "Debate in the Cortes October 31st, 1906 (extract)," FO 367/46, National Archives, London, UK, 3 (first and second quotes). For the Portuguese original, see *Diario da Camara dos Senhores Deputados*, 22.ª Sessão, October 31, 1906, 6; WAC to H. R. Fox Bourne, October 22, 1906, CP 5/38 (third quote); Burtt, "Report on the Condition of Coloured Labour," 3; JB to WAC, December 18, 1906, JDC, 279.

36. JB to WAC, December 15, 1906, 274; JB to WAC, December 18, 1906, JDC, 279 (first and second quotes), 280 (third quote); Burtt, "Report on the Condition of Coloured Labour," 23 (fourth through sixth quotes).

37. Burtt, "Report on the Condition of Coloured Labour," 4 (second through fourth quotes), 5 (first quote), 7.

38. Ibid., 7 (second quote), 17 (first quote), 21, 23, 24 (third and fourth quotes).

39. Ibid., 5 (first quote), 24 (second quote); Robert M. Burroughs, *Travel Writing and Atrocities: Eyewitness Accounts of Colonialism in the Congo, Angola, and the Putumayo* (New York: Routledge, 2011), 118.

40. Burtt, "Report on the Condition of Coloured Labour," 24 (first quote); "Debate in the Cortes," 1–4; WAC to Joseph Sturge, April 27, CP 4/5; WAC to Sturge, May 1, 1901, CP 4/6; WAC to William Albright, May 2, 1901, CP 4/4; Nevinson, *Modern Slavery*, 16–17 (second quote). See also José Paulo Monteiro Cancella, "Impressões de uma Viagem ás Ilhas de S. Thomé e Principe," *Boletim da Sociedade de Geographia de Lisboa*, série 19, no. 4–6 (1901): 1, 471–501.

CHAPTER 6: MOZAMBICAN MINERS

1. Malyn Newitt, *A History of Mozambique* (Bloomington: Indiana University Press, 1995), 25; Newitt, "British Travellers' Accounts of Portuguese Africa in the Nineteenth Century," *Revista de Estudos Anglo-Portugueses* 11 (2002): 125; Jeanne Marie Penvenne, *African Workers and Colonial Racism: Mozambican Strategies and Struggles in Lourenço Marques, 1877–1962* (Portsmouth, N.H.: Heinemann, 1995), 1, 32 (first and second quotes); José Capela, "O Ultimatum na Perspectiva de Moçambique," in *Moçambique: Navegações, Comércio e Técnicas*, Actas do Seminário, Maputo, November 25–28, 1996 ([Lisbon]: Comissão Nacional para as Comemorações dos Descobrimentos Portugueses, 1998), 266–67.

2. Newitt, *History of Mozambique*, 375 (fourth quote), 376; Penvenne, *African Workers and Colonial Racism*, 32; Carlos Santos Reis, *A População de Lourenço Marques em 1894 (Um Censo Inédito)* (Lisbon: Publicações do Centro de Estudos Demográficos, 1973), 21, 28 (the Chinese are listed as "Amarelo" [Yellow]); António Rita Ferreira, *O Movimento Migratório de Trabalhadores entre Moçambique e a África do Sul*, Estudos de Ciências Políticas e Socias, no. 67 (Lisbon: Junta de Investigações do Ultramar, Centro de Estudos Políticos e Socias, 1963), 45–46, 53; *Questões Africanas: A Questão do Maputo—Documentos* (Lisbon: Sociedade

de Geographia de Lisboa, 1890), 4; Vasco Pulido Valente, *Um Herói Português: Henrique Paiva Couceiro (1861–1944)*, 2nd ed. (Lisbon: Alêtheia Editores, 2006), 27 (first quote), 30 (second and third quotes); René Pélissier, *História de Moçambique: Formaçä e Oposição, 1854–1918*, vol. 2 (Lisbon: Editorial Estampa, 1994), 261–62.

3. Penvenne, *African Workers and Colonial Racism*, 33 (quote), 35; Reis, *População de Lourenço Marques em 1894*, 21; JB to WAC, December 25, 1906, JDC, 280, 295.

4. Penvenne, *African Workers and Colonial Racism*, 33; James Duffy, *A Question of Slavery: Labour Policies in Portuguese Africa and the British Protest, 1850–1920* (Cambridge, Mass.: Harvard University Press, 1967), 141.

5. Leroy Vail and Landeg White, *Capitalism and Colonialism in Mozambique: A Study of Quelimane District* (Minneapolis: University of Minnesota Press, 1980), 145, 162, 164; Duffy, *Question of Slavery*, 141; Patrick Harries, *Work, Culture, and Identity: Migrant Laborers in Mozambique and South Africa, c. 1860–1919* (Portsmouth, N.H.: Heinemann, 1994), 19. The British South Africa Company administered Southern Rhodesia from 1890 through 1923, when it became a British Crown Colony. Steven C. Rubert and R. Kent Rasmussen, eds., *Historical Dictionary of Zimbabwe*, 3rd ed. (Lanham, Md.: Scarecrow Press, 2001), 35–36.

6. On the structure of the prazos, see Vail and White, *Capitalism and Colonialism*, 8, 9–13; Newitt, *History of Mozambique*, 217–19, 237–42.

7. Newitt, *History of Mozambique*, 217–19, 237–42, 341, 365, 367–68; Vail and White, *Capitalism and Colonialism*, 162; Capela, "O Ultimatum," 270–72.

8. Newitt, *History of Mozambique*, 366, 367–73; Vail and White, *Capitalism and Colonialism*, 148–49, 155, 158, 161, 162; William Gervase Clarence-Smith, *The Third Portuguese Empire, 1825–1975: A Study in Economic Imperialism* (Manchester, UK: Manchester University Press, 1985), 102; Gregory Roger Pirio, "Commerce, Industry and Empire: The Making of Modern Portuguese Colonialism in Angola and Mozambique, 1890–1914" (Ph.D. diss., University of California–Los Angeles, 1982), 234, 266–67, 270, 272; JB to WAC, February 17, 1907, JDC, 304.

9. Alan H. Jeeves, *Migrant Labour in South Africa's Mining Economy: The Struggle for the Gold Mines' Labour Supply, 1890–1920* (Kingston, Canada: McGill-Queen's University Press, 1985), 188; Newitt, *History of Mozambique*, 360; Duffy, *Question of Slavery*, 142–43.

10. Vail and White, *Capitalism and Colonialism*, 164; Duffy, *Question of Slavery*, 142; Harries, *Work, Culture, and Identity*, 177 (quote), 178–79; Ferreira, *O Movimento Migratório de Trabalhadores*, 161–62; Hygino Durão, *Relatorio sobre os Abonos Feitos ao Pessoal da Curadoria dos Indigenas de Johannesburg que Não Estavam Incluidos nas Tabellas Orçamentos* (Lisbon: Ministério da Marinha e Colónias—Inspecção Geral de Fazenda das Colónias, 1911), 15; Jeeves, *Migrant Labour in South Africa's Mining Economy*, 188.

11. Lowell Satre, *Chocolate on Trial: Slavery, Politics, and the Ethics of Business* (Athens: Ohio University Press, 2005), 71; Harries, *Work, Culture, and Identity*, 154, 155; Newitt, *History of Mozambique*, 376, 378; Pélissier, *História de Moçambique*, 300–306, 316–23; Vail and White, *Colonialism and Capitalism*, 167; Duffy, *Question of Slavery*, 141, 146 (quote); Penvenne, *African Workers and Colonial Racism*, 24, 26, 63; Ferreira, *O Movimento Migratório de Trabalhadores*, 44, 51–53.

12. William A. Cadbury, *Labour in Portuguese West Africa*, 2nd ed. (London: George Routledge and Sons, 1910), 128 (quote).

13. Jeeves, *Migrant Labour in South Africa's Mining Economy*, 203; Duffy, *Question of Slavery*, 148, 149 (quote), 150–52.

14. The full poem appears in Joseph Burtt, *Sonnets and Other Poems* (London: Oliphants, n.d. [1929?]), 12; "Freire de Andrade, Alfredo Augusto," in *Grande Enciclopédia Portuguesa e Brasileira* (Lisbon: Editorial Enciclopédia, 1945), 11:830; Newitt, *History of Mozambique*, 350.

15. Burtt, *Sonnets*, 12 (first quote); "Freire de Andrade" in *Grande Enciclopédia*, 11:830; A. Freire d'Andrade, *Relatorios sobre Moçambique* (Lourenço Marques, Mozambique: Imprensa Nacional, 1907), 1:62–64, 285; Penvenne, *African Workers and Colonial Racism*, 63 (second quote).

16. Cadbury, *Labour in Portuguese West Africa*, 128 (quote); Governo Geral de Moçambique à Ministro e Secretario dos Negocios da Marinha e Ultramar, 24 de Outubro de 1907, AHU/SEMU/Moçambique/1.ª repartição—1.ª secção/Anos 1906–1907/Correspondência de Governadores/N.° 23/Oficio N.° 1885, de 13/12/1907.

17. JB to WAC, February 17, 1907, JDC, 291 (quotes); Transvaal Chamber of Mines, *Thirteenth Report for the Year 1902* (Johannesburg, South Africa: Argus Printing and Publishing, 1903), 96.

18. Kevin Grant, *A Civilised Savagery: Britain and the New Slaveries in Africa, 1884–1926* (New York: Routledge, 2005), 88; Leonard Thompson, *History of South Africa*, 3rd ed. (New Haven, Conn.: Yale Nota Bene/Yale University Press, 2000), 143–47; JB to WAC, February 17, 1907, JDC, 292 (quote); Harries, *Work, Culture, and Identity*, 111–12; Transvaal Labour Commission, *Report of the Transvaal Labour Commission: Together with Minority Report, Minutes of Proceedings and Evidence* (Johannesburg, South Africa: Argus Printing and Publishing, 1903), iii, xi.

19. WAC to JB, January 21, 1907, CP 5/60; JB to WAC, February 17, 1907, JDC, 293–94; Duffy, *Question of Slavery*, 154.

20. JB to WAC, February 18, 1907, JDC, 296, 297 (quotes); Harries, *Work, Culture, and Identity*, 113, 139, 140, 180, 182; Ferreira, *O Movimento Migratório de Trabalhadores*, 110.

21. Jeeves, *Migrant Labour in South Africa's Mining Economy*, 30, 66; Grant, *Civilised Savagery*, 89.

22. JB to WAC, February 18, 1907, JDC, 297; Thompson, *History of South Africa*, 147; Jeeves, *Migrant Labour in South Africa's Mining Economy*, 66.

23. JB to WAC, February 17, 1907, JDC, 293–94; JB to WAC, February 18, 1907, 300–301; JB to WAC, March 9, 1907, JDC, 308; Grant, *Civilised Savagery*, 87; *Report of the Coloured Labour Compound Commission Appointed to Enquire into the Cubic Amount of Air-Space in the Compounds of the Mines of the Witwatersrand* (Pretoria: Government Printing and Stationery Office, 1905), i (first quote), x (second and third quotes).

24. Harries, *Work, Culture, and Identity*, 110, 114, 126–27, 196–99; JB to WAC, February 17, 1907, JDC, 294, 296 (quote); JB to WAC, February 18, 1907, 300, 303; Ferreira, *O Movimento Migratório de Trabalhadores*, 113.

25. Grant, *Civilised Savagery*, 89, 91 (quote), 92.

26. Ibid., 91, 95, 99, 103.

27. Ibid., 97, 99, 101, 103–4.

28. Henrique Barahona, "Os Indigenas da Província de Moçambique e os Chinezes nas Minas da Rand," *Revista Portugueza Colónial e Marítima* 9° anno, 1° semester (1905–6): 118–21; Jeeves, *Migrant Labour in South Africa's Mining Economy*, 208–9.

29. JB to WAC, February 18, 1907, JDC, 301 (first and second quotes), 302, 308; JB to WAC, February 17, 1907, JDC, 293 (third quote).

1. Arnold Rowntree to CB, March 22, 1907, CP 5/65; CB to Fry and Sons Ltd., April 27, 1907, CP 5/68 (the bill was for £704 18s. 7½ d.); CB to Edward Grey, March 15, 1907, CP 5/62; CB to Grey, April 23, 1907, CP 5/74; CB to Stollwerck, April 27, 1907, CP 5/70; CP 1/8: "Cadbury Brothers, Limited, and Others v. The Standard Newspapers Limited," pt. 5 (December 3, 1909): 290; Lowell Satre, *Chocolate on Trial: Slavery, Politics, and the Ethics of Business* (Athens: Ohio University Press, 2005), 74 (quote); Eric Barrington to CB, May 2, 1907, CP 5/81.

2. JB to WAC, April 30, 1907, CP 5/78 (first and second quotes); Arnold S. Rowntree to CB, March 22, 1907, CP 5/65 (third through fifth quotes); Rowntree to CB, March 26, 1907, CP 5/67.

3. JB to WAC, April 30, 1907, CP 5/78; WAC to JB, April 25, 1907, CP 5/75 (first quote); WAC to Travers Buxton, February 20, 1907, CP 5/64; Travers Buxton to WAC, May 28, 1907, CP 5/100; Fox Bourne to WAC, April 29, 1907, CP 5/76 (second through fourth quotes); WAC to Fox Bourne, April 30, 1907, CP 5/77 (fifth and sixth quotes).

4. JB to WAC, May 30, 1907, CP 5/103 (quotes); A. H. de Oliveira Marques, *História de Portugal*, vol. 3, *Das Revoluções Liberais aos Nossos Dias*, 13th ed. (Lisbon: Editorial Presença, 1998), 59–60, 622.

5. WAC to JB, May 31, 1907, CP 5/104 (first through third quotes); WAC to Nevinson, May 31, 1907, CP 5/111; CP 1/8: "Cadbury Brothers, Limited, and Others v. The Standard Newspapers Limited," pt. 4 (December 2, 1909): 215; CB to Rowntree & Co., June 3, 1907, CP 5/107; CB to Rowntree & Co., June 4, 1907, CP 5/108; Rowntree to CB, June 5, 1907, CP 5/109 (fourth quote); CB to Under Secretary of State, June 10, 1907, CP 5/121.

6. Kevin Grant, *A Civilised Savagery: Britain and the New Slaveries in Africa, 1884–1926* (New York: Routledge, 2005), 127; Satre, *Chocolate on Trial*, 18, 112, 147; CP 1/8: "Cadbury Brothers, Limited, and Others v. The Standard Newspapers Limited," pt. 2 (November 30, 1909): 56, and pt. 5 (December 3, 1909): 281.

7. JB to WAC, June 8, 1907, CP 5/124 (Burtt refers to "English pharisaism") (quotes).

8. Fox Bourne to WAC, June 21, 1907, CP 5/129; CB to APS [draft], June 1907, CP 5/131 (first quote); Roderick J. Fry to CB, June 24, 1907, CP 5/133 (second quote); Rowntree to CB, June 24, 1907, CP 5/135; CB to Rowntree, June 25, 1907, CP 5/136; CB to Rowntree, July 5, 1907, CP 5/159; CB to Fry, July 5, 1907, CP 5/166; Fox Bourne to WAC, July 5, 1907, CP 5/151; WAC to Fox Bourne, July 8, 1907, CP 5/153 (third and fourth quotes); Fox Bourne to WAC, July 10, 1907, CP 5/155; CB to APS, July 11, 1907, CP 5/156; WAC to Fox Bourne, July 11, 1907, CP 5/157.

9. Joseph Burtt, "Report on the Condition of Coloured Labour Employed on the Cocoa Plantations of S. Thomé and Principe, and the Methods of Procuring It in Angola," December 24, 1906, FO 367/46: 10; Joseph Burtt and W. Claude Horton, *Report on the Conditions of Coloured Labour on the Cocoa Plantations of S. Thomé and Principe, and the Methods of Procuring It in Angola* (London: n.p., [July 4], 1907), 2–3, 4–5. A copy of the second report, dated July 14, 1907, was included as appendix A in William A. Cadbury's *Labour in Portuguese West Africa*, 2nd ed. (London: George Routledge and Sons, 1910), 103–31.

10. Burtt, "Report on the Condition of Coloured Labour," 5 (second quote), 8–9, 12 (fifth quote); Burtt and Horton, *Report on the Conditions of Coloured Labour,* 6 (third quote), 9 (fourth quote), 11 (sixth quote), 18 (first quote).

11. Burtt and Horton, *Report on the Conditions of Coloured Labour*, 13, 18 (quote); Satre, *Chocolate on Trial*, 91–93.

12. JB to WAC, July 17, 1907, CP 5/171 (quotes); WAC to JB, July 18, 1907, CP 5/172; CB to APS, August 2, 1907, CP 5/183; JB to WAC, August 21, 1907, CP 5, 193. Alfredo da Silva helped Burtt arrange the printing of the report. The phrasing of Burtt's letter to Cadbury, "A Portuguese Protestant Minister—a Senhor Silva—a reliable man and friend of Corte Real is getting it done by trustworthy men who print religious works for him," might call into question Richard Wall's family memory that his great-grandfather taught Burtt Portuguese in 1904–5. JB to WAC, September 3, 1907, CP 6/6; Richard Wall to Catherine Higgs, October 29, 2004.

13. JB to WAC, August 21, 1907, CP 5/193; Nevinson to Cross, [August 1907], CP 5/187 (first quote); Nevinson to H. W. Massingham, August 2, 1907, CP 5/188 (second quote); Henry W. Nevinson, "The Angola Slave Trade," *Fortnightly Review* 82 (September 1907): 488–97; Satre, *Chocolate on Trial*, 80–83.

14. Satre, *Chocolate on Trial*, 83–85; Cadbury, *Labour in Portuguese West Africa*, 132, 137, 139–40 (quote).

15. JB to WAC, October 7, 1907, CP 6/47 (quotes); Fox Bourne to CB, November 11, 1907, CP 6/38; Travers Buxton to WAC, November 1, 1907, CP 6/35; Satre, *Chocolate on Trial*, 90–91, 248n82. See also Consul of the "Legação de Portugal nos Estados Unidos" to the [Colonial minister], December 23, 1907, 71–43/7–1-908, Processo n° 43/1907, commenting on an article about Pienaar in the *New York Times*, and "Nota da Legação 30–12–07," 43/13–1-908, enclosing the article "Portuguese Legation Replies to Charges of Pienaar; Says Stories Are Ludicrous," in 3°P-A-3 M772–778, "Serviçais em S. Tomé, Diversos 1905/1911," Arquivo Histórico Diplomática, Lisbon (hereafter AHD).

16. JB to WAC, October 22, 1907, CP 6/51; WAC to JB, October 28, 1907, CP 6/60; WAC to Fry and Rowntree, November 19, 1907, CP 6/71; Satre, *Chocolate on Trial*, 94; James Duffy, *A Question of Slavery: Labour Policies in Portuguese Africa and the British Protest, 1850–1920* (Cambridge, Mass.: Harvard University Press. 1967), 197 (quote); "O Problema Colonial: O Que Diz o Sr. Ayres de Ornellas," *O Século*, October 3, 1907.

17. WAC to APS, November 9, 1907, CP 6/37; WAC to Fry and Rowntree, November 19, 1907, CP 6/71; WAC to JB, October 25, 1907, CP 6/52; WAC to Carl de Merck, November 12, 1907, CP 6/68; Alfredo Mendes da Silva, Henrique José Monteiro de Mendonça, Joaquim de Ornellas e Mattos, José Paulo Cancella, Nicolau MacNicoll, and Francisco Mantero to WAC, December 4, 1907, CP 6/77; CB to Rowntree, June 10, 1907, CP 5/117.

18. Jeronymo Paiva de Carvalho, *O Trabalho Indigena na Provincia de S. Thomé e Principe: Monographia de Defeza contra as Accusações Feitas no Estrangeiro* (Lisbon: Typographia do Commercio, 1907), 7–9, 10, 12: "individuos de capacidade restricta" (first quote), 13, 15: "Se isto é escravatura, então estamos completamente ás escuras sobre o problema da mão de obra nas colonias!" (second quote), 17.

19. WAC to APS, November 9, 1907, CP 6/37; JB to WAC, September 3, 1907, CP 6/6; JB to WAC, September 22, 1907, CP 6/8; JB to WAC, October 22, 1907, CP 6/51 (quote); Satre, *Chocolate on Trial*, 86.

20. WAC to [CB], November 18, 1907, CP 6/70; Cross to WAC, July 16, 1907, CP 5/168; W. Langley, F.O. to CB, October 25, 1907, CP 6/55; WAC to Clarke, October 28, 1907, CP 6/58; JB to WAC, September 3, 1907, CP 6/6 (quote); JB to WAC, August 26,

1907, CP 5/195 (quote); CB to F.O., October 8, 1907, CP 6/22; WAC to Fry and Rowntree, November 19, 1907, CP 6/71; Mendes da Silva et al. to WAC, December 4, 1907, CP 6/77; "O Cacau de S. Thomé: Os Nossos Agricultores e os Industriaes Inglezes," *O Século*, November 30, 1907.

21. Cadbury, *Labour in Portuguese West Africa*, 141–44, 145 (first quote); WAC to Fry and Rowntree, November 19, 1907, CP 6/71 (second quote).

22. Mendes da Silva et al., to WAC, December 4, 1907, CP 6/77 (quote); Satre, *Chocolate on Trial*, 96–97; Duffy, *Question of Slavery*, 197. On Burtt's failure to name his informants, see "Carta do Visconde d'Alte aos Principaes Importadores de Cacao" ("Letter from the Viscount d'Alte to the Principal Importers of Cocoa"), November 21, 1909, Processo n° 97/1909, in 3°P-A-3 M772–778, "Serviçais em S. Tomé," AHD.

23. Mendes da Silva et al., to WAC, December 4, 1907, CP 6/77 (first and second quotes); WAC to [CB], December 3, 1907, CP 6/80 (third and fourth quotes); Duffy, *Question of Slavery*, 198; Miguel Bandeiro Jerónimo, *Livros Brancos, Almas Negras: A "Missão Civilizadora" do Colonialismo Português c. 1870–1930* (Lisbon: Imprensa de Ciências Socias, 2010), 105–6.

24. WAC to [CB], December 3, 1907, CP 6/80 (first through third quotes); WAC to Mantero, December 19, 1907, CP 6/84 (fourth through seventh quotes). The original quote reads, "Mr. Cadbury's head in a charger"; Jerónimo, *Livros Brancos*, 107.

25. Douglas L. Wheeler, *Republican Portugal: A Political History, 1910–1926* (Madison: University of Wisconsin Press, 1978), 44; CB to Ornellas, February 5, 1908, CP 6/159 (quote); Ornellas to [WAC], February 9, 1908, CP 6/160. On the impact of photography on the cocoa controversy, see Jerónimo, *Livros Brancos*, 17–19; Robert M. Burroughs, *Travel Writing and Atrocities: Eyewitness Accounts of Colonialism in the Congo, Angola, and the Putumayo* (New York: Routledge, 2011), 110; and "Note on Sources," at the end of this notes section.

26. Duffy, *Question of Slavery*, 199; WAC to JB, April 7, 1908, CP 6/172 (first and second quotes); WAC to JB, February 10, 1908, CP 6/167 (third through ninth quotes); WAC to JB, June 10, 1908, CP 7/20; CB to Under Secretary of State, June 10, 1908, CP 7/21; Satre, *Chocolate on Trial*, 106.

27. José Paulo Monteiro Cancella to WAC, March 20, 1908, CP 6/170; Duffy, *Question of Slavery*, 198 (quote), 198n70, 199; Processo n° 24/1908 in 3°P-A-3 M772–778, "Serviçais em S. Tomé," AHD, contains correspondence relating to Cid's planned mission. See, for example, "Note Verbale," British Legation, March 6, 1908, 24/14–3-908, and "A Legação de Inglaterra" [from Lisbon], March 31, 1908, 24/31–3-908, as well as "Note Verbale," June 6, 1908, 24/9–6-08.

28. Satre, *Chocolate on Trial*, 106–7, 125; W. A. Woodward to Wragge & Co., May 14, 1908, CP 7/132; E. H. Johnstone to Wragge & Co., May 15, 1908, CP 7/134; WAC to [CB] Board, June 22, 1908, CP 7/32 (quotes).

29. WAC to Mantero, July 6, 1908, CP 7/38; Mantero to WAC, July 14, 1908, CP 7/39 (quotes).

30. Charles A. Swan, *The Slavery of To-day, or the Present Position of the Open Sore of Africa* (Glasgow, Scotland: Pickering and Inglis, 1909), 17; WAC to Charles Swan, July 6, 1908, CP 7/88; Swan to WAC, July 7, 1908, CP 7/89 (first and second quotes); Swan to WAC, July 15, 1907, CP 7/92; WAC to Swan, July 13, 1908, CP 7/91 (third quote); WAC to

Swan, July 27, 1908, CP 7/93 (fourth quote); Swan to WAC, August 4, 1908, CP 7/95 (fifth and sixth quotes); WAC to Swan, August 6, 1908, CP 7/96; Satre, *Chocolate on Trial*, 144.

31. WAC to [CB] directors, July 25, 1908, CP 7/73; Arnold Rowntree to WAC, July 17, 1908, CP 7/66 (first quote); WAC to Rowntree, July 20, 1908, CP 7/71 (second quote).

32. The text of the *Standard* article is reproduced in Satre, *Chocolate on Trial*, 227 (quotes), 228–29, see also 127, 128; Wragge & Co. to "The Standard," September 29, 1908, CP 7/138, and October 2, 1908, CP 7/140, and October 12, 1908, CP 7/144; Nevinson to "The Standard," October 6, 1908, CP 7/143. See also Gillian Wagner, *The Chocolate Conscience* (London: Chatto and Windus, 1987), 93–94.

33. W. A. Cadbury, "Record of Visit to West Africa 1908–09," CP 308, entries dated October 22 and 23, 1908; Cadbury, *Labour in Portuguese West Africa*, 13–14.

34. CP 308, entries dated November 2 and 5, 1909; WAC to [CB], October 27, 1908, CP 7/103. According to Duffy, *Question of Slavery*, 206, a British consul had not yet been assigned to the islands in 1908. See also Cadbury, *Labour in Portuguese West Africa*, 14, 31–43, 44, 47–49; MS 466 G/1/4, Diaries 1905–1909, William Adlington Cadbury Family Papers, Birmingham City Archives, Birmingham, UK (hereafter WAC Family Papers); William Gervase Clarence-Smith, *Cocoa and Chocolate, 1765–1914* (London: Routledge, 2000), 185 (quote).

35. Augusto Nascimento, "S. Tomé and Príncipe," in *O Império Africano 1890–1930*, ed. A. H. de Oliveira Marques, vol. 11 of *Nova História da Expansão Portuguesa*, ed. Joel Serrão and A. H. de Oliveira Marques (Lisbon: Editorial Estampa, 2001), 253; Cadbury, *Labour in Portuguese West Africa*, 15 (first and second quotes); "Campanha de Diffamação: Cadbury Espião ou Defensor do Cacao de S. Thomé?" *Portugal em Africa*, Ano 15, Supl. Colonial, n° 190 (1908): 340 (third quote), 341–42.

36. Cadbury, *Labour in Portuguese West Africa*, 15 (quote), 62, 63.

37. CP 308, entry dated November 16, 1908; Aida Faria Freudenthal, "Angola," in *O Império Africano*, 293–94, 451; Cadbury, *Labour in Portuguese West Africa*, 75, 77; Vasco Pulido Valente, *Um Herói Português: Henrique Paiva Couceiro (1861–1944)*, 2nd ed. (Lisbon: Alêtheia Editores, 2006), 48–51; Henrique Paiva Couceiro, *Angola (Dois Annos de Governo, Junho 1907–Junho 1909): Historia e Commentarios* (Lisbon: Editora a Nacional, 1910), 241–42.

38. CP 308, entry dated November 19, 1908; Cadbury, *Labour in Portuguese Africa*, 76, 77, 78 (quote).

39. CP 308, entry dated January 6, 1909; Cadbury, *Labour in Portuguese West Africa*, 78; WAC to Emmeline Cadbury, MS 466 G/3/7/1, January 3, 1909, WAC Family Papers; JB to John Cadbury, December 9, 1908, MS 466 G3/7/5, WAC Family Papers (quote); Emmeline Cadbury to WAC, January 17, 1908, MS 466 G/3/7/2, p. 13, WAC Family Papers.

40. CP 308, entry dated December 5, entry dated December 6, 1908 (first quote), entry dated December 21, 1908 (third quote), entries dated December 4 and 26, 1908 (at Novo Redondo); Cadbury, *Labour in Portuguese West Africa*, 78, 79 (second quote), 80–81, 85 (fifth quote), 90 (sixth quote), 92 (fourth quote); WAC to CB, November 25, 1908, CP 7/104 (seventh quote); CB to Fry, January 12, 1909, CP 7/113 (eighth quote).

41. CP 308, entries dated January 11 and 26, 1909; CP 308, WAC to [CB], two typed letters dated February 2 and 3, 1909, 79–86, 87 (quote); WAC to Emmeline Cadbury, January 3, 1909, MS 466 G/3/7/1, WAC Family Papers; Gwendolyn Mikell, *Cocoa and Chaos in Ghana* (Washington, D.C.: Howard University Press, 1992), 70; Processo n° 97/27–12–09

and "Portuguese Officials on Cocoa Slavery Reports," *Journal of Commerce*, New York, November 13, 1909, both in Processo n° 97/1909, 3°P-A-3 M772–778, "Serviçais em S. Tomé," AHD.

42. Satre, *Chocolate on Trial*, 116, 130, 139; Duffy, *Question of Slavery*, 216; Cadbury, *Labour in Portuguese West Africa*, 161–62; CB to [F.O.], March 15, 1909, CP 7/117; WAC to Mantero, March 15, 1909, CP 7/115 (quotes); Stollwerck to CB, March 19, 1909, CP 7/120; *Portugal em Africa*, April 22, 1909, 127, and May 7, 1909, 131, and "Supplemento Colonial," May 22, 1909, 145; William Gervase Clarence-Smith, *The Third Portuguese Empire, 1825–1975: A Study in Economic Imperialism* (Manchester, UK: Manchester University Press, 1985), 108; Ministerio dos Negocios da Marinha e Ultramar, *Serviço de Emigração de Operarios, Serviçaes e Trabalhadores para a Provincia de S. Thomé e Príncipe: Decreto de 31 de Dezembro de 1908* (Lisbon: Imprensa Nacional, 1909), 4; R. C. F. Maugham to [F.O.], March 3, 1909, CP 7/123 and CP 7/124; "Carta do Visconde d'Alte aos Principaes Importadores de Cacao."

43. Satre, *Chocolate on Trial*, 131, 132–33, 187 (Harris led the Anti-Slavery Society and APS, which amalgamated in 1910), 191–92; Nevinson to WAC, April 9, 1909, CP 7/125 (quotes).

44. Satre, *Chocolate on Trial*, 136; Jerónimo, *Livros Brancos*, 109, 116; Duffy, *Question of Slavery*, 205–7. A synopsis of Cid's recommendations appears in F. Villiers to Carlos Roma du Bocage [Colonial Ministry in Lisbon (?)], May 21, 1909, Processo n° 97/24-5-09 in 3°P-A-3 M772-778, "Serviçais em S. Tomé," AHD (quote). While living in Lisbon in 2006, I searched the collections of the Biblioteca Nacional, the Sociedade de Geografia da Lisboa, and the Arquivo Histórico Ultramarino for a copy of Francisco de Paula Cid's April 1909 report and could find neither a typescript nor a published report.

45. Swan, *Slavery of To-day*, 22–23 (quote), 27–36; Processo n° 97/27-12-09 in 3°P-A-3 M772-778, "Serviçais em S. Tomé," AHD; Duffy, *Question of Slavery*, 208–9; Satre, *Chocolate on Trial*, 144–45; Jerónimo, *Livros Brancos*, 18.

46. Satre, *Chocolate on Trial*, 134, 187–88; Stollwerck to CB, March 19, 1909, CP 7/120; "Against Slave System," *Boston Daily Globe*, September 27, 1909, 11; "Joseph Burtt Here to Battle against Slave Cocoa Trade," *Christian Science Monitor*, September 28, 1909, 1; Joseph Burtt, "How America Can Free the Portuguese Cocoa Slave: A Thrilling, Heart-Gripping Story of Twentieth Century Slavery Atrocities, and a Remedy," *Leslie's Weekly*, October 14, 1909, 368–69. See also Joseph Burtt, "My Success in America," *Leslie's Weekly*, December 16, 1909, 608.

47. Processo n° 97/16-11-09, letter dated December 4, 1909 (first quote); Processo n° 97/9-10-09 (second and third quotes), and "Declaração do Coronel Wyllie, Reproduzida em Centenas de Jornaes" ("Declaration of Colonel Wyllie, Reproduced in Hundreds of Newspapers"), enclosing an article dated November 25, 1909, titled "Denies Stories of Cruelty to Slaves" in 3°P-A-3 M772-778, "Serviçais em S. Tomé," AHD (fourth quote); Satre, *Chocolate on Trial*, 138.

48. "A Boycottage do Cacao," *Portugal em África*, November 7, 1909, 326 (quote), 327; "A Calúmnia de Escravatura," *Portugal em África*, December 7, 1909, 353; "Revista Colonial," *Portugal em África*, December 7, 1909, 363, 375–76. On the unlikelihood of American buyers boycotting, see also letter dated Washington, October 11, 1909, Processo n° 97/1909 in 3°P-A-3 M772-778, "Serviçais em S. Tomé," AHD. On Burtt as a propagandist, see Processo n° 97/27-12-09 in 3°P-A-3 M772-778, "Serviçais em S. Tomé," AHD; Satre, *Chocolate on Trial*, 134.

49. Grant, *Civilised Savagery*, 130; Satre, *Chocolate on Trial*, 153–56 (Satre offers a detailed discussion of the trial and verdict on 149–82). See also Marouf Hasian Jr., "Critical Memories of Crafted Virtues: The Cadbury Chocolate Scandals, Mediated Reputations, and Modern Globalized Slavery," *Journal of Communication Inquiry* 32 (2008): 259–64; Wagner, *Chocolate Conscience*, 94.

50. Wagner, *Chocolate Conscience*, 94, 97–98; Satre, *Chocolate on Trial*, 161–64; Grant, *Civilised Savagery*, 131; Hasian, "Critical Memories of Crafted Virtues," 262–63; Burroughs, *Travel Writing and Atrocities*, 116–17.

51. CP 1/8: "Printed Document: Proceedings at the 7 Days of the Trial," pt. 5, December 3, 1909, 288 (first quote), 289–92, 294 (second quote), 295.

52. Wagner, *Chocolate Conscience*, 99–100; Satre, *Chocolate on Trial*, 170 (quote).

53. Wagner, *Chocolate Conscience*, 101 (quotes); Satre, *Chocolate on Trial*, 174, 182.

54. CP 177: "Press Cuttings Relating to the Trial, 1907–1909"; CP 179/56: "Critical Letters after the Trial, Dec. 1909" (quotes). There are 257 letters of congratulation in CP 178, "Letters of Congratulation after the Trial, Dec. 1909," and 86 critical letters in CP 179.

55. Satre, *Chocolate on Trial*, 184–85, 264, 264nn2, 8; Cadbury, *Labour in Portuguese West Africa*, 102 (quote), 177; Grant, *Civilised Savagery*, 131 (quote), 132; Duffy, *Question of Slavery*, 209; Burroughs, *Travel Writing and Atrocities*, 115–17.

56. Duffy, *Question of Slavery*, 211–14; WAC, "A Private *Inside History* of the Connection of Cadbury Bros. Ltd., with African Slavery," November 5, 1949, CP 183; William A. Cadbury, "Angola and San Thomé," *Anti-Slavery Reporter and Aborigines' Friend*, series 6, vol. 10, no. 3 (1955): 43.

EPILOGUE: COCOA AND SLAVERY

1. William A. Cadbury, *Os Serviçaes de S. Thomé: Relatorio d'uma Visita ás Ilhas de S. Thomé e Príncipe e a Angola, Feita em 1908, para Observer as Condições da Mão d'Obra Empregada nas Roças de Cacao da Africa Portugueza*, trans. Alfredo da Silva (Lisbon: Livraria Bertrand, 1910), v, vi; "O Cacau de S. Thomé," 100, and "Portuguese Colonies: An Interview with Marquis de Valle-Flôr," 190 (quote), *Portugal em África*, 17 (1910); Cadbury distributed fifty copies of the photo album: W. A. Cadbury and Joseph Burtt, "Views Taken during a Visit to S. Thome and Angola, Portuguese West Africa in 1908–09," CP 242; Miguel Bandeiro Jerónimo, *Livros Brancos, Almas Negras: A "Missão Civilizadora" do Colonialismo Português c. 1870–1930* (Lisbon: Imprensa de Ciências Socias, 2010), 17–18.

2. Francisco Mantero, *Obras Completas*, vol. 1, *A Mão-de-Obra em S. Tomé e Príncipe* (Lisbon, [1954]), 179; "Monographia de S. Thomé," *Boletim do Centro Colonial de Lisboa*, ano 1, no. 12 (1910): 35; "O Livro do Sr. Mantero: A Mão d'Obra em S. Thomé e Principe," *Boletim do Centro Colonial de Lisboa*, ano 2, no. 4 (1910): 40; Mantero, *Manual Labour in S. Thomé and Principe*, trans. John Wyllie (Lisbon: Annuario Commercial, 1910), 92, 93 (quote); Marouf Hasian Jr., "Critical Memories of Crafted Virtues: The Cadbury Chocolate Scandals, Mediated Reputations, and Modern Globalized Slavery," *Journal of Communication Inquiry* 32, no. 3 (2008): 263–64; Jerónimo, *Livros Brancos*, 20.

3. Jerónimo, *Livros Brancos*, 124; James Duffy, *A Question of Slavery: Labour Policies in Portuguese Africa and the British Protest, 1850–1920* (Cambridge, Mass.: Harvard University Press, 1967), 212–13.

4. Duffy, *Question of Slavery,* 214–15; Lowell Satre, *Chocolate on Trial: Slavery, Politics, and the Ethics of Business* (Athens: Ohio University Press, 2005), 191, 192 (quotes).

5. Joseph Burtt, *The Voice of the Forest* (London: T. Fisher Unwin, 1911), 4, 5 (first quote), 26, 30, 135–36, 141–42, 226–30, 241 (second quote), 254–64. Burroughs suggests that Cadbury was embarrassed by the dedication and by the novel; Robert M. Burroughs, *Travel Writing and Atrocities: Eyewitness Accounts of Colonialism in the Congo, Angola, and the Putumayo* (New York: Routledge, 2011), 118, 119.

6. Duffy, *Question of Slavery,* 218–19, 223; Satre, *Chocolate on Trial,* 193, 198, 199, 278; William A. Cadbury and E. D. Morel, "The West African Slave Traffic: Britain's Duty towards Angola and San Thomé," *Nineteenth Century and After* 72 (October 1912): 837 (quote); A. Freire de Andrade, *Rapport présenté au Ministre des Colonies, à propos du livre Portuguese Slavery du Missionaire John Harris* (Lisbon: Imprimeire Nationale, 1914), 62.

7. "Freire de Andrade," in *Grande Enciclopédia Portuguesa e Brasileira* (Lisbon: Editorial Enciclopédia, 1945), 11:831. The English text of Freire de Andrade's reply to the 1912 white book was published under the title *Traducção do Relatorio sobre o Trabalho em S. Thomé e Principe Apresentatdo a S. Ex.ª O Ministro das Colonias* (Lisbon: Typographica—Bandeira and Brito, 1912), 1, 2, 3, 7 (quote), 9.

8. Andrade's response to Cadbury and Morel, in Portuguese and English, dated December 30, 1912, appeared as "A Questão dos Serviçaes: Carta de A. Freire d'Andrade," *Revista Colonial,* ano 1, no. 1 (1913): 10–19, and was reissued in pamphlet form as *A Questão dos Serviçaes de S. Thomé: Carta de A. Freire d'Andrade, Edição da Agencia Colonial* (Lisbon: Typ. Do Annuario Commerical, 1913), 2, 8, 12, 14 (quotes), 20, 26; Eric Allina, "Fallacious Mirrors: Colonial Anxiety and Images of African Labor in Mozambique, ca. 1929," *History in Africa* 24 (1997): 14.

9. Jerónimo Paiva de Carvalho, *Alma Negra: Depoimento sobre a Questão dos Serviçais de S. Tomé* (Porto, Portugal: Tipografia Progresso, 1912), "A existencia da escravatura nas ilhas é um facto," 5 (quote); Andrade, *Rapport présenté au Ministre,* 45, 46; Jerónimo, *Livros Brancos,* 130–32; *Slavery in West Africa: Portuguese Revelations.* Translated from a Pamphlet Published Last Year by Senhor Jeronimo Paiva de Carvalho, Formerly Curator on the Island of Principe (London: Anti-Slavery and Aborigines' Protection Society, n.d.), 2; Alfredo da Silva, *O Monstro da Escravatura: A Minha Defeza na Campanha Levantada a Proposito da Publicação do Folheto Alma Negra* (Porto, Portugal: Tipografia Mendonça, 1913), 34–35; Satre, *Chocolate on Trial,* 202. See also CP 309: "Jeronimo Paiva de Carvalho and Alfredo da Silva."

10. "Processo instaurado a Paiva de Carvalho pelo publicação do folheto 'Alma Negra,'" letters dated April 30, 1913 (27/1-5/913) and May 12, 1913 (27/13-5/913), both in Processo n° 27/1914, 3°P-A-3 M770-771, "Serviçais em S. Tomé, Campanha dos Chocolateiros 1913/1916," AHD; Jerónimo Paiva de Carvalho, *A Desafronta: Defesa de um Homem Injustamente Perseguido e Caluniada. A Questão dos Serviçais de S. Tomé* (Coimbra, Portugal: Tipografia Literária, 1916), 8; Andrade, *Rapport présenté au Ministre,* 45 (first quote), 46, 68, 78 (second quote, "M. Cadbury est un de nos accusateurs les plus acharnés"), 101–3, 104 (third quote); for a discussion of Cadbury and Carvalho, see 45–62, and for a sustained discussion of Harris, see 62–69. The report was published in French and Portuguese (*Relatório Feito pelo Director-Geral das Colónisa Acêrca do Livro Portuguese Slavery Escrito pelo Sr. John H. Harris* [Lisbon: Imprensa Nacional, 1913]) but not in English. See also Jerónimo, *Livros Brancos,* 131n76; Allina, "Fallacious Mirrors," 14–15.

11. Duffy, *Question of Slavery*, 126n48. The Viscount of Giraúl continued to defend Portugal's colonial alcohol policies; see Antonio Duarte Ramada Curto, Ayres Kopke, and Visconde de Giraúl, *L'Alcoolisme dans les Colonies Portugaises* (Lisbon: A Editora, 1910), 7, 12, 13, 14; William Gervase Clarence-Smith, *Slaves, Peasants and Capitalists in Southern Angola, 1840–1926* (Cambridge: Cambridge University Press, 1979), 41–42; Andrade, *Traducção do Relatorio sobre o Trabalho*, 14. On British attempts to control vagrancy in Kenya, see Frederick Cooper, *From Slaves to Squatters: Plantation Labor and Agriculture in Zanzibar and Coastal Kenya, 1890–1925* (New Haven, Conn.: Yale University Press, 1980), 116–21; Sociedade da Emigração para S. Thomé e Príncipe, *Relatorio da Direcção Parecer do Conselho Fiscal Lista dos Accionistas*, 2° anno (Lisbon, 1914), 3, 23; Augusto Nascimento, "S. Tomé e Príncipe," in *O Império Africano, 1890–1930*, ed. A. H. de Oliveira Marques, vol. 11 of *Nova História da Expansão Portuguesa*, ed. Joel Serrão and A. H. de Oliveira Marques (Lisbon: Editorial Estampa, 2001), 221.

12. Duffy, *Question of Slavery*, 226; Satre, *Chocolate on Trial*, 207 (quote); Cadbury, "Angola and San Thomé," *Anti-Slavery Reporter*, 43.

13. Joseph Burtt, "San Thomé," *Bournville Works Magazine* 15 (January–December 1917): 176, 177 (quote), 179; Antonio A. Corrêa Aguiar, *O Trabalho Indígena nas Ilhas de S. Tomé e Príncipe: Relatorio Apresentado ao Governo da Colónia—A Proposito de Alguns Reparos Feitos em Inglaterra sobre a Mortalidade, Recontratos, Repatriação e Estatistica dos Serviçais—Pelo Juiz de Direito e Curador Geral dos Serviçais e Colónos* (São Tomé: Imprensa Nacional, 1919), 20–21, 39–46 (death rates for Mozambican miners), 247, 248–50, 292–311, 321, 323, 325; Jerónimo, *Livros Brancos*, 137–39.

14. Duffy, *Question of Slavery*, 206; Satre, *Chocolate on Trial*, 208; William Gervase Clarence-Smith, *The Third Portuguese Empire, 1825–1975: A Study in Economic Imperialism* (Manchester, UK: Manchester University Press, 1985), 122; *Portugal em África*, May 22, 1909, 145; António J. Monteiro Filippe, "Notas sobre a Cultura do Cacau em S. Thomé," *Bróteria* 18 (1920): 174; Edmundo A. Dias, "A Evolução de S. Tomé e Príncipe," *Boletim da Agência Geral das Colonias* 5, no. 43 (1929): 173; [W. M. Hood], "Cocoa in West Africa: The Past, Present and Future of a Great Colonial Industry," *Bournville Works Magazine* 43, no. 2 (February 1945): 23; Orlando Bastos Villela, "O Caso do Cacau Escravo," *Indústria Portuguesa* 22, no. 259 (1949): 597.

15. Clarence-Smith, *Third Portuguese Empire*, 140; Eric Allina, *Slavery By Any Other Name: African Life under Company Rule in Colonial Mozambique* (Charlottesville: University of Virginia Press, 2012), 75–80; Jerónimo, *Livros Brancos*, 242–43; "Publicações e Aviso Oficias," *Boletim Oficial de S. Tomé e Príncipe*, n° 24 (June 13, 1925): 226 (quote), 227; Portuguese Delegation to the VIth Assembly of the League of Nations, *Some Observations on Professor Ross's Report: Submitted for the Information of the Temporary Slavery Commission of the League of Nations* (Geneva, Switzerland: Imprimerie du Journal de Genève, 1925), 5, 34–35; Allina, "Fallacious Mirrors," 15–16; Satre, *Chocolate on Trial*, 210.

16. Satre, *Chocolate on Trial*, 216; "Joseph Burtt," *Friend* 97 (May 19, 1939): 408–10; Joseph Burtt, *Sonnets and Other Poems* (London: Oliphants, n.d. [1929?]), 8–9, 12, 23–24, 45 (quote), 46–47.

17. Satre, *Chocolate on Trial*, 217 (first quote); Cadbury, "A Private Inside History," CP 183: 1, 2 (second quote), 3, 4 (third quote); Cadbury, "Angola and San Thomé," *Anti-Slavery Reporter*, 43–44.

18. Satre, *Chocolate on Trial*, 216; Kevin Shillington, *History of Africa*, 2nd rev. ed. (New York: Palgrave St. Martin's, 2005), 380, 388–408.

19. Satre, *Chocolate on Trial*, 221–22; Carol Off, *Bitter Chocolate: Investigating the Dark Side of the World's Most Seductive Sweet* (Toronto: Vintage Canada, 2007), 139–43, 144 (second quote), 151. See www.worldcocoafoundation.org/ (first quote); Órla Ryan, *Chocolate Nations: Living and Dying for Cocoa in West Africa* (London: Zed Books, 2011), 47, 55.

20. Off, *Bitter Chocolate*, 163, 165, 179–83; Ryan, *Chocolate Nations*, 71–72; "The World at a Glance: Abidjan, Ivory Coast: Cocoa Power Play," *Week* (February 4, 2011): 8; "Endgame in Côte d'Ivoire: Basement Blues," *Economist* (April 9, 2011): 53–54; "Ivory Coast's Turmoil," *Week* (April 15, 2011): 6; "Côte d'Ivoire's New President: The King of Kong," *Economist* (April 23, 2011): 51–52.

A NOTE ON SOURCES

1. "Transfer of West African papers from Cadbury Archives to University," T. Insull to Wynn Evans, August 1, 1972, Cadbury Research Library, Special Collections, University of Birmingham, Birmingham, UK; Catherine Higgs to Dorothy Woodson, January 28, 2007, Woodson to Higgs, January 29, 2007, and Higgs to Woodson, May 4, 2010, regarding the James Duffy Collection donated to the African Collection, Yale University, New Haven, Conn. James Duffy, *A Question of Slavery: Labour Policies in Portuguese Africa and the British Protest, 1850–1920* (Cambridge, Mass.: Harvard University Press, 1967), 195n59 (quote).

2. A. H. de Oliveira Marques, *Das Revoluções Liberais aos Nossos Dias*, vol. 3 of *História de Portugal*, 13th ed. (Lisbon: Editorial Presença, 1998), 188 (quote), 189. See also Oliveira Marques, "Introdução," in *O Império Africano, 1890–1930*, ed. A. H. de Oliveira Marques, vol. 11 of *Nova História da Expansão Portuguesa*, ed. Joel Serrão and A. H. de Oliveira Marques (Lisbon: Editorial Estampa, 2001), 71; Miguel Sousa Tavares, *Equador* (Lisbon: Oficina do Livro, 2003); Miguel Bandeiro Jerónimo, *Livros Brancos, Almas Negras: A "Missão Civilizadora" do Colonialismo Português c. 1870–1930* (Lisbon: Imprensa de Ciências Socias, 2010), 99–112.

3. Diogo Ramada Curto, "Prefácio," in *Livros Brancos*, 17–20; James R. Ryan, *Picturing Empire: Photography and the Visualization of the British Empire* (Chicago: University of Chicago Press, 1997), 12–13, 16–18, 19; Wolfram Hartmann, Jeremy Silvester, and Patricia Hayes, *The Colonising Camera: Photographs in the Making of Namibian History* (Cape Town: University of Cape Town Press, 1998); Paul S. Landau and Deborah D. Kaspin, eds., *Images and Empires: Visuality in Colonial and Postcolonial Africa* (Berkeley: University of California Press, 2002).

4. Copy 48 of 50 of Cadbury and Burtt, "Views taken during a visit to S. Thome and Angola," CP 242; CP 308, entry dated January 7, 1909; Jerónimo, *Livros Brancos*, 17–18; Mary Kingsley, *Travels in West Africa: Congo Français, Corisco and Cameroons*, 3rd ed. (1897; repr., London: Frank Cass, 1965), 340 (quote).

5. A. G. Gardiner, *Life of George Cadbury* (London: Cassell, 1923), chap. 13; Iolo A. Williams, *The Firm of Cadbury, 1831–1931* (London: Constable, 1931), chap. 8; Lowell Satre, *Chocolate on Trial: Slavery, Politics, and the Ethics of Business* (Athens: Ohio University Press, 2005), 212, 258n115, 264n5; Kevin Grant, *A Civilised Savagery: Britain and the New Slaveries in Africa, 1884–1926* (New York: Routledge, 2005), 113 (quote), 133; James Duffy,

Portuguese Africa (Cambridge, Mass.: Harvard University Press, 1959), 194–95, 204, 209–10. See also William Gervase Clarence-Smith, "The Hidden Costs of Labour on the Cocoa Plantations of São Tomé and Príncipe, 1875–1914," *Portuguese Studies* 6 (1990): 152–72 and "Labour Conditions in the Plantations of São Tomé and Príncipe, 1875–1914," *Slavery and Abolition* 14, no. 1 (1993): 149–67; Gillian Wagner, *The Chocolate Conscience* (London: Chatto and Windus, 1987), 93–94, 98–99, 101; Marouf Hasian Jr., "Critical Memories of Crafted Virtues: The Cadbury Chocolate Scandals, Mediated Reputations, and Modern Globalized Slavery," *Journal of Communication Inquiry* 32, no. 32 (2008): 249–70; Deborah Cadbury, *Chocolate Wars: The 150-Year Rivalry between the World's Greatest Chocolate Makers* (New York: Public Affairs, 2010), 173–13, 197–203; Robert M. Burroughs, *Travel Writing and Atrocities: Eyewitness Accounts of Colonialism in the Congo, Angola, and the Putumayo* (New York: Routledge, 2011), 98–121. See also Charles Dellheim, "The Creation of a Company Culture: *Cadburys, 1861–1931,*" *American Historical Review* 92, no. 1 (February 1987): 36, 42; Tony Hodges and Malyn Newitt, *São Tomé and Príncipe: From Plantation Colony to Micro-state* (Boulder, Colo.: Westview Press, 1988), 38–39, 63–64; Roger J. Southall, "Cadbury on the Gold Coast, 1907–1938: The Dilemma of the 'Model Firm' in a Colonial Economy" (Ph.D. diss., University of Birmingham, 1975).

SELECTED BIBLIOGRAPHY

MANUSCRIPTS AND ARCHIVAL COLLECTIONS

American Board of Commissioners for Foreign Missions. Papers. Houghton Library, Harvard University. Cambridge, Mass.

Arquivo Histórico Diplomática. Lisbon, Portugal.
  Serviçais em S. Tomé. Campanha dos Chocolateiros. 1913–1916.
  Serviçais em S. Tomé. Diversos 1905–1911.

Arquivo Histórico Nacional de Angola. Luanda, Angola.
  Catumbela. Concelho da Catumbela (1906).

Arquivo Histórico de São Tomé e Príncipe. São Tomé.
  Curadoria Geral dos Serviçais e Colonos (1904).
  Curadoria Geral dos Serviçais e Colonos (1905).

Arquivo Histórico Ultramarino. Lisbon, Portugal.
  Fundo Francisco Mantero.
  Secretaria do Estado Marinha e Ultramar. Gabineto do Ministro. 1° Repartição. 1° Secção. 1881–1911.

Secretaria do Estado Marinha e Ultramar. Moçambique. 1.ª Repartição—1.ª Secção. Correspondência de Governadores. 1906–1907.

Cadbury Papers. Cadbury Research Library. Special Collections. University of Birmingham. Birmingham, UK.

Cadbury, William Adlington. Family Papers. Birmingham City Archives. Birmingham, UK.

Duffy, James. Collection. African Collection. Yale University Library. New Haven, Conn.

Nevinson, Henry Woodd. Diaries. Bodleian Library. Oxford University. Oxford, UK.

PUBLISHED PAPERS AND REPORTS

United Kingdom

Foreign Office. *Correspondence Respecting Contract Labour in Portuguese West Africa*. Africa. No. 2. Cd. 6322. 1912.

Foreign Office. *Diplomatic and Consular Reports. Trade and Commerce of Angola for the Year 1899*. No. 2555. Cd. 429-13. February 1901.

Foreign Office. *Diplomatic and Consular Reports. Trade and Commerce of the Province of St. Thomé and Príncipe for the Year 1901*. No. 2922. Cd. 786-226. December 1902.

Foreign Office. *Further Correspondence Respecting Contract Labour in Portuguese West Africa*. Africa. No. 1. Cd. 7279. April 1914.

Foreign Office. *Further Correspondence Respecting Contract Labour in Portuguese West Africa*. Africa. No. 1. Cd. 8479. 1917–1918.

Portugal

Diário da Camara dos Senhores Deputados. Lisbon. 1906.

Ministerio dos Negocios da Marinha e Ultramar. *Serviço de Emigração de Operarios, Serviçaes e Trabalhadores para a Provincia de S. Thomé e Príncipe. Decreto de 31 de Dezembro de 1908.* Lisboa: Imprensa Nacional, 1909.

South Africa (British Colony of Transvaal)

Report of the Coloured Labour Compound Commission Appointed to Enquire into the Cubic Amount of Air-Space in the Compounds of the Mines of the Witwatersrand. Pretoria: Government Printing and Stationery Office, 1905.

Report of the Transvaal Labour Commission: Together with Minority Report, Minutes of Proceedings and Evidence. Johannesburg: Argus Printing and Publishing Company, Limited, 1903.

CONTEMPORARY SOURCES

Aguiar, Antonio A. Corrêa. *O Trabalho Indigena nas Ilhas de S. Tomé e Príncipe: Relatorio Apresentado ao Governo da Colónia—A Proposito de Alguns Reparos Feitos em Inglaterra sobre a Mortalidade, Recontratos, Repatriação e Estatistica dos Serviçais—Pelo Juiz de Direito e Curador Geral dos Serviçais e Colónos.* São Tomé: Imprensa Nacional, 1919.

American Board of Commissioners for Foreign Missions. *The Mission of the American Board to West Central Africa: Pioneer Work, 1881.* Boston: American Board of Commissioners for Foreign Missions, 1882.

Andrade, A. Freire de. *Rapport présenté au Ministre des Colonies, à propos du livre Portuguese Slavery du Missionaire John Harris.* Lisbon: Imprimeire Nationale, 1914.

———. *Relatorios sobre Moçambique.* 5 vols. Lourenço Marques, Mozambique: Imprensa Nacional, 1907.

———. *Traducção do Relatorio sobre o Trabalho em S. Thomé e Principe Apresentatdo a S. Ex.ᵃ O Ministro das Colonias.* Lisbon: Typographica—Bandeira and Brito, 1912.

Arnot, Fred S. *Bihé and Garenganze; or, Four Years Further Work and Travel in Central Africa.* London: J. E. Hawkins, 1893.

Barahona, Henrique. "Os Indigenas da Província de Moçambique e os Chinezes nas Minas da Rand." *Revista Portugueza Colónial e Marítima.* 9° anno. 1° semester (1905–6): 118–21.

Biker, Joachim Pedro Vieira Júdice. "Ilha de S. Thomé." *Revista Portugueza Colónial e Marítima* 1, no. 5 (1897–98): 307–10.

Burtt, Joseph. "How America Can Free the Portuguese Cocoa Slave: A Thrilling, Heart-Gripping Story of Twentieth Century Slavery Atrocities, and a Remedy." *Leslie's Weekly,* October 14, 1909, 368–69.

———. "Indentured and Forced Labour." Paper presented to the First Universal Races Congress, 1911. In *Papers on Inter-racial Problems,* edited by G. Spiller, 323–24. London: P. S. King and Son, 1911.

———. "My Success in America." *Leslie's Weekly,* December 16, 1909, 608.

———. *The People of Ararat.* London: Leonard and Virginia Woolf at the Hogarth Press, 1926.

———. "Report on the Condition of Coloured Labour Employed on the Cocoa Plantations of S. Thomé and Príncipe, and the Methods of Procuring It in Angola." December 24, 1906. FO 367/46. National Archives, London.

———. "The Slave and the Diplomat." *Friend* 54 (May 22, 1914): 356–57.

———. "Slave-Grown Cocoa." *Friend* 49 (September 17, 1909): 620–22.

———. "Slave Labour on Cocoa Plantations." *Contemporary Review* 96 (October 1909): 486–73.

———. "Slavery in S. Thome." *Friend* 50 (July 22, 1910): 485.

———. *Sonnets and Other Poems.* London: Oliphants, n.d. [1929].

———. *The Voice of the Forest.* London: T. Fisher Unwin, 1911.

Burtt, Joseph, and W. Claude Horton. *Report on the Conditions of Coloured Labour on the Cocoa Plantations of S. Thomé and Principe, and the Methods of Procuring It in Angola.* London: n.p. [July 4], 1907.

Cadbury, William A. "Angola and San Thomé." *Anti-Slavery Reporter and Aborigines' Friend.* Series 6, 10, no. 3 (1955): 42–43.

———. *Labour in Portuguese West Africa.* 2nd ed. London: George Routledge and Sons, 1910.

———. *Os Serviças de S. Thomé: Relatorio d'uma Visita ás Ilhas de S. Thomé e Príncipe e a Angola, Feita em 1908, para Observer as Condições da Mão d'Obra Empregada nas Roças de Cacao da Africa Portugueza.* Translated by Alfredo H. da Silva. Lisbon: Livraria Bertrand, 1910.

Cadbury, William A., and E. D. Morel. "The West African Slave Traffic: Britain's Duty towards Angola and San Thomé." *Nineteenth Century and After* 72 (October 1912): 836–51.

Campos, Ezequiel de. *Obras Publicas em S. Tomé e Príncipe: Subsidios para a Elaboracão e Realisação d'um Plano.* N.p: author's edition, [1914].

Cancella, José Paulo Monteiro. "Impressões de uma Viagem ás Ilhas de S. Thomé e Principe." *Boletim da Sociedade de Geographia da Lisboa,* série 19, no. 4–6 (1901): 471–501.

Carvalho, Jerónimo Paiva de. *Alma Negra: Depoimento sobre a Questão dos Serviçais de S. Tomé.* Porto, Portugal: Tipografia Progresso, 1912.

———. *A Desafronta: Defesa de um Homem Injustamente Perseguido e Caluniada—A Questão dos Serviçais de S. Tomé.* Coimbra, Portugal: Tipografia Literária, 1916.

———. *O Trabalho Indigena na Provincia de S. Thomé e Principe: Monographia de Defeza contra as Accusações Feitas no Estrangeiro.* Lisbon: Typographia do Commercio, 1907.

Chatelain, Heli, ed. *Folk-Tales of Angola: Fifty Tales, with Ki-Mbundu Text, Literal English Translation, Introduction, and Notes.* New York: Negro Universities Press, 1969 [1894].

Cid, Francisco de Paula. *Relatorio do Governador do Districto de Benguella, 1892.* Relatorios dos Governadores das Províncias Ultramarinas. Lisbon: Ministerio da Marinha e Ultramar, 1894.

Costa, Bernardo F. Bruto da. *Sleeping Sickness in the Island of Principe: Sanitation Statistics, Hospital Services, and Work of the Official Conservancy Brigade.* Translated by J. A. Wyllie. Lisbon: Centro Colonial, 1913.

Couceiro, Henrique Paiva. *Angola (Dous Annos de Governo, Junho 1907–Junho 1909): História e Commentários.* Lisbon: Editora a Nacional, 1910.

Curto, Antonio Duarte Ramada, Ayres Kopke, and Visconde de Giraúl. *L'Alcoolisme dans les Colonies Portugaises.* Lisbon: A Editora, 1910.

Durão, Hygino. *Relatorio sobre os Abonos Feitos ao Pessoal da Curadoria dos Indigenas de Johannesburg que Não Estavam Incluidos nas Tabellas Orçamentos*. Lisbon: Ministério da Marinha e Colónias, Inspecção Geral de Fazenda das Colónias, 1911.

A Famosa e Histórico Benguela: Catálogo dos Governadores (1779 a 1940). Edição do Govêrno da Província. Lisbon: Edições Cosmos, [1940].

Filippe, António J. Monteiro. "Notas sobre a Cultura do Cacau em S. Thomé." *Bróteria* 18 (1920): 174–80.

Giraúl, Visconde de. *Idéas Geraes sobre a Colonização Europeia da Provincia de Angola*. Lisbon: Imprensa Nacional, 1901.

Hartzell, Joseph C. *The African Mission of the Methodist Episcopal Church*. New York: Board of the Foreign Missions of the Methodist Episcopal Church, 1909.

Howard, Ebenezer. *Tomorrow: A Peaceful Path to Real Reform*. Original edition with commentary by Peter Hall, Dennis Hardy, and Colin Ward. New York: Routledge, 2003, [1898].

A Ilha de S. Thomé e o Trabalho Indigena. Separata da *Revista Portugueza Colonial e Maritima*. Lisbon: Livraria Ferin, 1907.

Johnston, Harry Hamilton. *A Comparative Study of the Bantu and Semi-Bantu Languages*. Vol. 1. Oxford: Clarendon Press, 1919.

"Joseph Burtt." *Friend* 97 (May 19, 1939): 408–10.

Kingsley, Mary. *Travels in West Africa: Congo Français, Corisco and Cameroons*. 3rd ed. London: Frank Cass, 1965, [1897].

Lecomte, Ernesto. *Methodo Pratico da Lingua Mbundu, Fallada no Districto de Benguella*. Lisbon: Imprensa Nacional, 1897.

Malheiro, Alexandre. *Chronicas do Bihé*. Lisbon: Livraria Ferreira, 1903.

Mantero, Francisco. *Manual Labour in S. Thomé and Principe*. Translated by John Wyllie. Lisbon: Annuario Commercial, 1910.

———. *A Mão-de-Obra em S. Tomé e Príncipe*. Vol. 1 of *Obras Completas*. Lisbon, [1954].

Mendonça, Henrique José Monteiro de. *The Boa Entrada Plantations, S. Thomé, Portuguese West Africa, "La Perle des Colonies Portuguaises."* Translated by J. A. Wyllie. Edinburgh: Oliphant Anderson and Ferrier, 1907.

———. *A Roça Boa Entrada, S. Thomé, Africa Occidental Portugueza, La perle des colonies portuguaises*. Lisbon: A Editora, 1906.

Nascimento, J. Pereira do. *Grammatica do Umbundu, ou Lingua de Benguella*. Lisbon: Imprensa Nacional, 1894.

Nascimento, J. Pereira do, and A. Alexandre de Mattos. *A Colonisação de Angola*. Lisbon, 1912.

Nevinson, Henry Woodd. "The Angola Slave Trade." *Fortnightly Review* 82 (September 1907): 488–97.

———. *A Modern Slavery*. London: Harper and Brothers Publishers, 1906.

———. "The New Slave Trade." *Harper's Monthly Magazine*. August 1905–February 1906.

Nevinson, Henry Woodd, and Ellis Roberts. *Fire of Life*. London: James Nisbet, 1935.

Ao País. Lisbon: Typographia, 1903.

Portuguese Delegation to the VIth Assembly of the League of Nations. *Some Observations on Professor Ross's Report: Submitted for the Information of the Temporary Slavery*

Commission of the League of Nations. Geneva, Switzerland: Imprimerie du Journal de Genève, 1925.

"A Questão dos Serviçaes: Carta de A. Freire d'Andrade." *Revista Colonial*, ano I, n°I (1913): 10–19. Reissued in pamphlet form as *A Questão dos Serviçaes de S. Thomé: Carta de A. Freire d'Andrade*, Edição da Agencia Colonial. Lisbon: Typ. do Annuario Commerical, 1913.

Questões Africanas: A Questão do Maputo: Documentos. Lisbon: Sociedade de Geographia de Lisboa, 1890.

Roçadas, J. A. Alves. *La main d'oeuvre indigène à Angola.* IIIe Congrès International d'Agriculture Tropicale. Lisbon: Editora Limitada, 1914.

Rowntree, B. Seebohm. *Poverty: A Study of Town Life.* London: Macmillan, 1901.

Sanders, W. H., and W. E. Fay. *Vocabulary of the Umbundu Language, Comprising Umbundu-English and English-Umbundu.* Boston: Beacon Press, 1885.

Silva, Alfredo da. *O Monstro da Escravatura: A Minha Defeza na Campanha Levantada a Proposito da Publicação do Folheto Alma Negra.* Porto, Portugal: Tipografia Mendonça, 1913.

Slavery in West Africa: Portuguese Revelations. Translated from a Pamphlet Published Last Year by Senhor Jeronimo Paiva de Carvalho, Formerly Curator on the Island of Principe. London: Anti-Slavery and Aborigines' Protection Society, n.d.

Sociedade da Emigração para S. Thomé e Príncipe. *Relatorio da Direcção Parecer do Conselho Fiscal Lista dos Accionistas.* 2° anno. Lisbon, 1914.

Street, Eugene E. *A Philosopher in Portugal.* London: T. Fisher Unwin, 1903.

Swan, Charles A. *The Slavery of To-day, or the Present Position of the Open Sore of Africa.* Glasgow, Scotland: Pickering and Inglis, 1909.

Transvaal Chamber of Mines. *Thirteenth Report for the Year 1902.* Johannesburg, South Africa: Argus Printing and Publishing, 1903.

Voz d'Angola Clamando no Deserto: Offerecida aos Amigos da Verdade pelos Naturaes. Lisbon: Typographia, 1901; repr., Lisbon: Edições 70, 1984.

NEWSPAPERS AND JOURNALS

Anti-Slavery Reporter
Boletim da Agência Geral das Colónias
Boletim da Sociedade de Geographia de Lisboa
Boletim do Centro Colonial de Lisboa
Boletim Oficial da Província de Angola
Boletim Oficial de S. Tomé e Príncipe
Boston Daily Globe
Bournville Works Magazine
Christian Science Monitor
The Economist
The Friend
Harper's Monthly Magazine
Leslie's Weekly
O Mundo Português
New York Times
Portugal em Africa

Revista Colonial
Revista Portugueza Colónial e Marítima
O Século
Times (London)
The Week

SECONDARY SOURCES

Alexander, Caroline. *One Dry Season: In the Footsteps of Mary Kingsley.* New York: Alfred A. Knopf, 1990.

Alexandre, Valetim. "The Colonial Empire." In *Contemporary Portugal: Politics, Society and Culture,* edited by António Costa Pinta. Boulder, Colo.: Social Science Monographs, 2003.

———. *Velho Brasil, Novas Áfricas: Portugal e o Império (1808–1975).* Porto, Portugal: Edições Afrontamento, 2000.

Allina, Eric. "Fallacious Mirrors: Colonial Anxiety and Images of African Labor in Mozambique, ca. 1929." In *History in Africa* 24 (1997): 9–52.

———. *Slavery By Any Other Name: African Life under Company Rule in Colonial Mozambique.* Charlottesville: University of Virginia Press, 2012.

American Board of Commissioners for Foreign Missions. *Papers of the American Board of Commissioners for Foreign Missions: Documents Administered by the Houghton Library of Harvard University—Guide to the Microfilm Collection.* Woodbridge, Conn.: Research Publications International, 1994.

Anderson, Benedict. *Imagined Communities: Reflections on the Origin and Spread of Nationalism.* Rev. ed. London: Verso, 1991.

Axelson, Eric. *Portugal and the Scramble for Africa, 1875–1891.* Johannesburg, South Africa: University of the Witwatersrand Press, 1967.

Bales, Kevin. *Disposable People: New Slavery in the Global Economy.* Rev. ed. Berkeley: University of California Press, 2004.

Bender, Gerald J. *Angola under the Portuguese: The Myth and the Reality.* Berkeley: University of California Press, 1978.

Birmingham, David. *A Concise History of Portugal.* Cambridge: Cambridge University Press, 1993.

———. *Empire in Africa: Angola and Its Neighbors.* Africa Series no. 84. Athens: Ohio University Press, 2006.

———. *Portugal and Africa.* Athens: Ohio University Press, 1999.

———. "Wagon Technology, Transport and Long-Distance Communication in Angola, 1885–1908." In *Angola on the Move: Transport Routes, Communications and History/Angola em Movimento: Vias de Transporte, Communicação e História,* edited by Beatrix Heintze and Achim von Oppen, 52–61. Frankfurt, Germany: Verlag Otto Lembeck, 2008.

Boeck, Guy de. *Les révoltes de la force publique sous Léopold II: Congo, 1895–1908.* Anvers, Belgium: Editions EPO, 1987.

Brettell, Caroline B. *Men Who Migrate, Women Who Wait: Population and History in a Portuguese Parish.* Princeton, N.J.: Princeton University Press, 1986.

Burroughs, Robert M. *Travel Writing and Atrocities: Eyewitness Accounts of Colonialism in the Congo, Angola, and the Putumayo.* New York: Routledge, 2011.

Bush, Julia. *Edwardian Ladies and Imperial Power.* London: Leicester University Press, 2000.

Cadbury, Deborah. *Chocolate Wars: The 150-Year Rivalry between the World's Greatest Chocolate Makers.* New York: Public Affairs, 2010.

Candido, Marianna P. "Trade, Slavery, and Migration in the Interior of Benguela: The Case of Caconda, 1830–1870." In *Angola on the Move: Transport Routes, Communications and History/Angola em Movimento: Vias de Transporte, Communicação e História,* edited by Beatrix Heintze and Achim von Oppen, 63–81. Frankfurt, Germany: Verlag Otto Lembek, 2008.

Capela, José. "*O Ultimatum* na Perspectiva de Moçambique." In *Moçambique: Navegações, Comércio e Técnicas,* Actas do Seminário, Maputo, November 25–28, 1996. [Lisbon]: Comissão Nacional para as Comemorações dos Descobrimentos Portugueses, 1998.

Carreira, António. *Cabo Verde (Aspectos Sociais, Secas e Fomes do Século XX).* 2nd ed. Lisbon: Biblioteca Ulmeiro, 1984.

Cell, John W. *The Highest Stage of White Supremacy: The Origins of Segregation in South Africa and the American South.* Cambridge: Cambridge University Press, 1982.

Childs, Gladwyn Murray. *Kinship and Character of the Ovimbundu.* Oxford: Oxford University Press, 1949; repr., London: Dawsons of Pall Mall, 1969.

Clarence-Smith, William Gervase. *Cocoa and Chocolate, 1765–1914.* London: Routledge, 2000.

———. "The Hidden Costs of Labour on the Cocoa Plantations of São Tomé and Príncipe, 1875–1914." *Portuguese Studies* 6 (1990): 152–72.

———. "Labour Conditions in the Plantations of São Tomé and Príncipe, 1875–1914." *Slavery and Abolition* 14, no. 1 (1993): 149–67.

———. *Slaves, Peasants and Capitalists in Southern Angola, 1840–1926.* Cambridge: Cambridge University Press, 1979.

———. *The Third Portuguese Empire, 1825–1975: A Study in Economic Imperialism.* Manchester, UK: Manchester University Press, 1985.

Collelo, Thomas, ed. *Angola: A Country Study.* 3rd ed. Washington, D.C.: Federal Research Division, Library of Congress, 1991.

Cooper, Frederick. "Conditions Analogous to Slavery." In *Beyond Slavery: Explorations of Race, Labor, and Citizenship in Post-emancipation Societies,* edited by Frederick Cooper, Thomas C. Holt, and Rebecca J. Scott, 107–49. Chapel Hill: University of North Carolina Press, 2000.

———. *From Slaves to Squatters: Plantation Labor and Agriculture in Zanzibar and Coastal Kenya, 1890–1925.* New Haven, Conn.: Yale University Press, 1980.

Corrado, Jacopo. "The Fall of a Creole Elite? Angola at the Turn of the Twentieth Century: The Decline of the Euro-African Urban Community." *Luso-Brazilian Review* 47, no. 2 (2010): 121–49.

Crosfield, John F. *A History of the Cadbury Family.* Vol. 2. London: privately published, 1985.

Cutileiro, José. *A Portuguese Rural Society.* Oxford: Clarendon Press, 1971.

Dellheim, Charles. "The Creation of a Company Culture: *Cadburys,* 1861–1931." *American Historical Review* 92, no. 1 (February 1987): 13–44.

Deutsch, Jan Georg. *Emancipation without Abolition in German East Africa c. 1884–1914.* Oxford: James Currey, 2006.

Dias, Edmundo A. "A Evolução de S. Tomé e Príncipe." *Boletim da Agência Geral das Colónias* ano 5, n° 43 (1929): 152–78.

Dias, Jill R. "Changing Patterns of Power in the Luanda Hinterland: The Impact of Trade and Colonization on the Mbundu, ca. 1845–1920." *Paideuma* 32 (1985): 285–318.

Dreschsler, Horst. "Germany and S. Angola, 1898–1903." In *Actas do Congresso Internacional dos Descobrimentos*, vol. 6. Lisbon: Commissão Executiva do V Centário do Morte do Infante D. Henrique, 1961.

Duffy, James. *Portuguese Africa*. Cambridge, Mass.: Harvard University Press, 1959.

———. *A Question of Slavery: Labour Policies in Portuguese Africa and the British Protest, 1850–1920*. Cambridge, Mass.: Harvard University Press, 1967.

Edwards, Adrian C. *The Ovimbundu under Two Sovereignties: A Study of Social Control and Social Change among a People of Angola*. London: Oxford University Press, 1962.

Espírito Santo, Carlos. *Enciclopédia Fundamental de São Tomé e Príncipe*. Lisbon: Cooperação, 2001.

———. *Torre de Razão*. 2 vols. Lisbon: Cooperação, 2000.

Esteves, Emmanuel. "As Vias de Communicação e Meios de Transporte como Factores de Globalização, de Estabilidade Política e de Transformação Económica e Social: O Caso do Caminho-de-ferro de Bengela (Benguela) (1889–1950)." In *Angola on the Move: Transport Routes, Communications and History/Angola em Movimento: Vias de Transporte, Communicação e História*, edited by Beatrix Heintze and Achim von Oppen, 99–118. Frankfurt, Germany: Verlag Otto Lembek, 2008.

Eyzaguirre, Pablo B. "Small Farmers and Estates in São Tomé, West Africa." Ph.D. diss., Yale University, 1986.

Ferguson, Niall. *Empire: How Britain Made the Modern World*. London: Penguin Books, 2003.

Ferreira, António Rita. *O Movimento Migratório de Trabalhadores entre Moçambique e a África do Sul*. Estudos de Ciências Políticas e Socias, no. 67. Lisbon: Junta de Investigações do Ultramar, Centro de Estudos Políticos e Socias, 1963.

Ferreira, Manuel. "Gente do Mundo Português: O Barão de Água-Izé Figurado Império." *O Mundo Português* 9, no. 98 (1942): 83–87.

Freudenthal, Aida Faria. "Angola." In *O Império Africano 1890–1930*, edited by A. H. de Oliveira Marques. Vol. 11 of *Nova História da Expansão Portuguesa*, edited by Joel Serrão and A. H. de Oliveira Marques. Lisbon: Editorial Estampa, 2001.

Gann, Lewis H. "History of Rhodesia and Nyasaland 1889–1953." In *Handbook to the Federation of Rhodesia and Nyasaland*, edited by William Verson Brelsford. London: Cassell, 1960.

Gaspar, José Maria. "A Colonização Branca em Angola e Moçambique." *Estudos de Ciências Politicas e Sociáis* 7 (1958).

Gay, Peter. *The Cultivation of Hatred*. Vol. 3 of *The Bourgeois Experience: Victoria to Freud*. New York: W. W. Norton, 1993.

———. *Education of the Senses*. Vol. 1 of *The Bourgeois Experience: Victoria to Freud*. New York: Oxford University Press, 1984.

———. *The Tender Passion*. Vol. 2 of *The Bourgeois Experience: Victoria to Freud*. New York: Oxford University Press, 1986.

Grande Enciclopédia Portuguesa e Brasileira. Lisbon: Editorial Enciclopédia, 1945.

Grant, Kevin. *A Civilised Savagery: Britain and the New Slaveries in Africa, 1884–1926*. New York: Routledge, 2005.

Guerreiro, Manuel Viegas. *Boers de Angola*. Separata de *Garcia de Orta*, Revista da Junta das Missões Geográficas e de Investigações do Ultramar, 6, no. 1 Lisbon, 1958.

Hammond, Dorothy, and Alta Jablow. *The Africa That Never Was: Four Centuries of British Writing about Africa*. New York: Twayne Publishers, 1970.

Hammond, Richard J. *Portugal and Africa, 1815–1910: A Study in Uneconomic Imperialism*. Stanford, Calif.: Stanford University Press, 1966.

Hardy, Dennis. *Alternative Communities in Nineteenth Century England*. London: Longman, 1979.

———. *Utopian England: Community Experiments, 1900–1945*. London: E. and F. N. Spon, 2000.

Harms, Robert W. "The End of Red Rubber: A Reassessment." *Journal of African History* 16, no. 1 (1975): 73–88.

———. *River of Wealth, River of Sorrow: The Central Zaire Basin in the Era of the Slave and Ivory Trade, 1500–1891*. New Haven, Conn.: Yale University Press, 1981.

Harries, Patrick. *Work, Culture, and Identity: Migrant Laborers in Mozambique and South Africa, c. 1860–1910*. Portsmouth, N.H.: Heinemann, 1994.

Hartmann, Wolfram, Jeremy Silvester, and Patricia Hayes. *The Colonising Camera: Photographs in the Making of Namibian History*. Cape Town: University of Cape Town Press, 1998.

Hasian, Marouf, Jr. "Critical Memories of Crafted Virtues: The Cadbury Chocolate Scandals, Mediated Reputations, and Modern Globalized Slavery." *Journal of Communication Inquiry* 32, no. 3 (2008): 249–70.

Heintze, Beatrix, and Achim von Oppen, eds. *Angola on the Move: Transport Routes, Communications and History/Angola em Movimento: Vias de Transporte, Communicação e História*. Frankfurt, Germany: Verlag Otto Lembeck, 2008.

Heywood, Linda. *Contested Power in Angola, 1840s to the Present*. Rochester, N.Y.: University of Rochester Press, 2000.

Hochschild, Adam. *King Leopold's Ghost: A Story of Greed, Terror, and Heroism in Colonial Africa*. Boston: Mariner Books, 1998.

Hodges, Tony, and Malyn Newitt. *São Tomé and Príncipe: From Plantation Colony to Microstate*. Boulder, Colo.: Westview Press, 1988.

[Hood, W. M.]. "Cocoa in West Africa: The Past, Present and Future of a Great Colonial Industry." *Bournville Works Magazine* 43, no. 2 (February 1945): 22–28.

Hopkins, Eric. *Birmingham: The Making of the Second City, 1850–1939*. Stroud, Gloucestershire, UK: Tempus Publishing, 2001.

Jeal, Tim. *Stanley: The Impossible Life of Africa's Greatest Explorer*. New Haven, Conn.: Yale University Press, 2007.

Jeeves, Alan H. *Migrant Labour in South Africa's Mining Economy: The Struggle for the Gold Mines' Labour Supply, 1890–1920*. Kingston, Canada: McGill-Queen's University Press, 1985.

Jerónimo, Miguel Bandeiro. *Livros Brancos, Almas Negras: A "Missão Civilizadora" do Colonialismo Português c. 1870–1930*. Lisbon: Imprensa de Ciências Socias, 2010.

John, Angela V. *War, Journalism and the Shaping of the Twentieth Century: The Life and Times of Henry W. Nevinson*. London: I. B. Tauris, 2006.

Kazamias, M. Andreas, ed. *Herbert Spencer on Education*. New York: Teacher's College Press, Columbia University, 1966.

Landau, Paul S., and Deborah D. Kaspin, eds. *Images and Empires: Visuality in Colonial and Postcolonial Africa.* Berkeley: University of California Press, 2002.

Lapa, Albino. *O Conselheiro Ramada Curto.* Colecção Pelo Império (no. 62). Vol. 2. Lisbon: Agência Geral das Colónias, 1940.

Lavradio, Marquez do. *Pedro Francisco Massano de Amorim.* Lisbon: Editorial Ática, 1941.

Loureiro, João. *Memórias de Angola.* Memória Portuguesa de África e do Oriente. Lisbon: Maisimagem-Comunicação Global, n.d.

———. *Memórias de Benguela e do Lobito.* Memória Portuguesa de África e do Oriente. Lisbon: Maisimagem-Comunicação Global, 2004.

———. *Memórias de Lourenço Marques: Uma Visão do Passado da Cidade de Maputo.* Memória Portuguesa de África e do Oriente. Lisbon: Maisimagem-Comunicação Global, 2003.

———. *Memórias de Moçambique.* 3ª edição. Memória Portuguesa de África e do Oriente. Lisbon: João Loureiro e Associados, 2001.

———. *Postais Antigos de S. Tomé e Príncipe.* Memória Portuguesa de África e do Oriente. Lisbon: Maisimagem-Comunicação Global, n.d.

Lovejoy, Paul E. *Transformations in Slavery: A History of Slavery in Africa.* Cambridge: Cambridge University Press, 1983.

Marques, João Pedro. *The Sounds of Silence: Nineteenth-Century Portugal and the Abolition of the Slave Trade.* Translated by Richard Wall. New York: Berghahn Books, 2005.

Matias, Nicásia Casimiro. "Os Boers Portugueses da Humpata: Um Fracasso da Política de Assimilação Portuguesa?" In *Actas do Seminário: Encontro de Povos e Culturas em Angola.* 282–299. Luanda: Comissão Nacional para as Comemorações dos Descobrimentos Portugueses, 1995.

Médard, Henri, and Shane Doyle, eds. *Slavery in the Great Lakes Region of East Africa.* Oxford: James Currey, 2007.

Meillassoux, Claude. "Female Slavery." In *Problems in African History: The Precolonial Centuries,* edited by Robert O. Collins, James McDonald Burns, and Erik Kristofer Ching, 174–80. New York: Markus Wiener Publishing, 1993.

Miers, Suzanne. *Britain and the Ending of the Slave Trade.* New York: Africana Publishing, 1975.

———. "Slavery to Freedom in Sub-Saharan Africa: Expectations and Reality." In *After Slavery: Emancipation and its Discontents,* edited by Howard Temperley, 237–640. London: Frank Cass, 2000.

Miers, Suzanne, and Igor Kopytoff. "Slavery in Africa." In *Problems in African History: The Precolonial Centuries,* edited by Robert O. Collins, James McDonald Burns, and Erik Kristofer Ching, 264–76. New York: Markus Wiener Publishing, 1993.

Mikell, Gwendolyn. *Cocoa and Chaos in Ghana.* Washington, D.C.: Howard University Press, 1992.

Miller, Joseph C. "From Group Mobility to Individual Movement: The Colonial Effort to Turn Back History." In *Angola on the Move: Transport Routes, Communications and History/Angola em Movimento: Vias de Transporte, Communicação e História,* edited by Beatrix Heintze and Achim von Oppen, 243–62. Frankfurt, Germany: Verlag Otto Lembek, 2008.

———. *Way of Death: Merchant Capitalism and the Angolan Slave Trade, 1730–1830.* Madison: University of Wisconsin Press, 1988.

Mónica, Maria Filomena. *Artesãos e Operários: Indústria, Capitalismo e Class Operária em Portugal (1870–1934)*. Lisbon: Edições do Instituto de Ciências Sociais da Universidade de Lisboa, 1986.

————. *A Formação da Classe Operária Portuguesa: Antologia da Imprensa Operária, 1850–1934*. Lisbon: Fundação Calouste Gulbenkian, 1982.

Nascimento, Augusto. "Cabindas em São Tomé." *Revista Internacional de Estudos Africanos* 14–15 (1991).

————. *Órfãos da Raça: Europeus entre a Fortuna e a Desventura no S. Tomé e Príncipe Colonial*. São Tomé: Instituto Camões, Centro Cultural Português em S. Tomé e Príncipe, 2002.

————. "A Passagem de *Coolies* por S. Tomé e Príncipe." *Arquipélago-História*, 2e série, 8 (2004).

————. *Poderes e Quotidiano nas Roças de S. Tomé e Príncipe de Finais de Oitocentos a Meados de Novecentos*. Lisbon: by the author, 2002.

————. "S. Tomé and Príncipe." In *O Império Africano, 1890–1930*, edited by A. H. de Oliveira Marques. Vol. 11 of *Nova História da Expansão Portuguesa*, edited by Joel Serrão and A. H. de Oliveira Marques. Lisbon: Editorial Estampa, 2001.

Neto, Maria da Conceição. "Hóspedes Incómodos: Portugueses e Americanos no Bailundo no Último Quartel do Século XIX." In *Actas do Seminário: Encontro de Povos e Culturas em Angola*. 377–89. Luanda: Comissão Nacional para as Comemorações dos Descobrimentos Portugueses, 1995.

Newitt, Malyn. "Angola in Historical Context." In *Angola: The Weight of History*, edited by Patrick Chabal and Nuno Vidal, 19–92. New York: Columbia University Press, 2008.

————. "British Travellers' Accounts of Portuguese Africa in the Nineteenth Century." *Revista de Estudos Anglo-Portugueses* 11 (2002): 103–29.

————. *A History of Mozambique*. Bloomington: Indiana University Press, 1995.

Nwaka, Geoffrey I. "Cadburys and the Dilemma of Colonial Trade in Africa, 1901–1910." *Bulletin de l'Institut Fondamental d'Afrique Noire* 42 (October 1980): 780–93.

Off, Carol. *Bitter Chocolate: Investigating the Dark Side of the World's Most Seductive Sweet*. Toronto: Vintage Canada, 2007.

Okuma, Thomas Masaji. *Angola in Ferment: The Background and Prospects of Angolan Nationalism*. Westport, Conn.: Greenwood Press, 1974 [1962].

Oliveira Marques, A. H. de. *Das Revoluções Liberais aos Nossos Dias*. Vol. 3 of *História de Portugal*. 13th ed. Lisbon: Editorial Presença, 1998.

Oliver, Roland A. *Sir Harry Johnston and the Scramble for Africa*. London: Chatto and Windus, 1957.

Peel, J. D. Y., ed. *Herbert Spencer on Social Evolution: Selected Writings*. Chicago: University of Chicago Press, 1972.

Pélissier, René. *História de Moçambique: Formaçã e Oposição, 1854–1918*. Vol. 2. Lisbon: Editorial Estampa, 1994.

Penvenne, Jeanne Marie. *African Workers and Colonial Racism: Mozambican Strategies and Struggles in Lourenço Marques, 1877–1962*. Portsmouth, N.H.: Heinemann, 1995.

Pirio, Gregory Roger. "Commerce, Industry and Empire: The Making of Modern Portuguese Colonialism in Angola and Mozambique, 1890–1914." Ph.D. diss., University of California–Los Angeles, 1982.

Pratt, Mary Louise. *Imperial Eyes: Travel Writing and Transculturation*. London: Routledge, 1992.

Price, Richard. *Labour in British Society: An Interpretative History*. London: Croom Helm, 1986.

Reis, Carlos Santos. *A População de Lourenço Marques em 1894 (Um Censo Inédito)*. Lisbon: Publicações do Centro de Estudos Demográficos, 1973.

Roberts, Andrew. "Portuguese Africa." In *The Cambridge History of Africa*, vol. 7, edited by John D. Fage, A. D. Roberts, and Roland A. Oliver, 494–536. Cambridge: Cambridge University Press, 1986.

Rubert, Steven C., and R. Kent Rasmussen, eds. *Historical Dictionary of Zimbabwe*. 3rd ed. Lanham, Md.: Scarecrow Press, 2001.

Ryan, James R. *Picturing Empire: Photography and the Visualization of the British Empire*. Chicago: University of Chicago Press, 1997.

Ryan, Órla. *Chocolate Nations: Living and Dying for Cocoa in West Africa*. London: Zed Books, 2011.

Santos, Maria Emília Madeira. "Em Busca dos Sítios do Poder na África Centro Ocidental: Homens e Caminhos, Exércitos e Estradas (1483–1915)." In *Angola on the Move: Transport Routes, Communications and History/Angola em Movimento: Vias de Transporte, Comunicação e História*, edited by Beatrix Heintze and Achim van Oppen, 26–40. Frankfurt, Germany: Verlag Otto Lembeck, 2008.

Satre, Lowell. *Chocolate on Trial: Slavery, Politics, and the Ethics of Business*. Athens: Ohio University Press, 2005.

Seibert, Gerhard. "Castaways, Autochthons, or Maroons? The Debate on the *Angolares* of São Tomé Island." In *Creole Societies in the Portuguese Colonial Empire*, edited by Philip J. Havik and Malyn Newitt, 105–16. Lusophone Studies 6. Bristol, UK: University of Bristol.

———. *Comrades, Clients and Cousins: Colonialism, Socialism and Democratization in São Tomé and Príncipe*. Leiden, The Netherlands: Brill, 2006.

Shaw, Nellie. *Whiteway: A Colony on the Cotswolds*. London: C. W. Daniel, 1935.

Shillington, Kevin. *History of Africa*. 2nd rev. ed. New York: Palgrave St. Martin's, 2005.

Soremekun, Fola. "A History of the American Board Missions in Angola, 1880–1940." Ph.D. diss., Northwestern University, 1965.

Statham, J. C. B. *Through Angola: A Coming Colony*. Edinburgh: William Blackwood and Sons, 1922.

Stoler, Ann Laura. *Carnal Knowledge and Imperial Power: Race and the Intimate in Colonial Rule*. Berkeley: University of California Press, 2002.

Summerton, Pauline. *Fishers of Men: The Missionary Influence of an Extended Family in Central Africa*. N.p.: Brethren Archivists and Historians Network, 2003.

Tavares, Miguel Sousa. *Equador Ilustrado*. Edição Limitada. Ilustrada com Postais da Época da Colecção de João Loureiro. [Lisbon]: Oficina do Livro, 2005.

Teixeira, Nuno Severiano. "Between Africa and Europe: Portuguese Foreign Policy, 1890–2000." In *Contemporary Portugal: Politics, Society and Culture*, edited by António Costa Pinto, 85–118. Boulder, Colo.: Social Science Monographs, 2003.

Tenreiro, Francisco. *A Ilha de São Tomé*. Memórias da Junta de Investigações do Ultramar 24. [Lisbon], 1961.

Thompson, Leonard. *History of South Africa*. 3rd ed. New Haven, Conn.: Yale Nota Bene / Yale University Press, 2000.

Thornton, John. "Sexual Demography." In *Problems in African History: The Precolonial Centuries*, edited by Robert O. Collins, James McDonald Burns, and Erik Kristofer Ching, 187–90. New York: Markus Wiener Publishing, 1993.

Torres, Adelino. *O Império Português entre o Real e o Imaginário*. Colecção Estudos sobre África 5. Lisbon: Escher, 1991.

Tucker, John T. *Angola: The Land of the Blacksmith Prince*. London: World Dominion Press, 1933.

Vail, Leroy, and Landeg White. *Capitalism and Colonialism in Mozambique: A Study of Quelimane District*. Minneapolis: University of Minnesota Press, 1980.

Valente, Vasco Pulido. *Um Herói Português: Henrique Paiva Couceiro (1861–1944)*. 2nd ed. Lisbon: Alêtheia Editores, 2006.

Vieira, Salomão. *Caminhos-de-Ferro em S. Tomé e Príncipe: O Caminho-de-Ferro do Estado e os Caminhos-de-Ferro das Roças*. São Tomé: IPAD, Intituto Camões-Centro Cultural Português em S. Tomé e Príncipe, Biblioteca Nacional de S. Tomé e Príncipe, 2005.

Villela, Orlando Bastos. "O Caso do Cacau Escravo." *Indústria Portuguesa*, ano 22, nº 259 (1949): 595–98.

Vos, Jelmer. "The Economics of the Kwango Rubber Trade, c. 1900." In *Angola on the Move: Transport Routes, Communications and History / Angola em Movimento: Vias de Transporte, Communicação e História*, edited by Beatrix Heintze and Achim von Oppen, 85–98. Frankfurt, Germany: Verlag Otto Lembek, 2008.

Wagner, Gillian. *The Chocolate Conscience*. London: Chatto and Windus, 1987.

Wheeler, Douglas L. *Republican Portugal: A Political History, 1910–1926*. Madison: University of Wisconsin Press, 1978.

Wheeler, Douglas L., and C. Diane Christensen. "To Rise with One Mind: The Bailundo War of 1902." In *Social Change in Angola*, edited by Franz W. Heimer, 53–92. Munich, Germany: Weltforum Verlag, 1973.

Wheeler, Douglas L., and René Pélissier. *Angola*. New York: Praeger Publishers, 1971.

Williams, Iolo A. *The Firm of Cadbury, 1831–1931*. London: Constable, 1931.

Williams, Rosa. "Migration and Miscegenation." In *Creole Societies in the Portuguese Colonial Empire*, edited by Philip J. Havik and Malyn Newitt, 155–70. Lusophone Studies 6. Bristol, UK: University of Bristol, 2007.

INTERNET SOURCES

www.measuringworth.com
www.1911encyclopedia.org
www.oxforddab.com
www.worldcocoafoundation.org

INDEX

Page numbers in italics denote illustrations.